THE POWER OF
FREE EXPRESSION
IN AMERICA

FIRST EDITION

Written and Edited by Frank Harris III and Jerry Dunklee
Southern Connecticut State University

cognella®
academic publishing

Bassim Hamadeh, CEO and Publisher
Michael Simpson, Vice President of Acquisitions
Jamie Giganti, Senior Managing Editor
Jess Busch, Senior Graphic Designer
John Remington, Senior Field Acquisitions Editor
Monika Dziamka, Project Editor
Brian Fahey, Licensing Specialist
Allie Kiekhofer, Interior Designer

First published in the United States of America in 2016 by Cognella, Inc.

Trademark Notice: Product or corporate names may be trademarks or registered trademarks, and are used only for identification and explanation without intent to infringe.

Cover image copyright © 2011 by Depositphotos / Yuriy_Vlasenko.

Printed in the United States of America

ISBN: 978-1-63189-333-9 (pbk) / 978-1-63189-334-6 (br)

www.cognella.com   800-200-3908

DEDICATION

This book is dedicated to the memory of Professor Robin Marshall Glassman—award-winning journalist, writing coach, founder of the Southern Connecticut State University journalism program, and a member of the Connecticut Journalism Hall of Fame. Throughout a 55-year career, she taught thousands of students and helped many fellow journalists with her particular grace, skill, and sensitivity.

CONTENTS

On any given day, Americans throughout this land will come across an issue involving the central element of this book—the First Amendment. It is arguably the most important amendment of the United States Constitution. Included are freedoms of speech, press, and religion, along with the right to assemble and petition the government for a redress of grievances.

This book explores and provides a basic examination of freedom of expression in America from before the first American newspaper hit the streets in 1690 to today's news media, the Internet and social media, and other forms of expression in the early morning of the 21st century.

Of all the subjects to study and learn, the First Amendment's freedom of expression is one that students will carry and use for a lifetime.

Frank Harris III and Jerry Dunklee
Southern Connecticut State University
New Haven, Connecticut
August 2015

Of all the inalienable rights Americans possess, there is one that rings like a bell: freedom of expression.

The First Amendment, the right to freely express one's thoughts, ideas and feelings—via the spoken or written word, the sign or symbol—is the one right that distinguishes America from most other countries and societies on this planet. It is central to the inalienable rights of life, liberty, and the pursuit of happiness. It is central to a healthy democracy. It is central to the lives of every American.

All Americans have a stake in learning about freedom of expression. Well-educated citizens must be able to read, view, and critically interpret the information contained in the morning newspaper, the weekly news magazines, the TV news, the TV news magazines, the radio, the Internet, social media, or right before their eyes. They must understand the structure and culture of the news and information media, and the techniques of manipulation. They must be aware of the importance of freedom of expression and the power that comes with it. They must be aware of the many issues of the day that will confront them as citizens in society. Most importantly, they must be able to articulate these ideas in a precise and cogent manner.

Though times have changed, the basic issues of conflict that arise between free speech and other rights ring as true in this age of social media and the Internet as it did in the age of the first printing press: Should there be absolute freedom of expression or limits? Should the press be censored in wartime? Should hate speech and adult websites be banned on the Internet? Can music lyrics be censored? Should books be published that instruct citizens on how to be hitmen? Can profane words be worn on jackets in public? Should journalists be expected to go easy on government officials during times of national crises? Should reporters be able to ask about the private lives of public officials? Should citizens relinquish their civil liberties in order to stop a potential domestic threat? Can citizens use their smartphones to video record police performing their duties? Should crime scene photos such as those from Newtown, Connecticut, be off-limits for journalists and the public?

Freedom of expression is a wonderful thing, yes, but with it comes conflict between those who want the freedom and power to express their views without restriction, and those who want to restrict that freedom and power at their discretion.

How much freedom is too much freedom? Should freedom be absolute, or should there be limits? The First Amendment of the U.S. Constitution says:

> *"Congress shall make no law respecting an establishment of religion, or prohibiting the free exercise thereof; or abridging the freedom of speech, or of the press; or the right of the people peaceably to assemble, and to petition the government for a redress of grievances."*

There are those who take this literally, so that when the First Amendment says Congress shall make no law, it means no law. This means, in essence, that people are free to express themselves, however they see fit.

Think about it. You can write whatever you want, say whatever you want about anyone. Are you OK with that? Remember, though, people can say whatever they want about you, too. So suppose someone says you are a thief? Or a child molester? Or you should be killed? Should freedom of speech protect a person's right to say that? How about if someone acts upon that person's suggestion and kills you? Should the person who carried out the act be solely accountable, or should the person who published, posted, or broadcast the message that encouraged or incited the act also be accountable? At what point between the words and action does accountability for the speaker, writer, publisher, broadcaster, or Internet poster begin and end?

Looking at another aspect of the literal interpretation of the First Amendment, if a man wants to hang a swastika in the window of his home or shop, he is able to do so? And if neighbors complain, and individuals and groups are offended? Well, what should happen? Whose rights should be valued—the individual to express himself, or, say, the person whose relatives died in the concentration camps?

According to the Absolutist Theory, that man and, in fact, all people, should have the right to write or say whatever they want. That is, to express themselves, regardless of how offensive it might be to someone else. What do you think?

The issues of the First Amendment involve a constant battle, a tug-of-war, a yin and yang concerning the realm and boundaries of free speech. Sometimes the conflict is between individual members of society, at other times it is between government and society, press and society, press and government.

This book, *The Power of Free Expression in America*, concentrates on the freedoms of speech and the press. We will also offer some history and law relating to religion, assembly, and petition, the other freedoms granted in the First Amendment. Equally important, we will provide you with the tools to articulate these ideas in a precise and cogent manner through a section on oral presentations.

In particular, this book will:

- Inform you of the historic background of press freedom in relation to the government.
- Acquaint you with the bases for freedom of expression.
- Teach you the First Amendment and the five theories relating to its application.

- Familiarize you with the role and duty of the press in relation to government.
- Apprise you of the conflicts between government and the press in war and peace.
- Introduce you to some major court cases involving press freedom and government.
- Inform you of the role and effect of advertising and corporate ownership on freedom of expression.
- Introduce you to how journalists gather and report stories.
- Familiarize you with the many freedom of expression vs. privacy and inflammatory speech issues.
- Foster the ability to critically read, view, and interpret the information contained in newspapers, magazines, broadcast news, and the Internet.
- Instruct you on honing your oral presentation skills so that you may effectively express your own thoughts and ideas.
- Provide you with the knowledge and ability to engage in critical discussion.

Every topic covered in *The Power of Free Expression in America* can be studied in more depth. If you become interested in the court cases, or in any of the myriad of First Amendment issues posed here, there are deep pools of information available in books and online. Dive in. It's a rewarding excursion into one of the most important of human activities—free expression.

PART I
Freedom of Expression

CHAPTER 1

The Historic Roots of Free Expression in America

Freedom of expression in America has not come easy. Although it is a recognized right for all Americans, it remains something that is fought over in the courts and in the streets today, as it was in the past. And what about the past? Where did freedom of expression originate? You may know that the fruits of freedom of expression in America stem from one of the many branches of the United States Constitution—the First Amendment. What you may not know is that the roots of such expression reach beyond American soil clear across the Atlantic to the nation that colonized America with the first settlement in Jamestown in 1607: England.

The freedom to express one's views has always been a challenge. While there are those in America who believe freedom is a natural right that all people are born with, it seems the other right—natural too, perhaps—is that there are people who want to limit that right, particularly when it comes to criticism of the powerful.

This, as said before, is a recurrent theme throughout history: The powerful seek to maintain their power by controlling the flow and substance of information.

In England, the powerful were those in the church and the Crown; people were not allowed to criticize or question either, lest it lead to severe punishment or death.

Consider this: You are born and you have thoughts and ideas and a voice and a pen and paper to express your thoughts and ideas, but you aren't allowed. Any ideas you have to improve the conditions or quality of life will get you in trouble, so you keep your mouth shut and take your thoughts and ideas to the grave. The downside to this is that if your ideas truly could have improved the quality of life, the world would never know because your voice was not allowed to be heard.

Surely it would seem that everyone should be in favor of freedom of expression. Why would anyone be against it?

All right. Let's look at it from another perspective. Say you are the person in power. You are the king or queen. You like having power. There is privilege with power. Of course, you don't want to give it up. You don't want to share. Why would you?

Figure 1-1. William Caxton

The Inland Printer Company / Copyright in the Public Domain.

But along comes this citizen who starts criticizing how you are running things. That's right, freedom of expression means hearing good ideas, yes, but criticism also comes with it. You're hearing it now. That person is freely telling you that the roads need fixing, the buildings are crumbling, and the common folk are paying too much in taxes while you reap the benefits. And by the way, you're doing a lousy job sitting on your throne.

OK. So how much of this do you take? Well, if no one listens, there's no problem. You could ignore that person or throw him or her in jail.

But suppose by letting this person speak, others start listening and agreeing, and soon, they too start speaking and clamoring for change—a change in how things are done, and a change in the leadership, meaning you. Now you've got a problem. You can lock everybody up and throw away the key, or you can make examples out of them by lining them up and removing their heads. Or, being the peace-loving kind of person that you are, you merely put them on display in some creative type of punishment so people will get the message that you're not taking any, uh, stuff, and this is what happens to those who criticize your authority.

This run-in with freedom of expression serves as a learning experience for you, too. You've learned that in order to prevent future occurrences, you need a set of laws designed to limit or ban freedom of expression. Or maybe it's just certain kinds of expression? You might say that it is against the law to criticize you or the Crown, and those who break this law will have hell to pay.

All right, step away from the throne and look at the situation from afar. Along comes William Caxton who, in 1476, sets up a printing press. It's the first in England. The importance of the printing press was immense. It changed the way people learned about events. Remember, at one point, the power to communicate rested mostly with the government and church. They controlled much of the flow of information. With the printing press, individual citizens had the power to print what he or she wanted and mass-produce it to communicate with masses of people. In essence, the printing press took away some of the Crown's power. Prior to this, as well, news spread by word-of-mouth from town to town. There were certain problems with this word-of-mouth communication if you think back to the game of telephone that was played or tested as kids. Remember how the final message would be radically different from the original message by the time it reached the last person? It might be embellished by a particular teller of the story, or key elements might be excluded by intent or accident.

Having the words on paper in a handbill or pamphlet, for instance, eliminated this to a large measure. Everyone who saw the posted message would see the same words, though these words were subject to interpretation and one's personal experience. In addition, the handbill could be passed along and read at another place and time.

You know that the people have the capacity to print and what they're going to print. What's the best thing to do? Control who can print. How? Find those who are friendly toward you. Why not? If you have someone who likes the way you are running something, whether it's a government or a business, the chances are that that person is not going to criticize you; and if there is criticism, it will be less than it would be if there was someone printing things without your control. So you make the printer feel good about you. Or, what the heck, you've got the power—you can make the printer fear you to the point of not printing anything that could remotely hurt you. This can be accomplished by making laws and setting up punishment for the violation of those laws.

Here are several ways the English did this:

- Bonding—Anyone wanting to print something must put down a large sum of money. (If the person prints something that the government disapproves of, then that person loses his money. And of course, if the person wants to publish again, he'd have to present another bond).
- Taxation—Those seeking to print must pay a tax. (The high cost of the tax, which was passed along to the readers, caused some printers to go out of business when readers would not pay the higher cost).
- Licensing—Those seeking to publish anything had to get prior approval and pay to get a license from the government. (The government could decide whether to grant a license and, at the same time, had the power to take it away. With such power hanging over their heads, those printing anything did so knowing that if they printed something critical, they could lose their license).

In England, anything published outside the realm of approval could get one into The Court of the Star Chamber, more commonly known as the Star Chamber. It was so named because of the star pattern that was painted on the ceiling of the room at Westminster Palace where its meetings were held. In 1487, more than a decade after the invention of the first printing press in England, the Star Chamber became a powerful entity that heard petitions of redress. It lasted for more than 150 years before its abolishment in 1641, building a notoriety that, to this day, is synonymous with secret proceedings and harsh punishment for those who came before it on charges of seditious libel or other transgressions. In such cases, the truth of whatever was said was no defense.

While the judges in the Star Chamber could not impose the death penalty on those found guilty, it could order torture, imprisonment, and fines.

As will be shown throughout history, those in power do not like to be criticized. Too much criticism can lead to attempts to remove them from power. So to stay in power, there comes the need to restrict or censor what can be printed or spoken.

For nearly 300 years after the invention of Caxton's printing press, England maintained effective control of the flow of information through its laws against what came to be known as seditious libel—that is, criticism of the government with the intent of inciting resistance or rebellion to its authority.

Licensing was one of the key forms of laws the English government used to censor the people. English poet John Milton referred to the law of licensing as "the greatest discouragement and affront that can be offered to learning." He spoke these words before the Parliament in England in 1644 in "A speech for the liberty of printers to be able to print without licensing." It was contained in the book *Areopagitica*.

John Milton's Areopagitica

Milton's speech against the law of licensing provides a foundation for freedom of expression. At the time of Milton's speech, England had over 350 years of censorship that made it a crime to speak against the government or the church. Once the printing press was established, the censorship became more pronounced, with licensing serving as the main cog in the wheel that steamrolled freedom of expression. A select group of printers in London were said to have a monopoly over all printing in the country.

Milton spoke long, and presumably passionately, about the order put forth by the government to regulate printing so that "no book, pamphlet, or paper shall be henceforth printed, unless the same be first approved and licensed" by the government or someone the government appointed. He spoke about the effect that this had on learning, serving, in fact, to discourage learning and putting the brakes on truth. Said Milton:

"Who kills a man kills a reasonable creature, God's image; but he who destroys a good book, kills reason itself ..."

Figure 1-2. John Milton

Understand that when one spoke of government approval for licensing a book or other publication, it literally meant a stamp was placed on the title page or elsewhere in the book indicating it had been reviewed and approved for publication by government authority. Then the person reviewing it would sign his name.

Now for someone who is knowledgeable in one's field, this could be considered an insulting experience, as Milton said in his speech. Chances are the person who was reviewing the document and approving it often had less knowledge than the writer. Combine this with the fact that the reviewer, or censor as he might be better called, had to read an endless number of documents, pamphlets, and books—often handwritten. Well, this could be a tiresome job that would place the censor in a not-to-kindly frame of mind to begin with.

Milton argued that licensing could not achieve its purpose, which, it seemed, was to protect the institutions and the people from thoughts and ideas that might corrupt them or lead to social or political upheaval.

He said it was important for people to know the evil as well as the good. That only from knowing that which is bad, can one know that which is good.

> "Since, therefore, the knowledge and survey of vice is in this world so necessary to the constituting of human virtue, and the scanning of error to the confirmation of truth, how can we more safely, and with less danger, scout into the regions of sin and falsity than by reading all manner of tractates and hearing all manner of reason?"

Certainly there are those who might argue against this view that unless one is exposed to evil and vice, one can never appreciate good and virtue. He pointed out, though, that even the Bible itself "relates blasphemy not nicely (and) describes the carnal sense of wicked men not unelegantly."

He said it is impossible to suppress the bad without suppressing that which is good.

Milton also said "if (writers) be not repulsed or slighted, must appear in print like a puny with his guardian, and his censor's hand on the back of his title … it cannot be but a dishonour and derogation to the author, to the book, to the privilege and dignity of learning."

Milton spoke of the dilution of the author's authority as a teacher when that author has to have approval of another to print his works:

> "And how can a man teach with authority, which is the life of teaching … whenas all he teaches, all he delivers, is but under the tuition, under the correction of his patriarchal licenser to blot or alter what precisely accords not with the hidebound humour which he calls his judgment … I endure not an instructor that comes to me under the wardship of an overseeing fist."

Milton, in a word, believed and trusted that good would win over evil, and truth would always trump the lie, which is why he spoke of the need to lift licensing.

"Let (truth) and falsehood grapple," he said. "Who ever knew Truth put to the worse, in a free and open encounter?"

There was great effort expended to manage the control of information, which attests to the power of the printing press. In many ways, the printing press did in 1476 what the Internet and the video camera did in the 1990s, and what the smartphone has done in recent years. In 1476, the printing press took a large chunk of the ability to communicate to the people out of the hands of the government and placed some of it in the hands of citizens. In the 1990s, the Internet and the video camera played that role. Continuing on through today, it is the Internet and the smartphone that have taken some of the control—arguably small—out of the hands of journalists and others and placed it in the hands of citizens. Indeed, the Internet is like a modern handbill posted at a tavern or town center, but with the capacity to reach countless people. News organizations and government organs recognize this power. The press often uses crowd sourcing to provide it with information; police organizations post notices on the Internet to spur citizen responses.

Traditionally, words and images have been gathered and distributed primarily by journalists. With smartphones in the hands of everyday people, there are more images made available to the public than ever before. Images that may never have been seen or heard are now seen and heard, courtesy of members of the public sending them in.

Consider what kicked off this public recording of events and submissions to news organizations: the police beating of Rodney King in March 1991. George Holliday was in his apartment when he heard the commotion in the street; he recorded the image of several white police officers beating an unarmed black man on his new video camera. The public saw it when the news media aired it. The result: outrage, a renewed awareness of police brutality and racism, and, well, the rest is history. An all-white jury found the officers innocent. Riots broke out in Los Angeles, and tension erupted in the country in response to the verdict. There followed another trial in which the officers were found guilty.

And if the image had never been shown?

Knowledge is power. It is an old saying, yes, but one as resiliently true today as it was whenever it was first said.

Exercises

1. In what year was the first British printing press set up?
2. Who set up the first British printing press?
3. What did the printing press allow one to do?
4. Prior to the printing press, who controlled the flow of information in England?
5. Why did the British government seek to restrict the printing press?
6. Name at least three means by which the British sought to limit or restrict the press. Describe each.
7. What was the Star Chamber?
8. True or false. British control of the press during the 300 years following the first printing press was generally successful.
9. What was the central theme of John Milton's *Areopagitica* and his speech before the English parliament in 1644?
10. Define what the following means: "Let [truth] and falsehood grapple; who ever knew truth put to the worse in a free and open encounter?"

For Critical Discussion or Writing

1. What parallels, if any, does the first printing press have with the video camera, smartphone, and the Internet?
2. If you were king or queen and there was someone writing negative material about you, what would you do?
3. John Milton believed that good would win over evil, and truth would always trump the lie. Do you believe this to be true? Do you trust enough in your belief to allow people to publish something that is a lie, but which others might believe is true?

CHAPTER 2

The Bases for Freedom

The bases for freedom of expression are centered in two areas that are some-times in conflict: the individual and society. Namely, where do the rights of the individual end and the rights of society begin, and to what extent do society's rights outweigh or supersede the rights of the individual?

The Individual's Rights to Freedom of Expression

One of the chief proponents for the rights of the individual to freedom of expression was John Locke, an English philosopher and scholar. In his *Two Treatises of Government*, published in 1690, Locke wrote that human beings were born free with inalienable rights.

"All men are naturally in … a state of perfect freedom to order their actions," as well as "a state of equality without subordination of subjection," he said. (He did not use "human beings," but said "man," which meant males not females, and certainly not those of African descent. Such was the thinking of the time.)

His treatise was a direct response to Robert Filmer's *Patriarcha*, which held that liberty was an unnatural right for people and governments. Filmer's position was that one person was given Divine authority to rule others with no criticism from those being ruled and no accountability to them. He compared the ruling king to that of a family in which the father exercises absolute control and requires obedience from his wife and the children, the latter who are born as slaves to their parents, particularly the father, whom children, by natural law, must obey. Said Filmer:

> *"If we compare the natural rights of a father with those of a king, we find them all one, without any difference at all but only in the latitude or extent of them: as the father over one family, so the king, as father over many families …"*

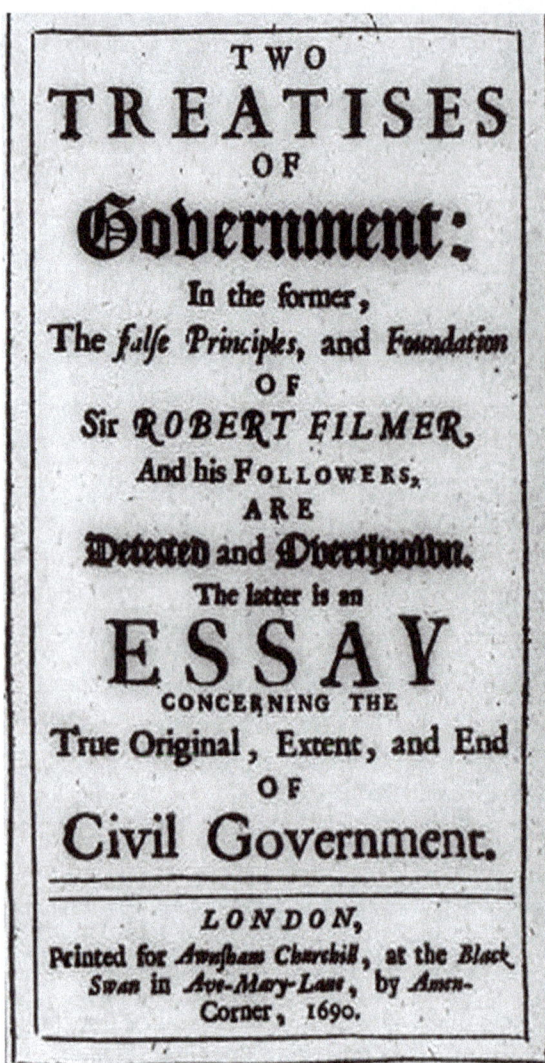

Figure 2-1. Two Treatises on Government

Copyright in the Public Domain.

Locke described Filmer's *Patriarcha* as a plea for all men to understand that they are born slaves and "ought to be so" with no right to question, criticize, let alone change those who are in power.

However, while Locke advocated liberty as a natural right, he presented contradictory statements on liberty when referencing liberty's polar extreme: slavery. In one passage, he said: "Slavery is so vile and miserable an estate of man, and so directly opposite to the generous temper and courage of our nation, that it is hardly to be conceived that an Englishman, much less a gentleman, should plead for it."

But later in the same treatise, he said: "There is another sort of servant which by a peculiar name we call slaves, who being captives taken in a just war are, by the right of Nature, subjected to the absolute dominion and arbitrary power of their masters. These men having, as I say, forfeited their lives and, with it, their liberties, and lost their estates, and being in the state of slavery, not capable of any property, cannot in that state be considered as any part of civil society, the chief end whereof is the preservation of property."

So even with the position that all are free or should be free, there were parameters that determined who was considered a man or worthy of the benefits of freedom. It should be noted that those who were without title or land were not considered under English law. Perhaps Locke himself, in his definition of political power, best explains this apparent contradiction, which was also presented in his treatise. Political power, he said, is "the right of making law." The power included in this is the right to set the parameters of whom the law shall apply and whom it shall not.

Flawed though it be—the argument of liberty for all but slaves—the foundation of freedom was set for the day when people would catch up and live up to the exalted principles espoused.

Society's Rights to Freedom of Expression and the Marketplace of Ideas

The concept of a "marketplace of ideas" is said to come from John Milton's view, expressed in *Areopagitica*, that everyone benefits from diverse ideas coming from diverse people. While he never used the words "marketplace of ideas" in *Areopagitica*, the words he did use helped others, hundreds of years later, infer from his words and place them in context. Here are Milton's words:

> "*There can no greater testimony appear, than when your prudent spirit acknowledges and obeys the voice of reason from what quarter so ever it be heard speaking.*"

Figure 2-2. John Locke

Copyright in the Public Domain.

This is a key concept to learn and remember. It simply says that every idea counts in society, no matter who offers the idea, no matter the content. This notion allows that even the ideas that may seem absurd have value; it is only with freedom of expression that any and all ideas can be put before the community, nation, or, in fact, anywhere, for discussion.

John Stuart Mill would echo Milton's views more than 200 years later in his book *On Liberty*, published in 1859.

> "*If all mankind minus one, were of one opinion, and only one person were of the contrary opinion, mankind would be no more justified in silencing that one person, than he, if he had the power, would be justified in silencing mankind … the peculiar evil of silencing the expression of an opinion is, that it is robbing the human race; posterity as well as the existing generation; those who dissent from the opinion, still more than those who hold it. If the opinion is right, they are deprived of the opportunity of exchanging error for truth: if wrong, they lose, what is almost as great a benefit, the clearer perception and livelier impression of truth, produced by its collision with error.*"

Again, the philosophy is every thought, every idea counts and should be heard.

Mill also wrote that the silencing of discussion is the assumption of infallibility. So if you believe your own ideas or thoughts cannot possibly be wrong or bested, why hear others' views? Not only does the silencing of discussion suggest infallibility, it suggests presumptuousness.

There are those who might disagree and say only those knowledgeable in a given area should have their ideas heard—that to hear every idea is a waste of valuable time. But consider, sometimes it is those who are neither experts nor knowledgeable in a specific field who, because of their lack of expertise or knowledge, can see solutions to problems that might otherwise go unnoticed or be

Figure 2-3. John Stuart Mill

Ernst Hader / Copyright in the Public Domain.

taken for granted by those who are the experts. Students new to journalism, for instance, are made aware of the advantage and disadvantage of being knowledgeable in a story they are about to cover. For instance, if a reporter is writing a story about a freedom movement among dissidents in a repressive regime, yes, it certainly would be helpful to know the background of the movement, the history of the country, its culture, religion, and a whole array of other facts. However, it does not guarantee that the story is going to be fair, accurate, or relevant. The disadvantage of being an expert is that one might not pose the questions that someone who does not have the knowledge might pose. Thus the public, whose knowledge may be minimal, misses the information it may need to understand, simply because the questions were not asked.

Being less than an expert in this example can be advantageous; it forces the journalist to ask questions that ensure her understanding of the facts, which can then be relayed to the audience. In order for the journalist to be able to write the story, the journalist must understand the important and relevant facts first.

But back to the marketplace of ideas and the notion that every idea counts. Think food. Think marketplace. Would you rather have just one type of food to choose to fill your basket, or would you rather have a variety?

This talk of food, of course, makes you hungry, so let's move to a food-free example of the value of the marketplace of ideas.

Let's say you and your classmates are locked in a room with no windows. Indeed, as much as you love your class and your classmates, you want to get out—fast. Maybe there is someone who is knowledgeable about doors and locks. Do you limit the ideas for getting out of the room solely to this one person, or do you open discussion to all? Does this include the one who's always disagreeing with your position? How about the one who listens to hip-hop or classical? The one who reeks of tobacco or perfume? The fat one, thin one, white one, brown one, and others you may not know? Hopefully, everyone gets a chance to have one's ideas heard. If you limit who can speak, you might be excluding the one idea that everyone else might not have considered—the one that might just help you get out of the room.

Freedom of Expression as a Safety Valve

What does this mean? It means that if people know they have freedom of expression to make their voices heard, they will be less likely to turn to violent means to make a change. Simply put, if people are denied their right to speak and write and otherwise express their views, they will become frustrated and angry and channel their energies toward violence. An example of this was South Africa under apartheid. Prior to its current black majority rule, a white minority ruled South Africa, and established rigid laws against the black majority in order to stay in power. Apartheid was much like segregation in America. The difference was that in America there existed the right to express one's opposition. In South Africa, the expression of ideas opposing apartheid was illegal and banned. This, followed with the violent government response to such activities as demonstrations, as well as written and oral expressions, led to the once-peaceful, nonviolent resistance turning toward violence. The late Nelson Mandela, who would become South Africa's first black president, and one who brought peace and reconciliation after apartheid's end, was, prior to this, arrested and jailed for years because he espoused violence when all other doors for free expression (and freedom itself) were closed. The theory is that as long as people believe they have the right to express themselves in support or against an authority or law, it serves as a safety valve to blow off steam and reduce the chance of violence.

Freedom of Expression as a Key to Self-Governance

The third value of freedom of expression for society is that a democratic government requires the knowledge of its citizens and the free flow of ideas so people can make informed decisions on choosing whom they will elect to represent them—hence, the value of debates among candidates, the value of citizens to pose questions of candidates for public office or those in office, and the value of journalists to pose questions, to dig and query.

There are those like Alexander Meiklejohn, a social philosopher and civil libertarian, who believe that this last value is the most important in a democracy—that freedom of expression leads to quality self-governance, that the First Amendment is designed to allow self-governance in a free and democratic society.

Freedom of Expression as a Watchdog

The news media are recognized as the Fourth Estate, meaning they are regarded as the unofficial fourth branch of government behind the three official branches: Legislative, Judicial, and Executive. The news media act as the watchdog of government, recognizing that power unchecked can be misused and abused. The news media's right to freedom of expression enables it to serve society as a watchdog for society's interest. This concept of a watchdog is quite simple: When a watchdog sees wrongdoing, it barks and lets those in the house know so they can make informed decisions. The watchdog keeps directing its eyes and nose toward government, companies, and citizens—always ready to bark.

Exercises

1. What is meant by the term, "the marketplace of ideas"?
2. What is meant by freedom of expression is a safety valve?
3. Why is freedom of expression said to be valuable in a democratic society?
4. The news media are recognized as the Fourth Estate. What does this mean? What are the three official branches of government?

For Critical Discussion or Writing

1. John Stuart Mill said that the peculiar evil of silencing the expression of an opinion is that it is robbing the human race. Explain what he meant. Do you agree?
2. What is one of the arguments against the marketplace of ideas? State your views.

CHAPTER 3

The American Colonies and the Press

The first newspaper hit the streets in the American colonies in September 1690. Published by Benjamin Harris, *Publick Occurrences Both Domestick and Forreign* was published just once and never again. Why "one and done"? The British authorities shut it down because Harris did not get prior approval, did not have a license, and did not fully appreciate the "mistake" of criticizing a government authority. As previously noted, the criticism of authority is a recurring theme throughout much of America's history that has sparked the greatest conflicts pertaining to free expression. The first major spark came with a printer named Zenger, a governor named Cosby, a newspaper, and a few political adversaries.

The Trial of John Peter Zenger

In 1734, printer John Peter Zenger printed the *New York Weekly Journal,* which contained articles critical of the unpopular colonial governor of New York, William Cosby. Zenger's publication was sponsored by Lewis Morris and James Alexander, political opponents of Cosby, and although Zenger did not write the articles, he was the printer, which meant he had technically committed the crime of seditious libel. Cosby, after receiving several attacks in the paper, apparently thought that by jailing the printer, of which it was said Zenger was one of only two in New York, he could stifle any and all criticism. Zenger languished in jail for a year before his trial came up. His case, however, became well known, and he had the good fortune of being represented by renowned criminal attorney Andrew Hamilton. As captured in the book, "A Brief Narrative of the (Trial) of John Peter Zenger of the New York Journal," published in 1736, a year after the trial, all odds were against Zenger.

Figure 3-1. Andrew Hamilton in Court Defending John Peter Zenger

He had confessed to publishing the article, and the attorney for the colonial government felt assured of a favorable verdict. But Hamilton stopped them with his words:

> *"I hope it is not our bare Printing and Publishing a Paper, that will make it a Libel: You will have something more to do, before you make my Client a Libeller; for the Words themselves must be libellous, that is, false, scandalous, and seditious or else we are not guilty …"*

In speaking before an American jury, Hamilton persuaded its members to look at the truth of what was said. His argument was that no one should be punished for publishing criticism of the government if that criticism is true. The jurors agreed, and even though he had violated the laws that were on the books, they found Zenger innocent through a process of jury "nullification." This simply meant that the jury ignored the law, which surely Zenger was guilty of, and found him innocent.

It was the first time truth was considered as a defense, and the first time someone was found innocent of seditious libel over the instructions of the judge. Politically, it was a triumph of the Americans over the British. While the trial's results neither eliminated nor changed the law of seditious libel, it galvanized public opinion against this form of government censorship, which made prosecuting such laws before colonial jurors a losing proposition. The British, though, quickly countered by bringing those accused of seditious libel before colonial legislatures and assemblies that were hostile to journalists.

The Relativity of Freedom

Despite licensing, taxation, and bonding, the British contended that freedom of the press existed. Sir William Blackstone, a compiler of common law, had a major influence on both English and American legal thinking. It was his definition of freedom of the press that holds true to this day: Freedom of the press is the absence of "previous restraints upon publications." And freedom of expression meant freedom from prior restraint. "The liberty of the press is indeed essential to the nature of a free state," he wrote in his *Commentaries on the Laws of England*, 1765–69, an important treatise on the common laws of England that influenced America's legal system, including the First Amendment.

However, he did not imply this meant absolute freedom of the press; he noted that there were consequences for publishing information that was "improper, mischievous, or illegal." Punishment for any "dangerous or offensive writings," he said, was reasonable and "necessary for the preservation of peace and good order, of government and religion, the only solid foundations of civil liberty."

The issue that arises time after time is what is deemed "dangerous," "offensive," "improper," "mischievous," or "illegal." Recall that prior to the Zenger case, it was illegal in the colonies to criticize a government official, regardless of whether what one was saying was the truth.

The colonies, however, had roughly the same laws as evident in England. Printers courted danger for publishing material that was deemed on the wrong side of government or social opinion. Freedom, thus, was and is relative. Indeed, freedom of expression can be a shifting box of sand. Looking at some of the practices of some of the previously mentioned Englishmen who spoke for freedom of expression, one can see just how relative and shifting freedom of expression can be.

Remember John Milton and his oratory on the value of freedom of expression without government licensing? Well, it is said, as a Puritan, he did not want free expression for the discussion of Catholicism or Atheism. Imagine that.

In addition, while he and John Locke were against censorship prior to publication, neither he nor Locke had a problem with punishment after publication, or the suppression of views they considered contrary to the morality and common good of society.

But the English did not have a monopoly on what some might call hypocrisy.

The Double Standard of Colonists Concerning Freedom of Expression

American colonists were often just as guilty of using freedom of expression only when it suited their interests, and against it when what was being expressed ran counter to their interests. Remember, that while there was a growing number of Americans who resented English rule, there were many Americans who were quite happy with the way the British were running things. Later, when the clear majority of American sentiment went against British rule, the ability of those to express opposing views became a dangerous proposition.

Call it "community censorship." It's when citizens know what the prevailing sentiment in a community is on an issue and conduct themselves accordingly—by not speaking or writing anything that might differ from the prevailing sentiment. It is important to note that community censorship is NOT the meting out of punishment on the person who made the "transgression." Rather, it is what results when a citizen knows what the community's sentiment is on an issue, having witnessed or heard of the punishment another citizen suffered as a result of speaking or writing something contrary to the community's sentiment.

John Stuart Mill spoke of something similar in the Introductory of his essays "On Liberty," when he referred to a "social tyranny" and its effect on the individual.

> *"Society practises a social tyranny more formidable than many kinds of political oppression, since, though not usually upheld by such extreme penalties, it leaves fewer means of escape, penetrating much more deeply into the details of life, and enslaving the soul itself."*

The setting of community standards of views may be quite subtle, or it might be overt. An example of the latter: An American stands up and says, "I support the British and their King." He's free to say it, but then, later in the evening, some people kick in his door and carry him out into the night where he is tarred and feathered. Or worse.

Word gets around. Fewer people feel free to express their views. No one wants tar, feathers, or worse.

Consequently, everyone knows what is or is not acceptable in certain communities and acts accordingly. For instance, at a New York Knicks game at Madison Square Garden, it might be uncool to stand up and go crazy over the Boston Celtics. Sure, a fan has a right to do it, but there may be a price to pay. Community censorship smothers the breath of free expression, leaving in its place the silence of self-censorship that wreaks havoc on any kind of meaningful marketplace of ideas.

In colonial America, the Americans who sought freedom from British rule, which included free speech, were quite willing to limit the free expression of fellow Americans who did not agree with their point of view. It was difficult for American printers to publish pro-British sentiments in many American cities after 1770, five years after the Stamp Act. Those who did were attacked, along with their printing presses, shops, and homes.

From colonial times to the present, those who sought to publish did so with varying degrees of risk to report what they considered news.

The Role of America's Journalists in Shaping the Nation

Ultimately, America's printers, the future journalists, played a major role in helping to secure America's independence from England. When the Stamp Act was passed in 1765, they printed words of protest that were passed around throughout the colonies, helping to galvanize support for the American cause. Were the stories objective? No. Nor were they neutral. During that time, printers made no pretense of objectivity or neutrality. They were either for or against something or someone, with papers often being sponsored by someone who wanted to present a particular view. Once independence was won, there came the U.S. Constitution and the desire for freedom of expression.

Interestingly, there was no national provision for freedom of expression in the original Articles of Confederation. Such provisions were made by the individual states to put into effect as they saw fit.

However, after recognizing that a nation comprised of states with their own sovereignty presented immense problems that strained the idea of one nation—there were states that had their own currency and laws—the representatives met to forge a new Constitution. Included in the new Constitution was a Bill of Rights that made provisions for what would become the First Amendment.

The First Amendment was originally the Third Amendment, but the two amendments preceding it were not ratified by the states. Once the amendments were passed, the nation was on its way, making America a unique young nation in an old world.

The words "Congress shall make no law ..." resonated throughout the land. But what exactly would it bring in the years ahead? Indeed, what exactly did it mean?

Exercises

1. Name the first newspaper published in America.
2. Who was its publisher?
3. In what year was it published?
4. Why was the paper banned?
5. Name the person involved in the most famous case of government censorship in the American colonies that led to a seditious libel trial.
6. Describe what led to the trial, and then describe its outcome.
7. What is jury nullification?
8. According to Sir William Blackstone, what does freedom of the press mean?
9. True or false. The patriots believed in freedom so much that they were open to the printing of pro-British sentiments, and such printers could print without fear.
10. What is community censorship and how did it work during colonial times?
11. True or false. The original Articles of the Confederation contained a national provision for freedom of expression.
12. The First Amendment was originally what numbered amendment?

For Critical Discussion or Writing

1. Should John Peter Zenger have been found innocent when he did, in fact, break the law?
2. Describe a current or recent example of jury nullification.
3. Describe a current or recent example of community censorship.
4. During colonial times, America's newspapers were clearly partisan; they presented a particular point of view and took sides. Should newspapers do that today on important issues and abandon all notions of neutrality.

CHAPTER 4

The First Amendment Legal Theories

Congress shall make no law respecting an establishment of religion, or prohibiting the free exercise thereof; or abridging the freedom of speech, or of the press; or the right of the people peaceably to assemble, and to petition the government for a redress of grievances.

First Amendment of the U.S. Constitution

The First Amendment provides five freedoms to Americans: freedom of religion, freedom of speech, freedom of the press, freedom to assemble, and freedom to petition.

With these freedoms, there emerges conflict as to the rights of the individual, society, and the government. How much freedom is too much freedom? What freedoms should be curtailed for the sake of society, government, and other individuals?

The Constitution of the United States gives the Supreme Court the task of deciding whether laws are constitutional. When Congress or a state or local branch of government passes a law, it may be challenged by citizens in the courts. Many significant court cases over the years have helped define various aspects of the Bill of Rights and other portions of the Constitution. The decisions by the Supreme Court hold the force of law and set precedents for government to follow in creating new law. Over the 200-plus years of the existence of the United States, most parts of the Constitution have been challenged and interpreted by the courts.

The Five Theories

When courts look at First Amendment cases, they apply one or more of the following interpretation theories or variations of them. Each of the theories has its supporters, and each has been used by the courts at one point in our history. But remember, scholars and the courts will continue to struggle with what the First Amendment means. As times change, as political movements and legal theories come and go, the way the First Amendment is interpreted will change too.

Absolutist Theory

This theory states that the Founding Fathers knew exactly what they were doing when they ratified the First Amendment. "No law" means no law should be made that would alter the freedoms provided by the First Amendment. Only two Supreme Court justices have supported the absolutist position, but there is a significant minority of journalists and scholars who are absolutists. Critics of the absolutists say there was not full freedom of expression in the 1790s, hence the Founders really did not mean to imply complete freedom.

Ad Hoc Balancing Theory

This theory says freedom of press and speech must be balanced with other conflicting rights in a constitutional society. For instance, the rights of the press must be balanced with the rights of the military to hold national security secrets that protect the American way of life. The courts erect an imaginary scale of justice. On one side they put the First Amendment and on the other the conflicting issue. They add evidence to each side of the scale. Whichever side is heavier, wins. In each case, the courts erect new scales for that particular case, hence the name "ad hoc." The decisions that result from this theory usually don't set precedents in law, and can be influenced by the personal bias of a judge.

Preferred Position Balancing Theory

This theory argues that because freedom of expression is so important to the U.S. form of government, the First Amendment should have a preferred position. So the court puts the imaginary scales back up, but it starts with the free press and freedom of speech weighing more. It's the role of those who wish to censor to bring a "heavy burden of proof" to their side of the case. This is an advantage to those who wish to criticize government because it requires government to produce serious reasons why the First Amendment is not as important as the other side. This theory has been used more regularly by the courts in the past 50 years.

Meiklejohnian Theory

Alexander Meiklejohn was a social philosopher at Yale. He asked the question, "What is the purpose of the First Amendment?" He answered that question by saying that the purpose is "successful self-government." He then divided expression into two categories: speech that relates to self-government and that which doesn't. He defined self-government speech quite broadly. He included criticism of government and all political speech and also history, science, geography, and other areas of study. One problem with the Meiklejohnian Theory is where to draw the line. Is a man walking nude down the street to protest laws about wearing clothes political speech? That is open to interpretation. Is a tabloid exposé of a Hollywood star political? The courts have favored Meiklejohnian Theory in several important First Amendment cases. The most applicable example is the landmark libel case of the *New York Times v. Sullivan*, which you will learn more about later. In that case, the Supreme Court ruled that because criticism of public officials is so important to the workings of our government, public officials must meet a heavier burden of proof to win libel cases.

Access Theory

This theory relates to powerful economic trends in the United States in the latter part of the 20th century that created large media conglomerates. It also considers the fact that government can be big and powerful. Access Theory says that the First Amendment is meaningless if the average person does not have a legitimate way to be heard in print, in radio, or TV. It argues that these media should be forced to open up to those with views not being represented in that medium. For instance, if you walked into the offices of the *Wall Street Journal* and told the editors that they must put your point of view in the paper, do you think they would agree to do it? Big media *can* ignore smaller voices. Access Theory wants to remedy this imbalance. The Supreme Court killed Access Theory in non-broadcast media in a case called *Miami Herald v. Tornillo*. The court said publishers could not be forced to present views they didn't want to present (more on this in Chapter 7). But Access Theory has had an impact on First Amendment law in broadcasting. We'll explain later in this book.

An important point to keep in mind when studying the legal issues surrounding the First Amendment is that most of the laws infringing on free expression have arisen during times of national stress and fear. The Alien and Sedition Acts were passed at a time when John Adams feared an invasion by the French, and worried about immigrants undermining the new democracy.

Exercises

1. There are five First Amendment theories or strategies that are used to develop a practical definition of freedom of the press when such freedom conflicts with other rights. Who uses these definitions?
2. Define the Absolutist Theory and a criticism of it.
3. What is the Ad Hoc Balancing Theory and a criticism of it.
4. What is the Preferred Position Balancing Theory?
5. What is the Meiklejohnian Theory on freedom of expression?
6. Define Access Theory.
7. Which theory has been used more commonly by the courts in the past 50 years?

For Critical Discussion or Writing

1. Which First Amendment theory do you think should be regularly applied?
2. Are you an absolutist? Why? Why not?

PART II
Religion

Chapter 5: The Freedom to Worship—or Not

The Freedom to Worship—or Not

The First Amendment says, "Congress shall make no law respecting an establishment of religion, or prohibiting the free exercise thereof ..."

This is the "Establishment Clause." It means that the government may not create, sponsor, or advocate for or against any religions. That, the Founders believed, should be up to individuals. Why did they include religion among the five freedoms? Perhaps it was because of history and what they had experienced.

The men in Philadelphia represented several religions; some seldom attended any church; some were pious; some were non-believers. There were Episcopalians, Methodists, Catholics, Lutherans, and a range of other faiths. Some were slaveholders, divorcees, hard-edged Revolutionary War veterans, gentlemen farmers, and merchants. Many of them, according to historians, drank a lot. These men, (all were male) did not see eye-to-eye on many things, including morality in their personal lives. But they did agree that the new government should not establish an official religion. This became known as the "separation of church and state." What has been the impact of this clause in the First Amendment?

An historic Protestant church on the City Green in New Haven, Connecticut

Polls on the Belief in God

Let's jump ahead to the 21st century before we go back to the creation of the Constitution and the Bill of Rights. For years international polling organizations have asked people in a number of countries if they believe in a god. The results are often surprising to

Images formatted in text boxes courtesy of Frank Harris III and Jerry Dunklee. Used with permission.

many Americans. According to a Pew Research Center poll of U.S. citizens released in 2015 just over 76 percent of Americans say they believe in a "supreme being." (That number has dropped in the early years of the 21st Century from over 90 percent in the late 20th Century. People who describe themselves as "unaffiliated," "agnostic," or "atheist" has increased in recent years to a total of about 23 percent according to Pew.)

But compare the 76 percent of believers in the U.S. to some other parts of the world. In Italy, the home of the Catholic Church and the Vatican, only about 40 percent say they believe in God. In France, the number is also in the low 40s. The percentages are similar in Britain, Germany, Spain, Japan and other countries. Why is that? Perhaps it is because of the Founding Fathers' decision to include freedom of religion in the First Amendment and the U.S. tradition of faith freedom that has evolved since 1791.

Religions in America

What have those few words in the First Amendment meant in the U.S.? Take a look. Hundreds of religions have been created here. Some made-in-America religions are The Church of Jesus Christ of Latter-day Saints (the Mormons), The Christian Scientists, The Seventh Day Adventists, Jehovah's Witnesses, Scientology, The Nation of Islam, Full Gospel, the Unitarians, and many others. There are huge Catholic cathedrals, Jewish temples, and tiny chapels in hospitals. There are churches connected to major religions and many with no affiliations. There are small storefront churches, which have faith tenets peculiar to just that church. America has "mega-churches," snake handlers, holy rollers, Jews for Jesus, those who speak in tongues, Rastafarians, Hare Krishnas, and Native American religions that pre-date the Bill of Rights. There is a significant variety of Protestant religions, from the United Church of Christ, Episcopalians, Lutherans, Methodists to Free Methodists, Southern Baptists, and the African Methodist Episcopal Church. There are Muslims, Sikhs, Hindus. Baha'i, and many more. It is truly miraculous that so many faiths can exist in one country.

Perhaps that is the reason why so many U.S. citizens say they believe in God. Under the First Amendment you can choose whatever "god" you wish, and it's not required that it be the same as that of your neighbor. The government may not impose its will on your choice of faith.

We should not forget that the First Amendment also permits citizens to belong to NO church or to choose to be Atheist.

How the Establishment Clause in the First Amendment should be interpreted has been the subject of thousands of court cases over the years of the Union. Some examples are:

Holy Transfiguration Orthodox Church in Westville, Connecticut.

- May governments—federal, state, or local—offer any support of religious schools?
- May symbols of just one religion be displayed in public buildings?
- May religious literature be passed out door-to-door?
- May members of a religion that believes only God heals be forced to permit their sick children to get medical aid?
- May a city deny a parade permit to a group based on its faith, or lack of it?
- Should evolution be taught in public schools or just the biblical story of the Creation?
- May religious groups meet in public school buildings?
- Should birth control be taught in public schools?
- May a business owner deny health insurance covering birth control to its employees if the employer's religion is against it?
- Should the Ten Commandments be displayed on public property? What about a cross?
- Should a Christmas crèche be permitted in the public square? What about a menorah to celebrate Hanukkah?
- Does the First Amendment permit official, school-sponsored prayer in public schools?

A storefront mosque in Hamden, Connecticut.

ABDUL-MAJID KARIM HASAN ISLAMIC CENTER

The Scopes Monkey Trial

One of the most famous of religious freedom court cases is the so-called "Scopes Monkey Trial" from 1925. The case developed in the town of Dayton, Tennessee, the heart of the Bible Belt, when in March 1925, Tennessee passed the Butler Act. This act made it unlawful for any teacher in any of the state's colleges, high schools, elementary schools—essentially any public school supported by the state's tax dollars—to teach any theory "that denies the story of the Divine Creation of man as taught in the Bible, and to teach instead that man has descended from a lower order of animals."

The act was sparked by the fear that the teaching of Darwinism, the theory that humans evolved from apes, would lead to a weakening in the belief in God. British naturalist Charles Darwin's theory that all humans evolved from a common ancestor directly contradicted the biblical teachings on the creation of life, where God was said to have created life. Tennessee's state representative John Washington Butler, the act's founder, was said to have been

A church spire dominates the sky in Fair Haven, Connecticut.

Figure 5-12. John T. Scopes

Bain News Service / Copyright in the Public Domain.

motivated to write the act when a visiting preacher told him of a woman who lost her faith after studying evolutionary biology at a university.

How does this tie to religious freedom granted by the First Amendment? When it says Congress shall make no law respecting an establishment of religion, it means no part of the government—federal, state, or local—can mandate how one worships or chooses not to worship. By Tennessee making it a law punishable with a fine of anywhere from $100 to $500 for those who violate it, it was mandating how individuals—in this case teachers—not only taught, but were required to teach based upon what the state believed was the proper religious way. In a word, the law put the state in the position of supporting a religious belief.

The state's position, on the other hand, was that it had a right to choose what is taught in schools, since state money was supporting them.

However, despite Tennessee's ban, the biology textbooks used in schools, and approved by the state, contained the very same Darwinian theory of evolution they had banned schools from teaching. So anyone teaching biology was in violation.

Enter John Scopes, 24, a science teacher at Dayton's Rhea County High School, and part-time coach of the football team. Scopes, of Kentucky, was just a year out of college when he agreed to challenge the law. Newspaper accounts of the day described him as no radical but just a biology teacher who came about being the center of what was called the legal case of the century in a rather unassuming way.

As described in the Middletown, Nebraska, Daily Herald on June 8, 1925:

"There was a crowd sitting around in Robbins drug store one afternoon last month," said Scopes, *"and the doctor here said that nobody could teach biology and not teach evolution. I wasn't there. I was playing tennis up at the high school with some of the boys, but the dispute got so hot that they sent for me.*

"When I got there I said that sure enough, the doctor was right. I told them any teacher—even a high school teacher teaching evolution is violating the law. I told them, sure enough, I was violating it."

So Dr. Rappleyea said. *"Let's take this thing to court, and we did. That's how it started."*

A Baptist church in New Haven, Connecticut.

What followed became what would today be called a circus and media frenzy, sparked by not just the issue of science versus religion, but the by townsfolk's desire to capitalize on the publicity by drawing people into town to spend. Hundreds of newspaper reporters and spectators descended upon the small town, which then scrambled to figure out where to put all the people. Initial proposals included holding the trial beneath a huge tent erected over the town's baseball diamond so that people could hear. Loudspeakers were erected. When the trial would begin several weeks later, WGN radio, owned by the Chicago Tribune, would broadcast the trial live to the nation—the first live broadcast of a trial.

A nondenominational church in New Haven, Connecticut.

The May 23, 1925 edition of the Brooklyn, New York, Daily Eagle, in the article "War Tents Sought to House Throngs Expected at Dayton, Tenn., for Scopes Trial," gives some indication of how the town of 2,500 was scrambling for accommodations:

> *"Little Dayton, faced with an impending influx of thousands for the trial of J.T. Scopes, charged with violating the State's new statute against the teaching of evolution in the public schools, began a hunt today for Army tents, amplifiers and Pullman car sidings, to care for the overflow crowds."*

Scopes himself, who was described as quiet and unassuming, would become more of an afterthought as passions stirred. Celebrity lawyers headed both the prosecution and the defense teams. However, Scopes did have this to say about the passions his act had sparked, as described in The (Helena, Montana) Independent Record of June 16, 1925:

> *"The question is not concerned with the truth, for truth can take care of itself," he writes. "Rather is it whether science will continue to enjoy the liberty it has had since the founding of our government or shall have to bow again to superstition and prejudice as in its infancy. My parents were Presbyterians and I was reared to believe in the doctrines of Christ. At 24, in my first year of teaching, I find I can be arrested for my beliefs. I studied evolution in the schools and universities. The pupils in my classes were not less Christians after studying evolution than they were before."*

The town and the state were ridiculed by much of the country, as evident in this May 27, 1925, editorial in The Bakersfield Californian: "When some people are not trying to make ridiculous laws, others are trying to make the laws ridiculous. Down in Tennessee they do both."

Or this one in The Bismarck (North Dakota) Tribune of June 5, 1925, titled "The Dark Ages." Said the editorial: "The trial of John T. Scopes in Dayton, Tenn., in which the validity of the Tennessee evolution law will be determined is a case that will be heard around the world. So astonishing is the fact that the state interferes with the teaching of science that even in the dark countries of Europe the case is creating a furore."

The commentary crossed international borders and covered not just the state of Tennessee, but America itself. In Germany, Dr. Theodor Wolff, editor-in-chief of the Berliner Tageblatt, considered an influential newspaper, said the whole issue demonstrated that America was less free than Germany.

A storefront church in New Haven, Connecticut.

Speaking in a special to the Brooklyn Daily Eagle of June 29, 1925, Wolff said: "How people can pass laws curtailing their freedom, and then boast about their freedom is incomprehensible. Besides, why all this excitement about the Darwinian theory?"

It is important to note that there was no question as to the guilt of Scopes under Tennessee law. The intent was to challenge the law itself. Even before the trial began on July 10, 1925, Scopes had already become an afterthought as the focus settled on the two prominent lawyers: William Jennings Bryant, a three-time candidate for the US presidency and a Christian fundamentalist who represented the state; and Clarence Darrow, an agnostic and renowned criminal lawyer who represented Scopes.

The trial would last eight days. It would take a jury less than ten minutes to find Scopes guilty and the state's ban constitutional. He was fined $100. The books containing the theory of evolution were removed. Scope's conviction would be set aside several months later based on a technicality and the state would opt not to retry him. The state of Tennessee won the case in the legal sense, but in public opinion, Tennessee and other states that had anti-evolution bans on their books were looked upon as backward-thinking people who were harming the education of their students. A play about the trial, Inherit the Wind, would become a hit in 1950; ten years later, a movie by the same name would win numerous awards.

Tennessee's ban would remain for the next four decades, until May 1967.

Epperson v. Arkansas

Forty years after the Scopes case, another 24-year-old biology teacher would challenge the law banning the teaching of evolution and requiring the teaching of creationism. This time it was in the neighboring state of Arkansas, which, two years after the Scopes trial had adopted its own law against teaching the evolution theory.

Arkansas's anti-evolution law, Initiated Act no. 1, was different from those of other states that enacted such laws during the 1920s. Rather than go before a state legislature, its law was put to a vote of Arkansas citizens, who overwhelmingly passed it.

Susan Epperson, a tenth-grade teacher at Little Rock, Arkansas's Central High School, had been teaching for just a couple of years when she filed suit on December 6, 1965, saying that Arkansas' anti-evolution law violated her First Amendment right of freedom of speech, as well as the Establishment Clause relating to religion.

"Teacher attacks 'Monkey Law,'" said the front-page headline of the next day's Northwest (Fayetteville) Arkansas Times.

In her statement, reprinted in newspapers across the country, Epperson said:

Figure 5-13. Susan Epperson challenged Arkansas' evolution law all the way to the U.S. Supreme Court in 1968.

"My mother is a public school librarian and my father has been a professor of biology for many years. They are both dedicated Christians who see no conflict between their belief in God and the scientific search for truth. I share this belief…

"As a responsible biology teacher, it is my duty to discuss with my students and to explain to them various scientific theories and hypotheses in order that they may be as educated and enlightened as possible about matters pertaining to science, including the theories of Darwin as set forth in 'On The Origin of Species' and in "The Descent of Man." However when I do this, I become an irresponsible citizen—a law violator—a criminal subject to fine and dismissal from my job. On the other hand, if I obey the law, I neglect the obligations of a responsible teacher of biology. This is the sure path to the perpetuation of ignorance, prejudice and bigotry."

America in the 1960s had changed significantly from the 1920s. Fewer of the nation's people and states clung to the anti-evolution beliefs or saw the teachings of Darwin as anathema to religion. Even within Arkansas schools, it was being taught despite the law that was on the books. A new textbook approved for use at Epperson's school had a chapter on Darwin's theories of evolution. However, as the law was still on the books, if she taught it, she would be in violation of the law. So, much like Scopes

A Catholic church in Wooster Square, New Haven, Connecticut

before, she became the person to test the law. Also like Scopes, she had the support of the American Civil Liberties Union. However, unlike Scopes, her suit was supported by the local Ministerial Association, the Arkansas Education Association, and the National Education Association. A parent with children in the school joined her lawsuit.

Epperson's trial proceeded without celebrity attorneys, tons of media coverage, spectators, or the circus-like atmosphere. The trial focused on the constitutionality of the law rather than questions of evolution and religion.

But it was not completely devoid of the religious fervor of its predecessor. The Indiana (Pennsylvania) Gazette of August 16, 1966, noted this from Arkansas Attorney General Bruce Bennett:

"Will our children be 'free' to choose their religion after their minds have been warped by anti-religious propaganda; or will they be forever captives of the Darwin theory, foisted upon them in their youth?"

The people in Arkansas made it a point to distance themselves from the notoriety and ridicule that became hallmark of Tennessee's Scopes trial.

In the local state court, she won. The state found the ban unconstitutional and newspapers had a field day, with these wire service words filling the editorial pages of newspapers across the land:

"It required 41 years but the monkeys have finally won a case in court."

The victory was short-lived, as the state appealed to the Arkansas Supreme Court, which initially refused to advance the appeal before ultimately overturning the local court ruling a short time later, effectively upholding the state's anti-evolution law.

The case then was appealed to the US Supreme Court in 1968. The court ruled unanimously against Arkansas. Justice Abe Fortas wrote the opinion, which said in part:

"...The overriding fact is that Arkansas' law selects from the body of knowledge a particular segment which it proscribes for the sole reason that it is deemed to conflict with a particular religious doctrine; that is, with a particular interpretation of the Book of Genesis by a particular religious group..."

Fortas also wrote: "...The state has no legitimate interest in protecting any or all religions from views distasteful to them..."

This decision basically voided all laws in the country that prevented the teaching of theories of evolution in public schools and universities.

This did not end the battle. A number of places around the U.S. passed laws that required "Creationism" be taught alongside the more science-based theories of the ways humans and other life evolved on Earth. Eventually these laws ended up challenged in the courts. In 1987 the U.S. Supreme Court ruled in the Louisiana case of *Edwards v. Aguillard* that requiring teaching of "Creation Science" is a violation of the First Amendment's prohibition against government involvement in promoting religious belief. The debate over this issue, as is true on many other religious freedom concerns, continues among individuals, religions, the press and in the courts.

A Recent Ruling

A synagogue in Hamden, Connecticut.

In 2014, the U.S. Supreme Court ruled in the case of *Town of Greece (N.Y.) v. Galloway* that a prayer to begin city council meetings in Greece, New York, was not a violation of the First Amendment, even though most of the prayers offered over the years were Christian and referred directly to Jesus Christ. In its decision the Court ruled, by a 5–4 majority, that the town did not offend the Establishment Clause because the Congress and various legislatures have done the same thing for years, that the prayer did not require participation by those in attendance, and that the town did not reveal a prejudice against minority faiths by deciding who may offer the prayer. In the opinion, Justice Anthony Kennedy wrote, in part:

> *"… the First Amendment is not a majority rule and government may not seek to define permissible categories of religious speech. In rejecting the suggestion that legislative prayer must be nonsectarian, the Court does not imply that no constraints remain on its content. The relevant constraint derives from the prayer's place at the opening of legislative sessions, where it is meant to lend gravity to the occasion and reflect values long part of the Nation's heritage. From the Nation's earliest days, invocations have been addressed to assemblies comprising many different creeds, striving for the idea that people of many faiths may be united in a community of tolerance and devotion, even if they disagree as to religious doctrine. The prayers delivered in Greece do not fall outside this tradition…"*

There are many more cases testing the limits of freedom of religion in the United States. Your instructor may wish to delve more deeply into one of those mentioned above, or one of the many others. They are all controversial. If you are curious and wish to study this in more depth there are numerous websites, books, and legal articles about religion, the First Amendment, and the separation of church and state.

Exercises

1. What is the "Establishment Clause"?
2. Why were the First Amendment authors concerned about freedom of religion?
3. What did the Supreme Court say about public prayer in *Town of Greece v. Galloway?*

For Critical Discussion or Writing

1. Do you think religious freedom should be as broad as it is in the United States?
2. What would life be like in the U.S. if religious freedoms were limited, as in Saudi Arabia today or England in the 1500s?

PART III
Speech

Chapter 6: Americans and Free Speech

Suffragist Lucy Burns advocating for a woman's right to vote before a crowd in Washington, D.C. She was one of 8,000 suffragists to march in Washington before Woodrow Wilson's 1913 presidential inauguration.

Americans and Free Speech

The Real Test of Freedom

It is easy to speak of freedom and the goodness of democracy when life is good and there are no threats or dangers to our individual or national well-being. But the real test of a free people is how they conduct themselves when fear creeps into their lives like a shadow. That is, how well do they balance safety and security with civil liberties for both citizens and noncitizens alike?

This is an important test for government as well as the citizens who elect their government officials.

Historically, when fear creeps in, people throughout the world often react disappointingly, if not shamefully. Such has been the case in the United States during times of strife. Despite the First Amendment guarantee of free expression, laws often get trampled, set aside, conveniently forgotten, changed, or replaced by new laws that test the sincerity and commitment to the Constitution. Twenty-two years after the Declaration of Independence, this fear was manifested with the first peacetime restriction of the First Amendment in 1798.

The Alien and Sedition Acts of 1798

While often cited as one act, The Alien and Sedition Acts were actually two separate acts passed at a time when there was a strong possibility of war with France, a reigning world power at the time.

Americans were fearful of the revolution in France, and of French subjects living in the U.S. who might pose a "danger of the public peace or safety" should they side with their homeland during a conflict." The Alien Act gave the president power to apprehend, restrain, secure, and remove them as "alien enemies"—if they weren't naturalized citizens. The Act also increased the length of time it took for them to become naturalized citizens.

The Sedition Act made it a crime to "write, print, utter, or publish" or procure someone else to write, print, utter, or publish "any false, scandalous, and malicious writings against the government of the United States … or to stir up sedition within the United States."

Remember what the First Amendment said regarding free speech and the press? There should be no law abridging the freedom of speech. Yet here, these acts made it unlawful to criticize the government. As it turned out, the Alien and Sedition Acts did not go well for President John Adams: He lost the presidency in 1800 to Thomas Jefferson. (See Chapter 7). Some questions to consider: Does the threat of war (there was no war on at the time) or an actual war call for a change in the First Amendment? How much can a citizen criticize politicians, the war effort, or anything else the government has set its sights on? Does a government have a right to restrict speech that might be harmful to its aims? It is a recurring debate that occurred as the country approached a new century, and, again, some 60 years later during this nation's Civil War. One person who personified this debate was Clement Vallandigham, an Ohio politician who opposed the Union cause.

Figure 6-1. Clement L. Vallandigham

Julian Vannerson / Copyright in the Public Domain.

Free Speech During the Civil War

In the spring of 1863, Vallandigham gave two speeches in Ohio in which he criticized the Union war effort, and ridiculed President Abraham Lincoln—all in violation of Major General Ambrose Burnside's General Orders 38 that made it a crime of treason to declare sympathy or support for the enemy under the penalty of being tried and either hanged "or sent beyond our lines into the lines of their friends."

Several days after Vallandigham delivered his speech in Mount Vernon, Ohio, 150 Union soldiers surrounded Vallandigham's house in the wee hours of the morning, kicked open the door, arrested him, and whisked him off to a military tribunal.

The following May 10, 1863, *Daily Ohio Statesman's* newspaper account describes the charges and court proceedings:

"… *Clement L. Vallandigham, a citizen of the State of Ohio, on or about the 1st day of May, 1863, at Mount Vernon, Knox county, Ohio, did publicly address a large meeting of citizens, and did utter sentiments, in words or in effect as follows, declaring the present war 'a wicked, cruel and unnecessary war; a war not being waged for the preservation of the Union; a war for the purpose of crushing out liberty and erecting a despotism; a war for the freedom of the blacks and the enslavement of the whites ...; [advising people] at the close of the speech to come up together at the ballot and hurl the tyrant from his throne.' He styled the President at another time as King Lincoln."*

Vallandigham defended his First Amendment right to speak critically of the government, secreting out a letter that he penciled after his arrest in which he said he was within his constitutional rights:

"It is words spoken to the people of Ohio in an open and public political meeting, lawfully and peaceably assembled, under the Constitution and upon full notice. It is words of criticism of the public policy of the public servants of the people, by which policy it was alleged that the welfare of the country was not promoted. It was an appeal to the people to change that policy, not by force, but by free elections and the ballot-box. It is not pretended that I counseled disobedience to the Constitution, or resistance to laws and lawful authority. I have not. Beyond this protest, I have nothing further to submit."

Vallandigham would, in fact, submit a writ of habeas corpus, seeking a civil, rather than a military, trial. However, Burnside, responded to Vallandigham's writ with his own views on the matter:

"If I were to indulge in wholesale criticisms of the policy of the Government, it would demoralize the army under my command ... We are in a state of civil war... If I were to find a man from the enemy's country distributing in my camps speeches of their public men, that tended to demoralize the troops, or to destroy their confidence in the constituted authorities of the Government, I would have him tried, and hung if found guilty, and all the rules of modern warfare would sustain me. Why should such speeches from our own public men be allowed?... the greater responsibility rests upon the public men and upon the public press, and it behooves them to be careful as to what they say ..."

So who was right? Who was wrong? It certainly seemed as if Vallandigham had a strong First Amendment argument. However, with Lincoln's blessing, and protests notwithstanding, the military tribunal retained jurisdiction and found Vallandigham guilty. Though Vallandigham was not hanged, Burnside's edict was partially fulfilled: The Union deported him to the Confederacy.

Figure 6-2. Brig. Gen. Ambrose Burnside

This was but one example of government free speech restrictions during the Civil War. It was from the North. What about the South?

It is important to note that when the South seceded from the Union, it took with it the same First Amendment from the U.S. Constitution, and incorporated it, word for word, as section 12, Article I of its Confederate Constitution.

It is also important to note that with this same First Amendment, the South was no less restrictive in muzzling free speech and dissent from its citizens than the North.

Following are some examples from the South, as well as the North, found in *The War of the Rebellion: a Compilation of the Official Records of the Union and Confederate Armies* that was assembled in the years after the Civil War.

The words presented illustrate the earnestness, rooted in fear, in demanding loyalty from their citizens and tolerating nothing less. Those arrested often desperately sought ways out of their predicament by writing letters, or having others write letters for them. This one was to the Confederate Secretary of War, Judah Benjamin:

> *"RICHMOND, December 16, 1861. Hon. J. P. BENJAMIN, Secretary of War. DEAR SIR: A man by the name of L. M. Rowley, late a resident of Florida, was taken up about a month since on suspicion of being disloyal and sent to Montgomery where he is now confined in jail. He has appealed to me to have his case investigated, denying as I understand him the allegation. I most respectfully ask of you the appointment of some person to act as commissioner in his case. Your obedient servant, JACKSON MORTON. [Indorsement.]"*

The one that follows is both a pep talk and orders from Major General Robert Patterson to his Union troops in the field on June 3, 1861: "You are going on American soil, to sustain the civil power, to relieve the oppressed, and to retake that which is unlawfully held. You must bear in mind you are going for the good of the whole country, and that while it is your duty to punish sedition, you must protect the loyal, and, should occasion offer, at once suppress servile insurrection."

Often, though, it was not just the government, but citizens themselves who restricted freedom of expression. Recall John Stuart Mill's words: "[Society] practices a social tyranny more formidable than many kinds of political oppression."

Consider this report from the *Charleston Mercury* of December 19, 1859, prior to the Civil War: "A workman on the new State House, named Powers, has been uttering seditious sentiments here without concealment, and on more than one occasion expressed his entire approval of John Brown's invasion. He was apprehended by the Mayor, and subjected to examination ... the Vigilance Committee took him in hand, stripped him to the waist, inflicted twenty-nine lashes and a coat of tar and feathers ..."

There was also this April 17, 1861, article in the *Nashville Union* describing a Philadelphia "mob of 200 boys [who] visited the residences of the secessionists, and compelled them to hoist the American flag" shortly after the Civil War began.

Do note that both sides' newspapers reported what the other side was doing to restrict their supporters' liberties.

Social Stress and Fear in the 20th Century

During the first 25 years of the 20th century, the United States was a cauldron of rapid change, heavy immigration, war, and political challenges. Think about the period. People were flooding into the United States from Ireland, Italy, Eastern Europe, and elsewhere. It was one of the largest waves of immigration in the country's history. World War I was raging in Europe, and the United States entered that conflict. The Russian Revolution rocked the world in 1917; when the communists took over in Russia, it frightened many Americans, especially capitalists who owned American factories, railroads, oil, construction companies, and other concerns. There was a significant socialist political movement in the United States. Eugene V. Debs, a socialist, ran for president in 1918 and garnered millions of votes. Workers' unions were being formed and challenged by owners and governments. The women's suffrage movement was going strong, resulting in women winning the right to vote when the 19th Amendment was ratified by the states in 1920. Prohibition began and illegal liquor became the focus of law enforcement. The first mass-produced automobiles chugged up and down the roads. Radio stations began springing up all over the country, bringing music and news to the cumbersome boxes people put in their living rooms and kitchens. The Jazz Age began bringing hot music to new-fangled phonographs. Dance crazes like the Black Bottom took the country by storm. In short, it was a time of immense change, and such foment often causes governments to pass laws to attempt to control events.

Such was the case when the federal government and many states passed a series of laws to prevent speech criticizing the government or the armed services. The federal laws were called the Espionage Act (1917) and the Sedition Act (1918). They banned speech, or banned printed materials that suggested the draft was wrong and urged people not to serve in the Army or Navy, or banned expression that might hurt the war effort.

Loyalty vs. Dissent

A key word that would resurface over the years regarding government and the First Amendment is "loyalty." Dissent from the majority is seen as being disloyal or against the common cause.

This concern about loyalty was evident in President Woodrow Wilson's 1915 State of the Union Address:

> *"There are citizens of the United States, I blush to admit, born under other flags but welcomed under our generous naturalization laws to the full freedom and opportunity of America, who have poured the poison of disloyalty into the very arteries of our national life ... Such creatures of passion, disloyalty, and anarchy must be crushed out."*

At this time, the nations of Europe were engaged in a war that America, which was neutral, would soon enter. It was still a nation of immigrants, many of them first- or second-generation Americans with strong ties to their countries of origin. For a large number of these immigrants, their homeland was Germany, and there was great suspicion as to where their loyalties would go. As the war raged on

Figure 6-3. Woodrow Wilson

with German submarine attacks on neutral nations, anti-German sentiment ran high. It ran so high that Representative J. M. C. Smith of Michigan introduced a bill to change the names of all cities, counties, streets, and other places that had German names to American names to show loyalty to America. Towns like "Berlin" or "Germany" came to be "Liberty," "Victory," or some other patriotic designation. This carried over to food. Sauerkraut, for instance, became "liberty cabbage." It carried over to removing German-related books from schools and libraries, banning the speaking or learning of German, or the playing of music created by Germans. On top of that, many Germans in America were arrested and placed in detention centers.

It was a period of massive unrest. Newspapers were filled with stories of draft resisters and protests and clashes with government troops and local police sent in to quell them. There were endless arrests and riots, and reports of plots to blow up munitions plants and other buildings used to supply arms and ammunition from a neutral America that was, nevertheless, providing arms to the side it favored. The threats of sabotage were real, as evidenced in the July 1916 Black Tom Island explosion in Jersey City,

New Jersey, in July 1916 that caused both loss of life and millions of dollars of damage to property and war materials.

Wilson called for new laws to deal with those considered disloyal. Then on April 6, 1917, America entered the war. America's entry into World War I was hugely unpopular. It was one of the most unpopular wars the nation has fought, rivaling that of Vietnam a half century later. Still, two months later, Wilson got the new law he wanted.

The Espionage Act

The Espionage Act made it a crime for anyone, while the country is at war, to promote "disloyalty" and resistance to the war effort or give support to the enemy.

> *"Whoever, when the United States is at war, shall willfully … cause or attempt to cause insubordination, disloyalty, mutiny, refusal of duty, in the military or naval forces of the United States, or shall willfully obstruct the recruiting or enlistment service of the United States, to the injury of the service or of the United States, shall be punished by a fine of not more than $10,000 or imprisonment for not more than twenty years, or both."*
>
> *Espionage Act: Title I, Section 3*
> *June 15, 1917*

While the Espionage Act had legitimate concerns aimed at preventing and punishing saboteurs, there were many who believed it went too far in squelching the right to free speech, particularly speech that criticized the government and its policies. The law gave government agencies a long leash to pursue not just those who might be physically trying to harm the country through blowing up munitions plants and other infrastructure but also those who expressed ideas contrary to the government's war efforts. Headlines tell the story of the tension and fear of the time, as these two that ran side by side in the August 4, 1917, edition of the *Washington Times*: "War Department has troops ready to quell trouble (from anti-draft riots)" and "Plot to blow up munition(s) train is frustrated."

The Arrest of Charles Schenck

It was not just Germans who were the targets of the Espionage Act, but socialists, anarchists, Bolshevists, radicals—anyone dissenting anywhere in the country. However, to be a German and a socialist opposed to the draft during this time was like waving a red cape before a bull. So when the *Philadelphia Evening Ledger* of Wednesday, August 29, 1917, reported the arrest of Charles T. Schenck at the Philadelphia Socialist Party headquarters on Arch Street, along with the confiscation of 15,000 anti-draft circulars, he drew little sympathy. Schenck was the general secretary of the party, and his case would work its way to the Supreme Court where his name would be etched into history. What exactly was in those circulars he was distributing?

On one side were the bold-lettered words: "LONG LIVE THE CONSTITUTION OF THE UNITED STATES. Wake Up, America! Your Liberties Are in Danger!" On the other side was "ASSERT YOUR RIGHTS!"

What followed on both sides of the circular were words intended to get Americans to resist the draft:

> *"No power was delegated to send our citizens away to foreign shores to shoot up the people of other lands, no mater what may be their internal or international dispute. The people of this country did not vote in favor of war … To draw this country into the horrors of the present war in Europe, to force the youth of this land into the shambles and bloody trenches of war-crazy nations, would be a crime the magnitude of which defies description … Will you be led astray by a propaganda of jingoism masquerading under the guise of patriotism? No specious or plausible pleas about a 'war for democracy' can becloud the issue. Democracy can not be shot into a nation … a conscript is little better than a convict. He is deprived of his liberty and of his right to think and act as a free man … He is deprived of all freedom of conscience in being forced to kill against his will … Do not submit to intimidation. You have a right to demand the repeal of any law. Exercise your rights of free speech, peaceful assemblage and petitioning the government for a redress of grievances. Come to the headquarters of the Socialist Party, 1326 Arch Street, and sign a petition to Congress for the repeal of the Conscription Act. Help us wipe out this stain upon the Constitution!"*

Figure 6-4. Enlistment Poster

Copyright in the Public Domain.

Figure 6-5. U.S. Infantry Soldiers on the March During World War I

U.S. Army Signal Corps / Copyright in the Public Domain.

Over the next several years, Americans would read of the arrests of those reported to have violated the Espionage Act, as in this *Richmond Times-Dispatch* article of September 1, 1917:

> *"William Yager and wife were arrested yesterday at their home in Dumbarton by Special Federal Agent Joseph Pollard and Sheriff Sydnor, of Henrico County, on the charge of violating the Espionage Act of the United States. It is understood that Yager made statements to aid the enemies of the United States in that he had exhorted people not to comply with the draft act."*

The climate was such that citizens were being arrested all over the country for expressing in words and on paper what many took to be their First Amendment right to dissent. But the government was saying "not during wartime." There must be loyalty to the cause.

Meanwhile, the war raged in Europe with America's soldiers marching right into it. The president demanded loyalty to keep the soldiers coming.

Then, one month later, on October 6, 1917, a representative from Wisconsin took the Senate floor and delivered a passionate three-hour speech addressing the issue.

La Follette's "Free Speech in Wartime"

Senator Robert M. La Follette, Sr., of Wisconsin, was a former governor of that state and among five senators to oppose America's entry into the war, convinced that those promoting American involvement were doing so for financial gains. Because of his opposition, he was vilified with calls for his arrest for violating the Espionage Act. One judge went as far as to say that he and the others who opposed the war were traitors who should be lined up and shot. Here are passages:

> *"I have in my possession numerous affidavits establishing the fact that people are being unlawfully arrested, thrown into jail, held incommunicado for days, only to be eventually discharged without ever having been taken into court, because they have committed no crime. Private residences are being invaded, loyal citizens of undoubted integrity and probity arrested, cross-examined, and the most sacred constitutional rights guaranteed to every American citizen are being violated.*

> *"It appears to be the purpose of those conducting this campaign to throw the country into a state of terror, to coerce public opinion, to stifle criticism, and suppress discussion of the great issues involved in this war.*

> *"I think all men recognize that in time of war the citizen must surrender some rights for the common good which he is entitled to enjoy in time of peace. But sir, the right to control their own Government according to constitutional forms is not one of the rights that the citizens of this country are called upon to surrender in time of war.*

> *"More than all, the citizen and his representative in Congress in time of war must maintain his right of free speech... More than in times of peace it is necessary that the channels for free public discussion of governmental policies shall be open and unclogged. I believe, Mr. President, that I am now touching upon the most important question in this country to-day—and that is the*

Figure 6-6. Robert La Follette

right of the citizens of this country and their representatives in Congress to discuss in an orderly way frankly and publicly and without fear, from the platform and through the press, every important phase of this war ...

"I say without fear of contradiction that there has never been a time for more than a century and a half when the right of free speech and free press and the right of the people to peaceably assemble for public discussion have been so violated among English-speaking people as they are violated to-day throughout the United States. To-day, in the land we have been wont to call the free United States, governors, mayors, and policeman are preventing or breaking up peaceable meetings called to discuss the questions growing out of this war, and judges and courts, with some notable and worthy exceptions, are failing to protect the citizens in their rights.

"It is no answer to say that when the war is over the citizen may once more resume his rights and feel some security in his liberty and his person ... now is precisely the time when the country needs the counsel of all its citizens. In time of war even more than in time of peace ...

"It is the citizen's duty to obey the law until it is repealed or declared unconstitutional. But he has the inalienable right to fight what he deems an obnoxious law or a wrong policy in the courts and at the ballot box."

His speech has been regarded as a classic oratorical argument for free speech during wartime, and he would, in later years, be recognized as one of the great senators because of it. However, at the time, anger and personal attacks intensified. Senator Joseph Robinson, of Arkansas, was so incensed he reportedly needed to be restrained from attacking La Follette as he spoke. In a rebuttal, Robinson questioned La Follette's loyalty and suggested he resign from the Senate, saying he would be best served with the Kaiser in Germany. There were calls for his expulsion. An investigation was also begun. Headlines across the country attacked him fiercely, such as this one in the next day's *New York Sun*:

"LA FOLLETTE IN 2-HOUR SPEECH ANGERS SENATE," "Avalanche of Bitter Criticism Follows Fightin' Bob's 'Defence.'" "CHEERS FOR HIS FOES," "Men Who Betray Their Flag Had

Better Seek Cover'—Robinson." "RESIGNATION DEMANDED," "Pro-Germanism in Congress Inquiry Is to Be Started To-morrow."

The newspaper editorials also lined up against him, as did this one in the *Washington Times* two days after his speech.

> *"Senator Robinson was right. It is inconceivable that any member of the highly endowed Upper House of the American Congress could speak for upward of three hours upon a subject of American welfare and not give expression to sincere and thorough love for country … [he failed] to denote loyalty and allegiance to America and its institutions and its flag. … God save this country from its La Follettes."*

Life would be hell for La Follette and his family. Few wanted to risk the wrath that came with siding or associating with him. Charges against him would be dropped a few years later, but until then, the campaign against dissenters continued.

A November 9, 1917, *Tacoma Times* story described the arrest of bookstore manager Franz Bostrom, "prominent socialist of Tacoma."

> *"Complaints had been made that he was exhibiting anti-war literature and pictures. A cartoon in his window, labeled 'The New Freedom,' and showing Uncle Sam horsewhipping Americans into an armed fortress while 'Justice' was tied to a post, was seized by the officers."*

The climate of heightened tensions, fear, and anger kept ratcheting up. A new law would soon take things to another level.

The Sedition Act of 1918

The Sedition Act punished anyone for publishing or speaking anything critical, profane, or disloyal about the government, its policies, symbols or institutions:

> *"… Whoever, when the United States is at war, shall willfully utter, print, write or publish any disloyal, profane, scurrilous, or abusive language about the form of government of the United States or the Constitution of the United States, or the military or naval forces of the United States, or the flag of the United States, or the uniform of the Army or Navy of the United States into contempt, scorn, contumely, or disrepute, or shall willfully utter, print, write, or publish any language intended to incite, provoke, or encourage resistance to the United States, or to promote the cause of its enemies, or shall willfully display the flag of any foreign enemy, or shall willfully by utterance, writing, printing, publication, or language spoken, urge, incite, or advocate any curtailment of production in this country of any thing or things, product or products, necessary or essential to the prosecution of the war in which the United States may be engaged, with intent by such curtailment to cripple or hinder the United States in the prosecution of war, and whoever shall willfully advocate, teach, defend, or suggest the doing of any of the acts or things in this section enumerated, and whoever shall by word or act support or favor the cause of any country with which the United States is at war or by word or act oppose the cause of the United States therein, shall be punished by a fine of*

Figure 6-7. Justice Oliver Wendell Holmes

not more than $10,000 or the imprisonment for not more than twenty years, or both."

Sedition Act
May 16, 1918

Schenck v. United States

Before the case would go to the U.S. Supreme Court, Charles Schenck, who under the law faced a fine of $10,000 and 20 years in prison, was given six months in the Mercer County jail. The person tried with him, Dr. Elizabeth Baer, who had a medical practice, was sentenced to 90 days.

In the *Philadelphia Evening Ledger* of March 12, 1918, just a day after receiving her sentence, Baer expressed no regret, and the sympathetically written piece referred to "a Joan of Arc quality about this gray-haired woman of fragile physique, whose life has yet been one of inveterate labor."

"Would I do it again? Most assuredly! …I am fighting for a principle and am prepared to pay the price—prison if necessary … I stand for three things I am proud to have my name allied with—socialism, suffrage and humanity," she declared.

The case, which bore Schenck's name but involved Baer as well, went to the Supreme Court on January 9, 1919, less than two months after the armistice was signed, ending all fighting. On March 3, 1919, four months before the Treaty of Versailles officially ended the war, the Court reached a unanimous decision. It upheld the lower court's conviction under the Espionage Act, although it avoided acting on the validity of the Act.

Justice Oliver Wendell Holmes, in delivering the ruling said: "We admit that in many places and in ordinary times the defendants in saying all that was said in the circular would have been within the constitutional rights. But the character of every act depends upon the circumstances in which it is done."

In this ruling, the Court also sailed right past La Follette's argument before the Senate two years earlier.

"When a nation is at war," Holmes said, "many things that might be said in time of peace are such a hindrance to its effort that their utterance will not be endured so long as men fight and that no Court could regard them as protected by any constitutional right."

In explaining the decision, he said that while people have free speech, there are limitations. Free speech does not grant one carte blanche to "falsely [shout] 'Fire'" in a theater. Despite this memorable phrase, it is another phrase that particularly related to the Court's ruling. Those words are "clear and present danger." Specifically, Holmes said, "The question in every case is whether the words are used in such circumstances and are of such a nature as to create a clear and present danger that they will bring about the substantive evils that Congress has a right to prevent."

Debs v. United States

On June 30, 1918, in Cleveland, Ohio, U.S. marshals arrested Eugene V. Debs, four-time Socialist Party candidate for the presidency of the United States. The arrest came two weeks after he delivered an anti-war speech at the State Convention of the Ohio Socialist Party in Canton, Ohio. During his speech he said the purpose of the war was "plunder" and the working class should not be "cannon fodder."

Following are excerpts:

"Wars throughout history have been waged for conquest and plunder. ... The master class has always declared the wars; the subject class has always fought the battles ... They have always taught and trained you to believe it to be your patriotic duty to go to war and to have yourselves slaughtered at their command ... and it cannot be repeated too often—that the working class who fight all the battles, the working class who make the supreme sacrifices, the working class who freely shed their blood and furnish the corpses, have never yet had a voice in either declaring war or making peace. It is the ruling class that invariably does both. They alone declare war and they alone make peace ... yours not to reason why, yours to do or die ... That is their motto and we object on the part of the awakening workers of this nation. If war is right let it be declared by the people. You who have your lives to lose, you certainly above all others have the right to decide the momentous issue of war or peace."

Figure 6-8. Eugene V. Debs

Said Edwin Wertz, the attorney representing the government following Debs' arrest: "No man is too big to be held responsible for his acts under the Espionage Act or any other law of the United States." Added Assistant Attorney Joseph Breitenstein: "Mr. Debs was indicted, not as a Socialist, but as a violator of the law of the United States because of things he said in his Canton speech."

Newspaper editorials, such as the July 3, 1918, edition of the *Washington Herald,* offered no solace: "Except in some pro-German cities, we do not believe that much sympathy will be wasted upon Mr. Debs … In time of war especially [the laws] mean exactly what they say."

On September 12, a Cleveland court found him guilty of violating the Espionage Act. At the next day's sentencing, he received 10 years from the judge who also offered this parting shot, as reported in the *Philadelphia Evening Public Ledger* of September 14: "Any one who strikes the sword from the hand of those young men or causes another young man to refuse to do his duty when called to serve by their side, or any one who obstructs the recruiting service, does just as much injury and wrong to our country as if he were a soldier in the ranks of the German army."

After the Cleveland court's ruling, Debs appealed his case to the Supreme Court. On March 10, 1919, the Court upheld the lower court's ruling, once again ruling unanimously, as in Schenck's case, with Justice Holmes again delivering the Court's opinion. Holmes, however, would have a change of heart in the next case involving free speech during wartime.

Abrams v. United States

The U.S. marshals and deputies kept coming and arresting, and still the dissent kept coming, not always directed at the government's war and draft policy. Shortly after Debs' arrest, pamphlets began fluttering from the rooftops of New York City's densely populated East Side attacking President Woodrow Wilson and the U.S. policy toward the Russian Bolshevists. In late August, following a riot the day before, Justice Department agents, military police, and New York City detectives tracked the source of the pamphlets to a house and arrested seven people. All of them were Russian immigrants in the country less than eight years. One of them was Jacob Abrams, a paper cutter.

"Copies of seditious pamphlets were found, as well as copies of *Blast*, an anarchist publication," said the *New York Sun* of August 25, 1918. The pamphlets were titled, "The Hypocrisy of the United States and Her Allies" and denounced America and allied troop intervention in Russia. It called President Wilson a "hypocrite" and a "coward" before adding, "The Russian revolution cries: Workers of the World—awake, arise, put down your enemies and mine."

At the arraignment several weeks later, the September 13 edition of the *Sun* described the interaction between one of the arrestees, Mollie Steimer, who said the indictments were an attack on free speech, and the judge, who replied: "Freedom of speech does not protect disloyalty. I am sorry for the people of New York because they have to deal with people who have no more conception of what free government means than a William goat has of the Gospel."

One month later, the seven defendants would be reduced to six after one of them died in the hospital several weeks after an alleged beating by police seeking to find out where the pamphlets had been printed.

At the trial, Abrams, testifying for himself and the other defendants, argued that as there was no declared war in the U.S. intervention in Russia, there was no violation of the Espionage or Sedition Act. The court ruled otherwise, finding five of the six guilty. Abrams received 20 years and a $1,000 fine. Combined, the five received 75 years and $4,500 in fines. On November 4, 1918, they applied for bail from the U.S. Supreme Court, asserting, again, their right to free speech, arguing that the language in their pamphlets was "no more bitter perhaps than is the language used by the Republicans in their campaign," and it was not used to aid Germany. The Court granted their appeal and they were released on bail. A year later, on November 11, 1919, the Supreme Court would uphold their conviction, saying the words of the pamphlet were "clearly an appeal to the 'workers' of this country to arise and put down by force the Government of the United States." "This," the court held, "is not an attempt to bring about a change of administration by candid discussion … the manifest purpose of such a publication was to create an attempt to defeat the war programme of the Government of the United States. …"

Unlike the Schenck and Debs cases, this was not a unanimous ruling. Justices Louis Brandeis and Oliver Wendell Holmes dissented. Said Holmes:

> *"But as against dangers peculiar to war, as against others, the principle of the right to free speech is always the same. It is only the present danger of immediate evil or an intent to bring it about that warrants Congress in setting a limit to the expression of opinion where private rights are not concerned. Congress certainly cannot forbid all efforts to change the mind of the country.*
>
> *"In this case, sentences of twenty years' imprisonment have been imposed for the publishing of two leaflets that I believe the defendant has as much right to publish as the Government has to publish the Constitution of the United States, now vainly invoked by them.*
>
> *"… we should be eternally vigilant against attempts to check the expression of opinions that we loathe and believe to be fraught with death unless they so imminently threaten immediate interference with the lawful and pressing purposes of the law that an immediate check is required to save the country."*

Amid these three cases, and despite the cessation of hostilities with the end of World War I, there remained a tense, explosive situation in America. Americans feared Russians and the revolution. They feared the radicals, the Bolshevists, the anarchists, the socialists, the foreigners; and, in the middle of it all, was the antagonism with America's blacks, then called Negroes, with lynchings and race riots breaking out in major cities during the so-called Red Summer of 1919, remembered for the blood that was shed.

The End of the Espionage and Sedition Acts?

The Espionage Act and the Sedition Act would lead to the arrests of over 2,000 people. The Sedition Act was repealed by Congress in 1920. The Espionage Act remains in effect though its power has been restricted by legislation and court decisions. The passions that led to the enactment of these two bills, however, continue.

Gitlow v. New York

On a Saturday night in New York, federal agents raided 71 Communist Party headquarters in New York, arresting nearly 1,000 radicals. Over 950 were released, according to the *New York Tribune* of

Figure 6-9. Benjamin Gitlow

Copyright in the Public Domain.

November 10, 1919, in a story reported the next day. One who was not released was Benjamin Gitlow, a former Socialist Party New York assemblyman who was charged with being a communist leader. Two revolvers and six cartridges were reportedly found in his home, which also served as his office. James Larkin, described as "an agitator for Irish freedom who helped form the Left Wing branch of Socialist Party," was also among those not released.

They were arrested for violating New York State's anti-anarchy laws by publishing a magazine titled *The Revolutionary Age*, which government counsels said "advises, advocates, and teaches the doctrine that organized government should be overthrown by force and violence or by unlawful means." In particular, they would focus on the article, "The Left Wing Manifesto."

Said Chief Magistrate William McAdoo in the *New York Tribune* of November 15, 1919: "Well-meaning gentlemen tell us that we should not interfere with the incendiary when he is preparing the torch; we should only apprehend him when he is setting fire to the building. This statute is a preventative measure. It is intended to head off those mad and cruel men at the beginning of their careers. It is intended to put out a fire with a bucket of water which might later on not yield to the contents of the reservoir."

Addressing the New York jury in the trial court in early February 1920, Gitlow, who served as the business agent for the publication, acknowledged that in the eyes of society he was a revolutionary.

"I wish you to realize that I believe in these principles," he said, as reported in the February 5, 1920, edition of the *New York Tribune*. "I will fight for these principles. My life is devoted to them. I ask no clemency. Regardless of your verdict, I maintain these principles are correct."

The next day, the jury returned its verdict: He was found guilty of advocating in his magazine for the overthrow of the government. Judge Bartow Weeks addressed the jury, thanking them, and adding: "There must be a right for this organized state to protect itself. If citizens who accept the benefit of organized government do not recognize the government that protects them can only be overthrown by lawful means, then it is difficult to see how civilization can be maintained."

Gitlow was sentenced to five to 10 years in Sing-Sing, part of it as hard labor. In November 1922, the Supreme Court agreed to review his case. Three years later, in June 1925, the Supreme Court upheld his conviction. Justices Holmes and Brandeis again dissented, with Holmes saying there was no immediate danger that Gitlow's publication would lead to an overthrow. Several months later in December, New York's Governor Al Smith pardoned Gitlow, saying he'd been punished enough.

The 14th Amendment

The Court, in a small portion of its decision in *Gitlow v. New York*, made a major change in the way future courts could judge laws that might infringe on the First Amendment. Gitlow had argued that the 14th Amendment, passed right after the Civil War to prevent states from treating former slaves unequally, and its so-called "due process" clause, applied to First Amendment cases. That is, no state could pass a law that set First Amendment rights at a level below the rights granted under the federal Constitution. That one small part of the court's opinion has had a major impact on First Amendment cases since 1925. It means that states and municipal governments must respect freedom of speech, press, and religion.

Figure 6-10. Charlotte Anita Whitney

Copyright in the Public Domain.

Whitney v. United States

Similar to the Gitlow case, *Whitney v. United States* (1927) involved free speech pertaining to overthrowing the government. Justice Louis Brandeis, despite concurring with upholding the conviction of Anita Whitney for violating a California law that made it a crime to help establish a group whose goal was the violent overthrow of the government, wrote powerful words in defense of free speech:

> *"Men feared witches and burnt women. It is the function of speech to free men from the bondage of irrational fears.*

> *"Those who won our independence by revolution were not cowards. They did not fear political change. They did not exalt order at the cost of liberty. To courageous, self-reliant men, with confidence in the power of free and fearless reasoning applied through the processes of popular government, no danger flowing from speech can be deemed clear and present, unless the incidence of the evil apprehended is so imminent that it may befall before there is opportunity for full discussion. If there be time to expose through discussion the falsehood and fallacies, to avert the evil by the processes of education, the remedy to be applied is more speech, not enforced silence."*

Pearl Harbor and Japanese Americans

The major fear of Americans during time of war or conflict has been the loyalties of recent immigrants from the very nations with which America might go to war. This heightened even more following the

Figure 6-11. Japanese Plane Attacking Pearl Harbor

Japanese attack on Pearl Harbor. The December 7, 1941, attack left nearly 2,400 Americans dead, nearly 1,200 wounded, and plunged America into the Second World War.

As with the Germans in America during World War I, the fear was that these Japanese living in America would be loyal to their home country and spy against the United States. Unlike the German immigrants, who could visibly blend with the general white population, the Japanese were of a different racial group from the majority and stood out because of their physical features.

Three months after Pearl Harbor, President Franklin D. Roosevelt signed Executive Order 9066, effectively removing 120,000 Japanese Americans from their homes and into internment camps. Not only was movement restricted but so was freedom of speech. Only decades later in the 1990s, did the U.S. government make amends to its Japanese American citizens for taking away not just their liberty but also their land and other property.

The Smith Act

Prior to the start of World War II, America was still focused on rooting out communism, socialism, or any form of radicalism that advocated overthrowing the government. Following the war, the United States became embroiled in another kind of war: the Cold War. The American government's objective in the Cold War was to stop the spread of communism around the globe. In the late 1940s, Senator Joseph McCarthy began attempting to root out alleged communists and their sympathizers from government as well as parts of private society, including universities, Hollywood, radio, TV, and the publishing industry. The Alien Registration Act of 1940, better known as the Smith Act (named for its author, Representative Howard W. Smith of Virginia), made it unlawful to not only advocate the overthrow of the government but to be a member of a group that advocated such a belief. Said the Act:

Figure 6-12. Roy Takeno, editor of the Manzanar Free Press, reads his paper in front of the newspaper office at the Manzanar War Relocation Center. He was one of thousands of Japanese-Americans sent to internment camps after the Japanese attack at Pearl Harbor.

Ansel Adams / Library of Congress.

> *"Whoever knowingly or willfully advocates, abets, advises, or teaches the duty, necessity, desirability, or propriety of overthrowing or destroying the government of the United States or the government of any State, Territory, District or Possession thereof, or the government of any political subdivision therein, by force or violence, or by the assassination of any officer of any such government; or*

> *"Whoever, with intent to cause the overthrow or destruction of any such government, prints, publishes, edits, issues, circulates, sells, distributes, or publicly displays any written or printed matter advocating, advising, or teaching the duty, necessity, desirability, or propriety of overthrowing or destroying any government in the United States by force or violence, or attempts to do so; or*

> *"Whoever organizes or helps or attempts to organize any society, group, or assembly of persons who teach, advocate, or encourage the overthrow or destruction of any such government by force or violence; or becomes or is a member of, or affiliates with, any such society, group, or assembly of persons, knowing the purposes thereof—*

> *"Shall be fined under this title or imprisoned not more than twenty years, or both, and shall be ineligible for employment by the United States or any department or agency thereof, for the five years next following his conviction."*

In the late 1940s and into the 1950s, it was common to see headlines such as this one in the July 21, 1948, *Gettysburg Times:* "Twelve Communist leaders, representing the Party's high command in America, were under indictment today on charges of advocating the violent overthrow of the United States government."

Or this from the *Portsmouth (New Hampshire) Herald* of September 17, 1952: "The Justice Department announced today the arrest of 18 Midwest and West Coast Communist Party leaders on charges of conspiring to advocate overthrow of the government by force and violence."

The names would follow. And if any "Negroes" (using the common reference of the time) were involved, that information would be mentioned as well. Though blacks were few in number in the Communist Party in America, the charge of being communist-inspired and driven would be a common early accusation leveled at civil rights organizations of the 1950s and 1960s.

The depth of fear grew, particularly in the early 1950s, when a senator from Wisconsin, Joseph McCarthy, began accusing people of being communists. A charge such as this adversely affected everyday Americans, as well as prominent politicians and actors and anyone who refused before a Congressional committee to identify those whom they knew to be communists.

Such arrests would appear regularly in the news of that time. One person who remembers it on a personal level is Alfred Marder, 93, of New Haven, Connecticut. On May 29, 1954, FBI agents arrested Marder, then 32 and chairman of the New Haven section of the Communist Party, on charges of teaching and advocating the overthrow of the US government. At the time, he, along with the seven others arrested in Connecticut and New York, were among the 109 people who had been arrested under the Smith Act since July 1948.

Said Marder in an interview on November 21, 2014: "On one Saturday morning I had an apron on and I was cleaning the house and the FBI came, arrested me and nine others as a violation of the Smith Act. Now people have to know what the Smith Act was. The Smith Act was a conspiracy to teach. It wasn't necessarily to prove any act. It was what you talked about and what you taught was the overthrow or conspiracy to overthrow the US government. I was arrested. Jailed for a little while. Bailed out. And then (five) months—a trial on the Smith Act. And all they produced during that whole (five) months were witnesses that read excerpts from books from Karl Marx, from Lenin, from other eminent Communists and scholars to prove that that's what we were doing. In all (five) months not one witness was able to say that I either taught or used the language that was in any way connected (to a conspiracy to overthrow the government). So I was eventually acquitted. I was the only one in the United States that was acquitted (by a jury) in the Smith Act."

He noted that others were acquitted after appeals, but he was the only one acquitted by a jury.

Figure 6-13. Alfred L. Marder, 93, of New Haven, Conn., describes his experience of being arrested and tried under the Smith Act during the McCarthy Era of the 1950s.

Photo courtesy of Frank Harris III.

He remembers the difficulty of finding lawyers to take the case, which had him knocking on doors and, as noted in the September 24, 1954, edition of the Bridgeport Telegram ("Accused State Reds Appeal for Lawyers") sending mimeographs (copies) of letters of appeal to hundreds of lawyers.

"This trial," said Marder, "was part of the whole McCarthy period. This was to create the atmosphere that we were spies and we weren't people who were involved in the struggle here for a better life. They were out to isolate the Communists just as they did the trade unionists of that period and anyone connected with—this was the same

Figure 6-14. March on Washington

Rowland Scherman / Copyright in the Public Domain.

road with (Paul) Robeson and (W. E. B.) DuBois and others because you had to smash the people's struggles. You had to isolate them from the community and so you can do what you want to with them. So that was the issue. So those who were willing to stand up and fight had to be eliminated."

The Supreme Court in Yates v. United States 354 U.S. 298 (1957) would restrict the application of the Smith Act to the actual instigation of acts to overthrow the government, rather than words that advocate or teach it as an abstract principle or doctrine. This led to the federal courts throwing out the convictions of those charged under the act, including the five convicted in New Haven.

The 1960s was a turbulent time in the United States. There were civil rights protests and demonstrations, including the huge "March on Washington" in 1963 that gave us Martin Luther King's "I Have A Dream" speech. As the U.S. involvement in Vietnam expanded, there were constant protests around the country, both against and for the war. Some protested military service by burning their draft cards in public. The Supreme Court eventually ruled against that tactic. (See Chapter 8.)

There were occasions where protestors burned the American flag. There were major riots in several American cities, including Los Angeles (the Watts section), Detroit, Newark, and Washington, D.C. The Women's Rights movement was renewed through demonstrations and press reports.

The assertion of rights by gays and lesbians began to percolate in the culture. The courts actually expanded several First Amendment freedoms during this period, rather than restrict them as it had during other periods of national strife.

The Patriot Act

When two hijacked American commercial jets were crashed into New York's twin towers on September 11, 2001, it sent a chill through Americans like none before. While the attack on Pearl

Figure 6-15. World Trade Center on September 11

Harbor 60 years earlier shocked the nation, it occurred away from the American mainland, and aside from a few iconic photographs, Americans were shielded from the carnage.

The attack that came to be known as 9/11, however, was captured in real-time with both video and still cameras. The nation saw people die right before its eyes, and heard of more carnage at the Pentagon and a field in Pennsylvania, short of what many believe was the intended target, the White House.

In 1941, the attackers were from Japan, which led to a wave of suspicion directed against Japanese Americans living in America on the West Coast. In 2001, the attackers were from the Middle East. What would be the government's reaction to the nation's citizens of Arab descent and Islamic faith? What would be the people's reaction?

On September 20, 2001, President George W. Bush delivered a speech to the American people before the Joint Session of Congress. Among the words he presented were the following: "The enemy of America is not our many Muslim friends. It is not our many Arab friends. Our enemy is a radical network of terrorists and every government that supports them."

It was the government's response that set the tone for the nation. It did not mean that Arabs and those of the Muslim faith were not stopped and searched more closely and that rights were not violated. But it set the tone away from a repeat of what occurred after Pearl Harbor.

Still, throughout America's history, there have been events that have tested the commitment of the nation's government and people to its Constitution and democratic principles in many areas of life, particularly the First Amendment. The events of 9/11 would bring about the same:

> *"… As of today, we're changing the laws governing information-sharing … we're changing the culture of our various agencies that fight terrorism. The existing law was written in the era of rotary telephones. This new law that I sign today will allow surveillance of all communications used by terrorists, including e-mails, the Internet, and cell phones …*
>
> *"… This legislation is essential not only to pursuing and punishing terrorists but also preventing more atrocities in the hands of the evil ones. This government will enforce this law with all the urgency of a nation at war."*
>
> *President George W. Bush*
> *Remarks at signing of Patriot Act, Anti-Terrorism Legislation*
> *October 26, 2001*

Since the Patriot Act of 2001, there has been considerable debate as to whether laws quickly passed one month after the attack gave too much power to the president, leading to encroachments on Americans' civil liberties. Much of the debate centered on government surveillance.

For instance, should a citizen's books and other material checked from a public library, as well as Internet searches conducted on a computer in a public library, be subject to government scrutiny? This leads to other considerations, such as whether the awareness that one's readings and research can be subject to government surveillance serves as a de facto prior restraint on an individual's quest for knowledge and information? If so, does that restricted quest for knowledge and information weaken what each individual can contribute to the marketplace of ideas?

With this new law came the challenge of balancing safety with civil liberties. How much of one's right to privacy should a citizen be asked or required to surrender to ensure the safety of the greater public and individual good?

How does this affect our First Amendment right of free expression?

The effect of knowing your emails, phone calls, Internet searches, and a host of other records are accessible—if not at the moment, then at some point in the future—can have a chilling effect that stifles free expression. Of course, there is the argument that if you have nothing to hide, then why not throw open the doors to privacy and let the government in? Indeed, with our increased connection to the Internet, smart phones, and other electronic devices that are in turn accessed by commercial companies—our interests, associations, purchases, and connections are already out there.

If privacy is an illusion, then is free speech also a thing of the past?

In June 2013, 12 years after The Patriot Act, government contractor Edward Snowden, along with several others, released classified information about America's National Security Agency surveillance programs. The NSA, it was revealed, was collecting and making records of every citizen's phone calls in the United States. The government was outraged at the security breach, which some considered treason. Snowden, fearing prosecution, fled the country. Others were outraged that their privacy had been violated and hailed Snowden as a hero in the same vein as Daniel Ellsberg, who released the Pentagon Papers in 1971. However Snowden is regarded, the release of the classified information led to an appeal court ruling in May 2015 that the NSA's mass collection of Americans' phone records was an overreach of what was originally intended when the Patriot Act was passed. A month later, after much debate, lawmakers from different political spectrums voted to block the renewal of the Patriot Act.

USA Freedom Act

This Act evolved from the Patriot Act. It has been hailed by some as safeguarding Americans' civil liberties while at the same time working against terrorism. On the other side of the coin, others have insisted the Act does not go far enough in protecting Americans' civil liberties. Still others say it makes America vulnerable to terrorists.

The Act now bans the mass collection of phone records by the federal government. But phone companies must keep the records for a period of time and the government can get a court order to see a record if it believes there is a national security risk. The change indicates Americans' willingness to step from under the shadows of the fear caused by the attacks of Sept. 11, 2001, but the debate over privacy versus government surveillance under the banner of counter-terrorism will undoubtedly continue.

Exercises

1. When did a major First Amendment issue first reach the Supreme Court?
2. What was U.S. society like in the first part of the 20th Century?
3. What did the Espionage Act of 1917 and the Sedition Act of 1918 ban?
4. The first time the Supreme Court seriously considered whether a prosecution for sedition violated the First Amendment was in 1919 in a case involving Charles Schenck. Describe what led to his prosecution.
5. What famous words did Justice Oliver Wendell Holmes use in expressing his views about Schenck's First Amendment rights to print words critical of the government and its policies? The words became tied with American sedition law for years.
6. True or false. Holmes modified his position in cases that followed Schenck.
7. Who was Eugene V. Debs and why was he prosecuted?
8. Who was Benjamin Gitlow and what did he say that got him convicted?
9. What amendment did Gitlow claim in his defense, which said "no state shall deprive any person of life, liberty, or property without due process of law"?
10. What did the Smith Act of 1940 make it a crime to do?
11. What were some of the issues being protested during the 1960s?
12. When was the Patriot Act passed in the United States, and what did it do?
13. What is the name of the new Act that followed after the Patriot Act was not renewed in spring 2015?

For Critical Discussion or Writing

1. Should a person be able to say what he or she wants to say without fear of being arrested?
2. Years ago, there was a book that provided instructions on how to be a hitman. Should such a book be allowed to be published?
3. Should citizens be able to criticize the president or government policies in times of national crises?
4. Take a position for or against Robert La Follette's "Free Speech in Wartime."
5. Should speech on the Internet be controlled by government because too many people get hurt by online rumors today?

PART IV
Press

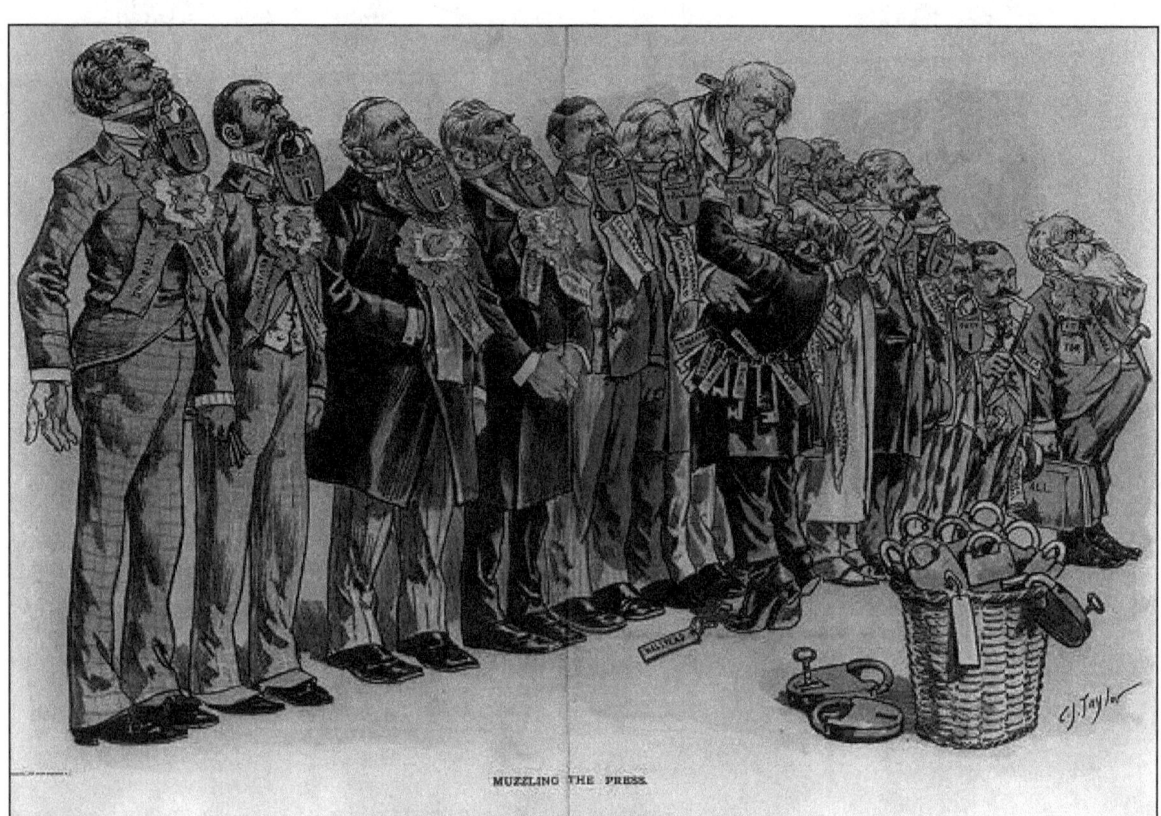

MUZZLING THE PRESS.

President Benjamin Harrison Placing Muzzles on Various Newsmen, 1889

CHAPTER 7

The Right to a Free Press

America's Press: Born Not Free

The first government actions to weaken the press in America came when the nation was under British colonial rule and the First Amendment was 101 years away. A newspaper needed a license and permission to publish, with the understanding that anything published would not criticize governmental authority. So America's press was born not free. This was hammered home when America's first newspaper, *Publick Occurrences Both Domestick and Forreign*, violated this understanding and, as noted in an earlier chapter, was shut down after one issue.

The First Amendment—with its provision that Congress shall make no law abridging the freedom of the press—clearly provided for press freedom among the five freedoms covered. While there are protections, freedom, as it relates to the press, has always been relative. Is that the way it should be? Unless one believes in the Absolutist Theory, should there not be some limitations placed on the press? When? How long? What kind? These are some of the questions that arise when government seeks to slap restrictions on the press, and the press seeks to summon forth a reminder of the Constitution's First Amendment.

The Sedition Act of 1798 and the Press

America's newspapers reached people in distant places, including England, where the people of that nation kept abreast of what was going on in its former colonies. One month after passage of the Sedition Act, *The London Evening Mail* of August 13, 1798, wrote:

"American papers have been received in town to the 6th (of this month) by which it appears, that a Bill, formed on the principle of the Treason and Sedition Acts, which have produced such beneficial effects in this country (England) has been brought into the American Senate, to prevent conspiracies against Government and Legislature of the United States, and to restrain the licentiousness of the press.

Several months later, *The London Observer* of January 27, 1799, noted that petitions were presented to Congress against the Alien and Sedition Acts based on the principle that Congress forbade any laws to abridge free speech or the liberty of the press. What followed was a bill passed that would allow state judges to "discharge persons" arrested under the Sedition Act.

The *Maryland Gazette* (Annapolis), noting the opposition to the Sedition Act in its July 3, 1800 edition, said the Act provided government with a power that was not granted by the Constitution, and one that was "expressly and positively forbidden" by the First Amendment that "leveled against the right of freely examining public characters and measures, and of free communication thereon; which has ever been justly deemed the only effectual guardian of every other right."

Newspaper editors were frequent targets of the Sedition Act. After the Act was allowed to expire on March 3, 1801, many editors reflected on how it had affected them, as in this September 13, 1802, note in *The North-Carolina Journal*: "It is known that one of the editors of this paper was condemned under the Sedition Act, to pay a fine of $200."

The act drew loud criticism. President John Adams, who signed the Sedition Act, saw his reputation severely damaged by its passage. Most historians believe it was one of the main reasons that Adams lost the presidency to Thomas Jefferson in 1800.

The Sedition Act was gone, but not before leaving an indelible mark on the idea that freedom of the press was absolute and untouchable.

The Press During the Civil War

The press played an important role during the Civil War by providing Americans with news of the war. News reporters would accompany the troops on various campaigns, writing about what they witnessed on the battlefield.

The generals read the newspapers and were aware of how they were perceived or would be perceived. This was evident in General Thomas West Sherman's message to Major General George B. McClellan on January 2, 1862, as noted in *The War of the Rebellion: a Compilation of the Official Records of the Union and Confederate Armies:* "… I must act militarily, and not to please the superficial nonsensical views of the public press, by which I have been soundly berated for not playing the militiaman and egotistical soldier."

The soldiers and politicians of both the North and South read each other's papers to gauge what the other side was doing militarily, as in this message from Confederate General G. T. Beauregard to General Samuel Cooper on May 20, 1863: "I have observed a newspaper reference to important changes on foot in the North in the armament of the monitors, which I apprehend deserve some considerations on our side."

Figure 7-1. New York Herald Tribune Reporters in the Field

Copyright in the Public Domain.

Figure 7-2. President Lincoln Visiting General McClelland and Troops

Copyright in the Public Domain.

Figure 7-3. Confederate Gen. Pierre G.T. Beauregard kept abreast of the news in Northern newspapers.

Figure 7-4. Simon Cameron, U.S. Secretary of War

They also followed the newspapers to assess the morale of soldiers and citizens and a range of other doings on the other side—all solid reasons for the respective governments to place restrictions on the press to ensure it did not print anything to harm morale or reveal military information that might be useful to the enemy.

The other reason was to avoid negative criticism of the government's policy.

In *Abraham Lincoln and Press Suppression Reconsidered*, author David Bulla cited the Civil War as the time of the largest newspaper suppression in America's history. The suppression was greater in the North, where anti-war sentiment was strong, than in the South, where those opposed to the war generally yielded to community censorship. In the North there were numerous Copperhead newspapers and citizens to read them. (Copperhead referred to the snake that sneaks and strikes without warning. In this context, it referred to citizens in the North who sympathized with the South, opposed the war, and/or favored a negotiated settlement with the South.) While both the North and South demanded strict loyalty from the press, the North accounted for the larger share of the more than 300 newspapers that were shut down during the Civil War.

Figure 7-5. Allan Pinkerton and Men

The North kept close tabs on newspapers with questionable loyalty, as noted in this message from David H. Carr, a U.S. Marshal in New Haven, Connecticut, to Simon Cameron, Secretary of War, on September 11, 1861:

> *"I have stopped the sale, keeping for sale or circulation of that damnable secession sheet the* New York Daily News *in the State of Connecticut."*

The aforementioned message was one of many found in *The War of the Rebellion: a Compilation of the Official Records of the Union and Confederate Armies* that was assembled in the years after the Civil War.

Two days later, shortly after midnight in Baltimore, Maryland, federal agents, under the orders of Secretary of State William Seward, arrested Francis Key Howard, an editor of the *Baltimore Exchange* newspaper, and T. W. Hall, of *The South* newspaper, for making what were deemed disloyal comments in their respective papers. Their homes were searched, as were their editorial offices. Allan Pinkerton, head of the Union's Intelligence Service, (the forerunner of the U.S. Secret Service) oversaw the arrest.

"I construed the order to search for and seize correspondence of a treasonable nature in the possession of the parties arrested," said Pinkerton in a message to Secretary of State Seward, "[as] sufficient warrant for me to enter and search the editorial and press rooms of the *Exchange* and *South*."

Key Howard, the grandson of Francis Scott Key, who wrote the *Star Spangled Banner*, would spend 14 months in jail. He documented his experience in his book, *Fourteen Months in the American Bastille*.

> *"We saw that Mr. Lincoln desired, by arbitrary measures to silence everything like opposition to his schemes and we felt under obligation to thwart his iniquitous project ... it was the duty of each of us ... to continue to denounce and protest against Mr. Lincoln's proceedings."*

When the Union Army took New Orleans, it issued a proclamation on May 1, 1862, that forbade any newspaper, handbill, or pamphlet from describing troop movements, or writing anything that spoke ill of the federal government. It also required all articles of war news, editorial comments, and correspondence to be submitted for approval before publication.

But the South had its own suppression of the press, as noted by this general order from Confederate Major Manning Marius Kimmell on July 4, 1862:

> *"The publication of any article in the newspapers in reference to the movements of the troops is prohibited, and if the editor or proprietor of any newspaper published in any of the counties herein before designated shall publish any editorial article or copy into his paper any article or paragraph calculated to impair confidence in any of the commanding officers whom the President may see fit to place over the troops, such editor or proprietor shall be subject to fine and imprisonment, and the publication of the paper shall be thereafter suspended."*

While it was understandable why both war departments would forbid newspaper editors and publishers from reporting information about troop movements, much of the clampdown had to do with criticism of the government and/or its policies. It is interesting that both governments had citizens and soldiers under surveillance to note what they were writing and speaking, to whom they were writing and speaking, and in what activities they were engaged. This involved reading newspapers, attending meetings and speeches, and following suspected disloyal persons, as evident in this dispatch from May 8, 1861, to Captain George L. Hartsuff at Key West:

> *"The newspaper called the* Key of the Gulf *I suppressed, because it was uttering treasonable and threatening language against the judiciary and other United States officers. I directed the mayor to inform the editor (a Mr. Ward) that he was under military surveillance, and that the fact of his not being in the cells of this fort for treason was simply a matter as to expediency and proper point of time."*

And this from the New Haven marshal:

> *"There is on the Naugatuck Railroad a newspaper traveling agent by the name of George A. Hubbell, a noisy secessionist, in a spot where he is doing great mischief by his treasonable talk, and also by his disobedience of this wholesome order of our Government ... all I want is an order from yourself or Seward to arrest and take him to some of the forts in New York."*

The government's suppression of newspapers on both sides of the Mason-Dixon Line clearly shows that the Civil War was fought not just on the battlefields but in the pages of the newspapers. For journalists, the prospect of being charged with disloyalty over something they wrote had a chilling effect on their reporting, which, in turn, meant that the public was denied full and accurate information from which to participate in the market of ideas on the important topic of war and peace. When the Civil War ended with Lee's surrender at Appomattox Courthouse, the press would again face restrictions in the new century with the First World War.

The Press and World War I

World War I was described as "The War in to End all Wars." Obviously, it did not quite work out that way; wars have continued to march through the footsteps of time with no end in sight. And the press? Well, if the Civil War involved the most press restrictions in America's history, then the restrictions faced in the First World War certainly weren't far behind. Beginning with the Espionage Act of 1917, and followed by the Sedition Act of 1918, the government under President Woodrow Wilson placed restrictions on the press that would label them disloyal and subject to arrest if they published anything critical of the government or its war policy.

Some papers did not succumb without a fight. The *Chicago Tribune* of April 17, 1917, had this to say about the Espionage Act:

> *"Congress is asked again to pass an espionage bill for purposes of war emergency. The bill has certain superficial qualities of merit and other qualities of downright malevolence to the essential of democratic government.*
>
> *"It would be theoretically possible under this bill for a government to suspend temporarily the publication of any newspaper which presumed to publish criticism of gross defects in the handling of the troops ... an attempt could be made to punish critics of the administration, no matter how valuable and important the criticism was ...*
>
> *"When a stupid bureaucracy tries to conceal itself from criticism by penalizing the critic, it attacks democracy by refusing to allow the formation of an intelligent opinion.*
>
> *"Any newspaper which would divulge military secrets of importance to the enemy ought to be suspended and its editors ought to be punished. But a newspaper which is*

ESPIONAGE ACT IS NOW PASSED

By Vote of 60 to 10 Senate Adopts This Very Important Measure.

Washington, Feb. 20.—The administration espionage bill, providing severe penalties for spying on matters of national defense and punishing conspiracies to violate American neutrality, was passed today by the senate 60 to 10.

The bill takes in 14 separate measures suggested by the department of justice. Senators opposing it declared its terms so stringent as to imperil American liberty of speech and of the press. It has not passed the house

Figure 7-6. News Clip of Espionage Act

kept from telling the people how their troops are mishandled is helping the enemy and not betraying the republic.

"So far as the Tribune *is concerned it welcomes a sensible censorship, but, law or no law, if the embalmed beef scandal is repeated in this war in which we are about to engage, if typhoid camps are erected again, and if men willing to sacrifice themselves for cause are sacrificed without cause, the facts will be told and the responsible editors will accept the penalty.*

"Congress may do what it wants to do to cover up incompetence, but self-respecting journalism will ignore the penalties, accept punishment, tell the truth, do what good may be done by telling the truth, and accept the verdict of the people."

The *Washington Post* also weighed in a month later in its May 7, 1917, issue with the headline, "Newspapers, to Succeed, Must Print All the News Available: William R. Hearst Asserts that Censorship Clause in Espionage Bill is Blow at Constitution and Rights of People—Says Congress and Party that Passes it Will be Swept from Power."

The editorial by Hearst assailed President Wilson, asking why would he, heretofore a "great" president, wish to be an autocratic, dictatorial president. He compared America's new bill to England's policy of censorship that England acknowledged was a mistake. Hearst said the bill was "un-American," "unconstitutional," and a huge mistake from which the American people would suffer.

Many newspapers compared the Espionage Act to the Alien and Sedition Acts of 1798, incorrectly noting that it was the nearest press censorship (forgetting about the censorship during the Civil War.)

SOCIALIST PAPER IS BARRED FROM THE U. S. MAILS

WASHINGTON, July 7.—The mails have been barred to the Appeal To Reason, Socialist weekly, of Girard, Kansas, for opposition to the war.

Figure 7-7. Socialist Paper Barred Clip

The shouts and howls about the Espionage Act extended beyond the big city newspapers.

Those violating the order faced charges of treason, as the editors of the German-language newspaper called *Tageblatt* learned. As reported in the *Chicago Daily Tribune* of September 21, 1917, five staff members of the Philadelphia-based newspaper were arraigned on espionage charges for allegedly "making and conveying false reports to promote the success of the enemies of the United States." (With the Sedition Act that came later, some states like Nebraska required publishers of foreign language newspapers to provide the state council with the correct translations.)

The Post Office also intervened by holding any newspaper from delivery that was deemed critical of the administration. The June 29, 1917, *Topeka Daily Capitol* referred to Georgia Editor

Thomas E. Watson's weekly newspaper, *The Jeffersonian*, that was being held up for "attacking the army draft."

Headlines regularly described newspapers being barred from publication for criticizing the war, the draft, the president—anything relating to the U.S. war effort. Here is one example from the *Lima (Ohio) News* of July 7, 1917, with the headline: "Socialist Paper Barred from the U.S. Mails." It was followed by the words explaining why it was barred—"for opposition to the war."

Scores of publications across the nation also were barred from the U.S. mail for publishing articles against the Selective Service law that drafted Americans into the armed services. These included *The Masses*, *The American Socialist*, *The Appeal to Reason*, *The Blast*, *The People's Press*, *The Michigan Socialist*, *The Socialist News*, *St. Louis Labor*, *Social Revolution*, *The Rebel*, and *The Jeffersonian*.

Some publications, such as *The Appeal*, had a single issue barred and were not notified of what particular passage or article led to its violation of the Espionage or Sedition Act.

There were newspapers, however, that supported the Sedition Act, such as *The Harrisburg Telegraph*, which, in its April 12, 1918, editorial, wrote the headline: "Traitors to the Rear," and followed it with this: "All disloyalty to the government at this time should be suppressed without regard to anything save the good of the nation."

On the Frontline

If journalists at home were on a short leash, consider the restrictions that reporters on the battlefield faced. Renowned muckraker George Seldes, who was 104 years old when he died in 1995, spent a few of those years as a war correspondent in the First World War. In *Tell the Truth and Run*, a film documentary about his life as a journalist, Seldes described how the military expected and demanded reporters to support the war effort. That meant no negative publicity or criticism that might hurt the fight.

In his first of many books, *You Can't Print That*, he recounted how government censors required him to pass every story by them. Once, when he witnessed American soldiers marching off to the trenches singing a popular hit song of two years before, he wrote about it and submitted it to the censors. Said Seldes: "… I did my best to draw this picture of heroic soldiers going back to the trenches singing, ironically, *I Didn't Raise my Boy to be a Soldier*, and laughing as they marched. I thought it grand wartime stuff." (The song was a hit in 1915 before America entered the war. The irony is that it was written by a pacifist—Alfred Bryan—and was now being sung by these soldiers going off to battle.) Some of the lyrics were:

> "I didn't raise my boy to be a soldier,
>
> I brought him up to be my pride and joy.
>
> Who dares to place a musket on his shoulder,
>
> To shoot some other mother's darling boy? …
>
> Let nations arbitrate their future troubles,

It's time to lay the sword and gun away.

There'd be no war today, if mothers all would say,

I didn't raise my boy to be a soldier."

"Needless to say, the military censor thought it wasn't so grand a story, saying it was 'damned pacifist propaganda'" said Seldes. And despite it being true, told Seldes "you can't print that."

One of the interesting elements in Seldes' book was his reference to military actions using "we" and "our." Back then, journalists were given uniforms and many of the privileges as officers. As noted in the film *Tell the Truth and Run*, once you have the uniform on, impartiality ceases and it becomes "us," "we," and "our." Is that a bad thing? Shouldn't American journalists be supporting American soldiers during a war? If they don't, shouldn't they be censored?

In Chapter 6, we outlined the powerful forces of war, immigration, and social change at work in the United States during the early 20th century that led to passage of the Espionage and Sedition Acts. With the Supreme Court rulings permitting government restrictions on speech and press in the Schenck, Abrams, and Gitlow cases, freedom of expression had come under a shadow. But that trend was about to change in major ways because of a case of press censorship in the state of Minnesota.

Near v. Minnesota: Prior Restraint

As you will recall, prior restraint involves government passing laws that prevent speech or publication in advance. Note that the Espionage Act and its cousins in state laws were clearly examples of the government attempting to prevent expression that it didn't like. Note also that the Supreme Court upheld these laws. So, how can the First Amendment clearly state, "Congress shall make no law ..." and the Court at the time rule that these laws were legal? That question, whether prior restraint is ever acceptable, leads to a case out of Minnesota that was decided by the Supreme Court in 1931.

Here was the situation: Minnesota had a state law that said no one could publish material that was "... malicious, scandalous or defamatory ..." The law said such a publication was a nuisance. A newspaper in St. Paul, Minnesota, published a series of stories alleging that the local police and politicians were taking bribes from the mob to ignore violations of prohibition, gambling, and racketeering. The articles were particularly critical of the police chief in Minneapolis. The paper was charged under the state law and found guilty in the state courts. The publishers appealed to the Supreme Court. The case is called *Near v. Minnesota* and is the landmark legal ruling in relation to the borders of prior restraint in the United States. The court ruled in favor of the newspaper. It said that the state law was unconstitutional, and, in addition, the Court set rules to define what kinds of prior restraint the government might legally engage in. The court laid out the following categories in which prior restraint could be constitutional. These are still the bedrock of prior restraint limits:

- National security in time of war
- Protection of the Fair Trial rights of the accused
- Obscenity

- Libel and Invasion of Privacy
- Speech that might cause a riot (incite violence)

Prior restraint is unconstitutional except if one of the above exceptions can be proven in court. Since *Near v. Minnesota,* it has been difficult for government to censor the news media.

What do the exceptions mean? How does one define "national security? What is "obscene"? Let's look at some of the cases that have defined the limits of the law.

National Security

It is clear that most Americans and the Congress are concerned about national security, especially since the attacks on September 11, 2001, on New York and the Pentagon. Troop movements, battle plans, intelligence sources, and the location of important security buildings are just some of the things many people think should be kept secret. But there are many gray areas. How long should secrets be kept? Should things the government did 30 years ago, such as helping overthrow a foreign government or testing biological weapons, now be made public? How much secrecy should surround a decision made by a president to attack another country? Should plans be kept from Congress? Wouldn't that undermine our democratic form of government? Do government agencies sometimes classify material as secret to protect the agency and its superiors from embarrassment, rather than a real concern about national security?

There are too many questions about what national security is to deal with all of them in this book. Each day's news might bring another issue to the forefront. As these cases arise, the issue in each will be how to balance national security with the right of the press under the First Amendment to report about it, and the right of the people to know what their government is doing.

Though journalists are sometimes blamed for revealing sensitive information, there is little credible evidence they have done that. During World War II, journalists traveled with the troops on land, air, and sea, and reported to the public back home. Battle plans, strategy, troop strength, and other critical issues were not reported in advance of military actions. In 1961, the *New York Times* and NBC knew in advance about the planned invasion of Cuba by a group of Cuban exiles, supported heavily by the U.S. That attack, which came to be known as the Bay of Pigs invasion, was not reported by the journalists who knew of the plans. (There has long been speculation that if it had been reported, it might have averted what became a major fiasco and a humiliating defeat for the exiles.)

The press has been blamed by some for the U.S. loss in Vietnam. The Army's own history of that conflict deflates that argument. That war caused tremendous division in the country, and the press reported on both the war effort in Vietnam and the demonstrations and political skirmishes at home. But the press, while trying to report the reality of Vietnam, did not reveal, for instance, national secrets, troop movements, intelligence reports, or the targets of coming raids.

One of the most difficult issues for citizens and journalists is whether, during a war, reporters should be patriotic supporters of the country, no matter what it does in the war, or simply try to report the truth of the conflict as best they can, whether it's positive or negative.

The "truth," of course, is slippery. Politicians and military officers don't always want the public to know everything; part of the "truth" might make them look bad. When American soldiers killed civilians in Vietnam at a place called My Lai, for example, the Army tried to cover up the facts.

Citizens are often irritated at the press for bringing them bad news, especially if a war is not going well. Journalists are accused of being unpatriotic if, for instance, they report an event when a U.S. bomb kills innocent civilians. Is a journalist a journalist first or an American first? The question is one of truth. Are journalists truly serving the nation if they abdicate their role of keeping some distance between the stories they cover and the people in them?

Harking back to what the *Chicago Tribune* editorial said about reporting: self-respecting journalism requires they report the truth.

When we try to define national security, it is complicated by the nature of government, the feelings of the public about the messenger (i.e., the press), and what the First Amendment really means. With this brief discussion in mind, let's take a look at some of the court cases that have dealt with national security.

The Pentagon Papers

The first case to really test the national security exception outlined in *Near v. Minnesota* was the Pentagon Papers case heard by the Supreme Court in 1971 during the Nixon administration. Very briefly, here's a summary of what happened.

The Pentagon Papers was a long, government-contracted, history of the U.S. involvement in Vietnam. It was prepared by the Rand Corporation for the government, and was classified. One of the people who worked at Rand, a man named Daniel Ellsberg, believed the public should know the history, which dated back to the 1930s. His involvement with the study led him to be against the war. He leaked the Pentagon Papers to several news media outlets, including the *New York Times* and the *Washington Post*. The *New York Times* and then the *Washington Post* began publishing parts of the long history. The Nixon administration, citing national security, went to court to stop publication. The first judge to hear the case ordered publication to cease. The *Times* appealed, and the case, because of its sensitive nature, went quickly up to the Supreme Court. The Court ruled in 1971, by a vote of 6–3, against the Nixon administration, and for continued publication of the Pentagon Papers. The justices said the government had not "met the heavy burden of proof required" to infringe on the right of a free press to publish the study.

In short, they said publication would not cause a serious enough national security problem. The Pentagon Papers were published. It was touted, at the time, as a great victory for the press, and the public's right to know what the government is doing. It was a victory, but not as substantial a triumph as some claimed. All nine justices wrote different opinions (a very rare occurrence) as to why or why not the Pentagon Papers should be published. And the court agreed that it might be permissible to permit prior restraint for national security reasons in some other case. We have not seen that case yet.

Progressive Magazine

If you could figure out how to build an H-bomb would you publish the plans? Would that be a serious breach of national security? That question was tested in the late 1970s by the *Progressive Magazine*, a left-of-center political magazine with a long history of investigative reporting with offices in Madison, Wisconsin.

A freelance reporter named Howard Morland went to public libraries, the libraries of military bases around the Midwest that were open to the general public, and talked with physicists. From this easily attainable public information, he wrote a story about how to build an H-bomb called "The H-bomb Secret: How We Got It, Why We're Telling It." The magazine's stated intention was to show that nuclear secrets were not being well protected. It argued that if one freelance reporter could put together the details in a few months, the spies of hostile countries or terrorist groups could clearly discover the information. Morland and his editor at the *Progressive* sent the article, before publication, to the Department of Energy, which handles all of the nuclear energy and weapons issues in the U.S. They asked the D.O.E. to tell them if the article's facts about building the bomb were correct. The D.O.E. told them they would be glad to rewrite the article to make sure national security was not affected. The magazine declined the offer. The D.O.E. went to court to stop publication. The federal judge ruled against publication. He said he didn't want dictators like Idi Amin, then the military ruler of Uganda, to get plans for the bomb. Then other papers published stories with similar information. This put the court and the D.O.E. in a difficult legal position. How could they stop the *Progressive* from publishing material they said affected national security when the same material had already been published? The D.O.E. withdrew its case. The *Progressive* published the story.

(*Just a note here*: Even if you had the plans for building a hydrogen bomb, you would still need some impressive and expensive technology to do so. You need very precise metal milling tools, specific kinds of metal alloys that are difficult to get, and you would need the refined nuclear fuel that is supposed to be protected carefully by the nations that make it. Most experts say it requires a large amount of money, technical expertise, and time to actually build a bomb. They say it's unlikely it could be done in someone's garage or basement.)

Other Kinds of Government-Sponsored Prior Restraint

Book Banning

Book banning is common in the United States. School boards, libraries, and city councils sometimes decide to ban a particular book. Often the reason is alleged obscenity. Sometimes it's racial, religious, or political sensitivity. Among the books that have been banned in one part of the country or another are Mark Twain's *The Adventures of Huckleberry Finn*, Madeline L'Engle's *A Wrinkle in Time*, Maya Angelou's *I Know Why The Caged Bird Sings*, books that talk about gay relationships, sex, and many others. We have included in the Appendix of this book a list of the 100 most banned books in the

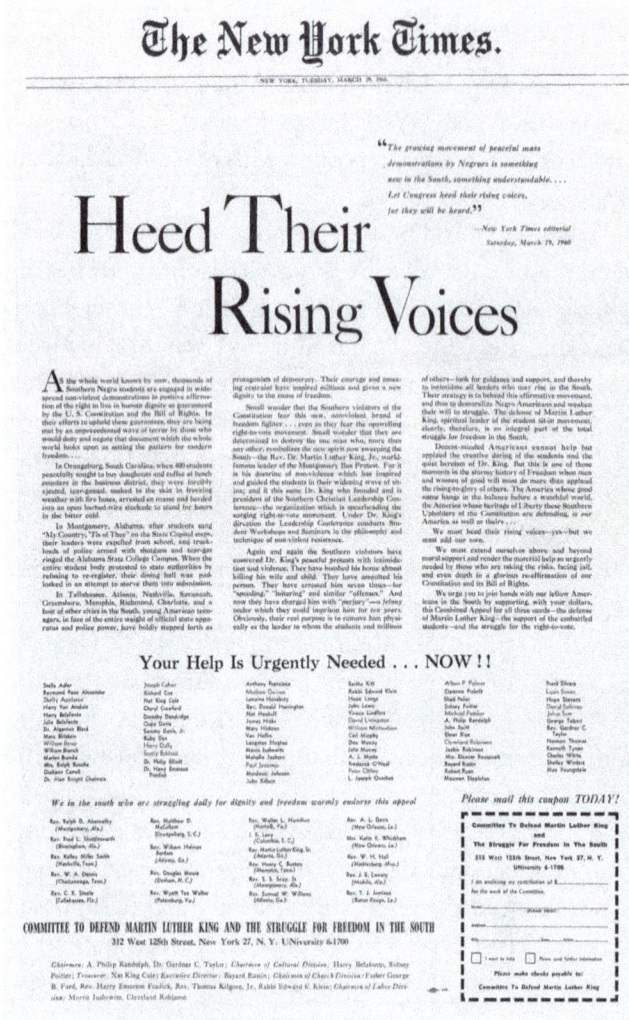

Figure 7-8. Heed Their Rising Voices

Copyright in the Public Domain.

U.S. compiled by the American Library Association. Some titles like *James and the Giant Peach* may surprise you.

Miami Herald v. Tornillo

Can a citizen go to a newspaper or other forms of news media and demand it publish a point of view the publisher disagrees with? This question relates directly to access theory. Since many media are so big, shouldn't they provide some space for ideas from people who don't own a newspaper, video company, or magazine? Are the First Amendment rights of "little people" less valuable because they don't have the means to publish their views in a way many other people will see them?

The access theory was tested in a case out of Florida. A man named Pat Tornillo, who was running for public office and whom the *Miami Herald* had criticized, wanted the paper to publish his reply to its criticism. Florida had a "right-of-reply" law requiring newspapers to publish replies when they attacked candidates in editorials. The *Miami Herald* refused. Tornillo took the paper to court. Tornillo won in the state courts, but the newspaper appealed to the U.S. Supreme Court. In a unanimous decision in 1974, the Court overturned the state law, saying that the newspaper had the First Amendment right to control what it publishes without any interference from government. The decision said, in part, "… press responsibility is not mandated by the Constitution and like many other virtues it cannot be legislated …" The Court said the First Amendment does not permit a government to order a newspaper publisher to print, or not print, something.

This ruling killed the access theory in all media, except broadcast and parts of cable television. We discuss how access theory is still relevant in these areas in Chapter 14: The Internet. The section on "Access Theory and Internet Comments" addresses the Federal Communications Commission and its ability to regulate some aspects of electronic media.

Sullivan v. New York Times

People often wonder why celebrities and famous politicians don't sue the press for libel more often; the tabloids seem to always be printing or broadcasting nasty things about them. There are several reasons for this reality. One is simply that stars like publicity and even negative stories or photos can keep them in the public spotlight. That can mean they will earn more money.

The legal reality is a different matter. First, what is libel?

Libel is the publication of FALSE information about someone that causes financial loss, damage to reputation, and mental anguish or suffering and humiliation. The principle defense against libel is the truth. If what is published is true, it cannot be libelous. Another is the opinion defense. Opinions (i.e., "I think Madonna is stupid."), are not libelous. There is an important defense for court cases and other government activities called the "privilege doctrine." It says you can publish anything said in "official actions by official bodies" even if it's false without fear of being sued for libel.

The principle case that defined the current libel law is *Sullivan v. New York Times*. The decision is considered a landmark for First Amendment law, and one of the most important freedom of the press decisions in the history of the United States.

Here's what happened. The *New York Times*, in the early 1960s during the height of the civil rights battles in the South, published an advertisement called "Heed Their Rising Voices" purchased by a collection of ministers and civil rights supporters. The ad accused public officials in several Southern states of brutality and breaking the law. It mentioned violence and Dr. Martin Luther King Jr. It called on the rest of the country to help those who were being attacked by dogs, fire hoses, and the police, and jailed for their marches and other actions in favor of equal rights for blacks. Several statements in the ad were incorrect. One of the cities mentioned in the ad was Montgomery, Alabama, where there had been confrontations at Alabama State College. Its public safety commissioner at the time was a man named L. B. Sullivan. He was not mentioned in the ad by name, but did supervise the police there. He sued the *New York Times* and several of the people who signed the ad. In the Alabama courts, he won, and the *New York Times* was ordered to pay him $500,000. The *Times* appealed to the Supreme Court.

In 1964, the Court ruled in favor of the *New York Times*. The decision set the rules for public officials attempting to sue for libel in the U.S. The Court was concerned that if public officials could sue the news media and win easily, it would "chill" First Amendment-protected expression in the country. The opinion said that the *New York Times* had been "at most, guilty of negligence in publishing the ad without verifying its accuracy. To subject the media to liability for honest mistakes or mere negligence which resulted in the defamation of public officials would inevitably lead to self-censorship regarding criticism of official conduct."

This, the Court said, would interfere with a "profound national commitment to the principle that debate on public issues should be uninhibited, robust and wide open." In short, the Court didn't want public officials who were criticized to be able to sue the news media out of existence. Public officials are people elected or appointed to office. They include most government workers, such as police officers, firefighters, or parks supervisors. The Court established the following rules:

First, a public official has to prove regular libel, defined above. Then, that public official has to prove one of two things: a) that the story was published with knowledge it was false (the publisher knew it was false, but published it anyway), or, b) that it was published with "reckless disregard of the truth." (This generally means the reporter was sloppy with the facts and/or didn't follow the normal standards of journalism). If one or both of these exist, the Court said the story was published with "actual malice" and a public official could win a libel judgment.

The Supreme Court said actual malice equaled knowledge of falsity or reckless disregard. But since Sullivan, several cases have helped refine the definition. The lawyers for the plaintiff (the person suing the media) will try to prove the "intent" of the reporter or editor. That usually means they will try to show that the publication was out to "get" the public official or public figure.

Of course, all of this has to be proven in court. That is not easy, and that's exactly what the Supreme Court intended. Our freedom to criticize the government, both by the news media and the public, has been enhanced by this decision. It is still possible for a public official to win a libel case, but it must be a compelling case of journalistic malpractice to do so.

A few years after the Sullivan decision, the Court added public figures to the law. A public figure is anyone who is in the public eye for one reason or another. These include movie and TV stars, DJs, journalists, singers, artists, people who lobby publicly for a cause, notorious criminals, or others who are often quoted in the press. This means "celebrities" must prove all the steps outlined above to win a libel case. Several famous people have won such cases, but it is a difficult task.

One of the realities of being public officials or public figures is that they have substantial power. They can call press conferences to dispute what's been written about them and many reporters will show up. This power acts as a balance to negative stories about the rich and famous. If a person who is not famous or powerful calls a press conference, it's doubtful anyone from the news media will show up. But it is much easier for private citizens to prove they have been libeled.

Section Note: Issues of law and issues of ethics are often technically separate. What is legal might not be ethical and what is ethical might not be legal. With journalism ethics, be aware that ethics and law often intertwine. As you learn about First Amendment law, notice that the legal issues and the ethical realities are often woven into each other.

High School Freedom of Expression

In the late 1980s, a student newspaper in Hazelwood, Missouri, tried to publish several stories that dealt with teenage pregnancy, and the impact of divorce on high school students. The principal of the school refused to permit the paper to print the stories. The students took the principal to court. The case made its way to the Supreme Court, and, in *Hazelwood v. Kuhlmeier*, the Court ruled that public schools have the right to censor high school expression. The decision said:

> *"We hold that educators do not offend the First Amendment by exercising editorial controls over the style and content of student speech in school-sponsored expressive activities so long as their actions are reasonably related to legitimate pedagogical concerns."*

The Court also said that the school owns the presses, hence can control what is published. Those who disagree with the Court's ruling say the public pays for the presses through its tax dollars, hence the school's officials don't own them.

In a much-quoted dissent, Justice William Brennan wrote:

> "… The young men and women of Hazelwood East expected a civics lesson, but not the one the court teaches them today. … Such unthinking contempt for individual rights is intolerable from any state official. It is particularly insidious from [a school principal] to whom the public entrusts the task of inculcating in its youth an appreciation for the cherished democratic liberties that our Constitution guarantees."

Since this decision, the number of cases of high school press censorship has increased significantly. The ruling not only relates to newspapers, but theatrical productions, yearbooks, TV and radio broadcasts, art exhibits, and any other kind of "expressive" student activity.

Several states have passed laws restoring speech freedom to high school students under their state constitutions. The states include Massachusetts, California, Arkansas, Iowa, and Oregon. The Student Press Law Center is an excellent resource on high school and college press freedom issues. (www.splc.org)

Exercises

1. What is prior restraint?
2. Which president passed the Alien and Sedition Acts, and how did he do in the next election?
3. How did freedom of the press fare in the North during the Civil War?
4. What got journalist George Seldes in trouble during WWI?
5. Describe the *Near v. Minnesota* case.
6. The Court ruled in favor of a newspaper's right to publish critical stories without prior restraint. Cite several instances in which the court said that the government *could* pass laws preventing speech or publication in advance.
7. Describe the Pentagon Papers case.
8. Describe the *Progressive Magazine* case.
9. What did the Supreme Court decide in the *Miami Herald v. Tornillo* case?
10. The Supreme Court, in the *New York Times v. Sullivan* case, set a new standard about libeling public officials. What is that standard?
11. What did the Supreme Court say in the case of *Hazelwood v. Kuhlmeier* about why public schools are permitted to restrict student rights?

For Critical Discussion or Writing

1. Do you think the courts haven granted the mainstream press too much freedom in the U.S., too little, or is it about right?
2. Do you think the government should control the press during times of national crises?
3. Should public high school expression like newspapers, plays, and art shows be censored by school officials, or should high school students have more First Amendment freedoms?

CHAPTER 8

Prior Restraint: Nipping it in the Bud

Prior restraint is unconstitutional except in the case of national security in time of war, protection of the fair trial rights of the accused, obscenity, libel, invasion of privacy, and speech that might incite violence. The issues of press restrictions were discussed in the previous chapter, but there are additional issues revolving around national security as well as the other areas of prior restraint decided in *Near v. Minnesota*.

Intelligence Agencies

There is a federal law that makes it illegal for a current or former intelligence agent to speak or write about his or her activities. Those who work for the various intelligence agencies in the United States sign an agreement that they will not reveal secrets, and will clear all speeches or written material with the agency they work or worked for in advance. The idea, of course, is to prevent secrets from becoming public knowledge, but it seemed like a violation of First Amendment rights to some of the employees who wanted to write about their lives in spycraft. Two cases were judged in the courts in the 1970s and '80s to decide the issue.

In one, *United States. v. Marchetti* (1972) the former CIA agent Victor Marchetti was ordered to submit a book he was writing about his CIA work to the agency for prior review. He appealed that decision, and after a trial held in secret because of the nature of the material being discussed, Marchetti basically lost. The Court did say the government could only censor classified information, so Marchetti was able to publish the non-classified parts of what he had written.

In *Snepp v. United States* (1980) former CIA agent Frank Snepp wrote a book critical of the agency's work in Vietnam. He didn't get prior approval. The government took him to court and Snepp lost. He was ordered to turn over all the profits from his book to the government.

The Supreme Court in the Snepp case ruled that the issue was not a First Amendment conflict, but one of contract law. That is, Snepp signed a contract to submit all writing to the CIA in advance and did not do so. The Court said he had broken his contract with the CIA.

Even politically appointed officials in the intelligence services must sign contracts, and have their writings undergo prior review by the agency. Admiral Stansfield Turner, who was CIA director during the administration of Jimmy Carter in the late 1970s, had to undergo a review of his book about his leadership of the agency. He has said that parts of his book were censored. He told co-author Jerry Dunklee, in a radio interview in the early 1980s, that he felt that the parts censored did not reveal any secrets because he was very careful. But, he said, the censored parts would have embarrassed some people in the government. Turner questioned the scope of the law, and worried that important historical analysis of what intelligence agencies have done would be lost to future decision makers and the public. The law stands today. Agents and former agents may not write or speak about their work without prior review by the government agency for which they worked.

More recent examples of breaches in national security are the cases of Chelsea (Bradley) Manning and Edward Snowden. Manning was an Army intelligence analyst who leaked a large number of government documents and videos to WikiLeaks in 2010. He was convicted by a military court under the Espionage Act and is serving 35 years in prison.

Snowden is a former CIA employee who, as a private contractor for the National Security Agency, leaked numerous classified documents about government spying to several journalists. He is a fugitive from U.S. justice, living in Russia. Some view Snowden as a "whistleblower" who revealed that the U.S. government was spying on its own citizens as well as leaders of other countries. Others say he is a "criminal" who stole secrets and should be convicted for his actions.

The press continues to write stories based on Snowden's leaks. There have been no government efforts, to date, by the federal government to bring charges against any of the press outlets that have published or posted these stories.

Sixth Amendment: Fair Trial vs. Free Press

The Constitution grants freedom of speech and press, but it also grants the right to a fair trial in the Sixth Amendment. The Sixth Amendment says:

> *"In all criminal prosecutions, the accused shall enjoy the right to a speedy and public trial, by an impartial jury of the State and district wherein the crime shall have been committed, which district shall have been previously ascertained by law, and to be informed of the nature and cause of the accusations; to be confronted with the witnesses against him; to have compulsory process for obtaining witnesses in his favor, and to have the Assistance of Counsel for his defence."*

What happens when fair trial and free press rights conflict? Remember, *Near v. Minnesota* said prior restraint might be acceptable to protect the fair trial rights of the accused. Here's an example of the problem:

There's a murder of a famous man's wife. He is arrested by the police and charged with the killing. He says he's innocent. The case attracts a tremendous amount of attention. The press covers the story extensively. Many stories, published before his trial, include opinions from various sources that the man is guilty. Some say he's guilty because he hired an expensive attorney. Other speculation includes rumors that he was cheating on his wife, that they had arguments, and that she had allegedly talked with friends about leaving him.

Before a trial has occurred, the press is filled with reports about the case that imply his guilt. The press reports "evidence," much of it hearsay, that could not be legally admitted at the trial.

When members of a jury are chosen, how can we be sure they have not been severely prejudiced by the press reports?

When the actual trial begins, the news media cover it minute-by-minute. Radio, TV, magazines, and newspapers all have crews at the courthouse. Sometimes they are intrusive, coming in and out of the courtroom at will and making noise.

No, this is not the O. J. Simpson case. It's the earlier famous case of Sam Sheppard, the doctor who was accused of killing his wife in the 1950s. The TV series and the movie, *The Fugitive*, were loosely based on the case. Shepard was convicted in his first trial and he appealed to the Supreme Court. (His lawyer was a young F. Lee Bailey who later worked as one of O. J. Simpson's attorneys.) Twelve years after his conviction, the Supreme Court, in 1966, decided Shepard should have a new trial. At that trial he was acquitted. What the Court decided set a series of precedents about conducting fair trials. The rules they established put most of the obligation for making sure a trial is fair on the government.

The Court said the courthouse is state property and hence the government can control access to it. This means that the judge can order press "pool" coverage (only permitting a few reporters into the trial at once), thus limiting the distraction too many reporters at once might cause. The judge can grant a continuance: delay the trial for several months to allow passions to cool. The judge can grant a change of venue: move the trial to another place where pre-trial publicity has not been as extensive. The judge can order the witnesses, lawyers, the defendant, and other court officers not to speak about the case: these are often called "gag" orders. The judge can also order the press to be careful in its coverage of a case. Judges will always question potential jurors to see if they've learned very much about a case from the news media, or have some other bias that would prevent them from being fair. If you've gone for jury duty you may have faced this questioning by the judge, prosecution, and defense attorneys. It's called Voir Dire.

There are several other ways the Court can work to make sure a fair trial for an accused person occurs, but the Supreme Court said specifically in the Shepard case that "it was not necessary to comment on a recalcitrant press."

They were, in effect, saying that this was not a First Amendment issue, but one of the government's responsibilities to insure a fair trial.

This does not excuse poor behavior on the part of reporters. The press has an ethical responsibility to use caution when reporting about a crime, arrest, and trial. Journalists should not convict or acquit a defendant. Only the courts do that.

The public should understand that both the defense and prosecution try to "spin" reporters to their side, especially if the judge has not issued a gag order on the lawyers. They often work to try the case in the "court of public opinion," and reporters should be careful not to fall into that trap. When the public perceives the press going over the line, the public should complain and use its First Amendment rights to criticize journalists who are not doing a good job.

Obscenity

Obscenity has always been subject to government censorship. *Near v. Minnesota* just continued that tradition. There is a long history in the United States of many kinds of material being censored because some level of government considered it obscene. These include material, such as birth control information, family planning, many kinds of art, magazines that show too much skin for some people's taste, books that deal with sex, public sculpture, and exotic dancing. The problem is defining what is obscene. One person's obscenity is another person's art. The courts have struggled with the issue, and there are a vast number of cases that deal with obscenity. Remember, the First Amendment says "Congress shall make no law …" so how can the courts square that wording with permitting censorship of material considered to be obscene?

The Supreme Court, in a landmark case in the 1950s, took on this problem. In *Roth v. United States*, Samuel Roth was actually found guilty of distributing obscene material, (a book, some advertising, and a circular), under a federal law. But the Court's decision defined obscenity for the first time. The ruling says:

> "… whether to the average person, applying contemporary community standards, the dominant theme of the material taken as a whole appeals to the prurient interest. … Whether the work depicts or describes, in a patently offensive way, sexual conduct specifically defined by the applicable state law, and whether the work, taken as a whole, lacks serious literary, artistic, political, or scientific merit."

The Court also said that in order to prosecute someone, prosecutors must follow certain rules. The censor must start judicial proceedings, and may stop the offending expression on an interim basis only after an initial hearing in which the parties can present their case. The publisher must be granted a speedy trial if the material is originally declared obscene and censored at the first hearing so a final decision can be made in the courts as quickly as possible.

Of course, while the Court rendered its definition of obscenity, it's still open to interpretation. What is an average person? What are contemporary community standards? Are the standards in New York City the same as those in a small town in the Midwest? What is patently offensive? What has serious literary or artistic merit?

There are hundreds of cases that deal with this issue. Those who wish to pursue study of this area of law will find a treasure trove of articles, books, and websites that talk about what obscene means.

A few illustrations:

- In 2001, a video store in Salt Lake City was charged under local statutes with obscenity for renting and selling X-rated videos. The defense used the Supreme Court's definition of obscenity, particularly the part that talks about contemporary community standards. The video store's lawyer pointed out to the jury that the same videos were available for viewing in hotels all over Salt Lake City. How, he asked, could his client be charged with a crime when the same material was available on the TVs of most hotel rooms in town? The jury deliberated less than an hour and acquitted the video store owner.

- With cable TV, TV networks, the Internet, national magazines, movies, and CDs, is the community the whole nation? Or could a rap singer be tried for obscenity because a CD he recorded was for sale in a small New England town, even though he recorded it in Los Angeles and had never visited the town in question?

- What does artistic merit mean? In 1990, city officials in Cincinnati, Ohio, ordered a show of Robert Mapplethorpe photos closed because they said it was obscene. Mapplethorpe was a famous art photographer whose photos often contained explicit gay images. The museum fought back in the courts. The Court eventually ruled that the exhibit was art, not obscene, and that it could continue to be open to adults.

Children and Obscenity

One of the most common and understandable views in American society is that adults must protect children from material that is too "adult" for them. The laws that prevent a magazine store from displaying centerfolds in its front window where children might see them are constitutional. So are the laws that prevent minors from renting X-rated videos. Child pornography is legally obscene in almost all cases. But where are the lines when we try to protect children? Congress has passed laws to protect children from online indecency three times. Each time, the courts have ruled the laws unconstitutional because they were too broad, and might prevent adults from viewing material clearly legal for them. You know that actual children being used in child pornography is a crime for which many adults have gone to jail. But the courts ruled in 2002 that creating virtual child pornography, that is, not using real children but computer-generated images, is legal because no actual child was harmed. Violent video games have also been a target of legislators. In 2001, the Supreme Court threw out a California law that restricted the sale of violent games to minors. Justice Antonin Scalia wrote in his majority opinion, there was "no tradition in this country of especially restricting children's access to depictions of violence. … Grimm's Fairy Tales, for example, are grim indeed."

Like many areas of First Amendment law, especially related to the relatively new Internet, society is moving quickly and the courts cannot keep up with all of the issues. The law is in flux, and will continue to be that way, because of the new technologies and the difficulty of defining obscenity.

Inciting Violence

This prior restraint exception was written into *Near v. Minnesota* at a time when large political rallies and demonstrations on public property were more common. A person who wanted to influence public opinion would literally stand on a wooden box on a street and preach his or her message to the passersby. In our history, some of these "speeches" resulted in a mob forming and violence occurring. It is unlikely that the news media could be charged with inciting violence because most of us read the news alone or watch TV in small groups, not in the public square. But there is an example of this issue in New York City in 1998. Mayor Rudolph Giuliani attempted to institute crowd size and control rules on an event called the "Million Youth March." The marchers were scheduled to meet in Harlem. The year before, at a similar gathering, there had been clashes with the police. The mayor said he was trying to prevent more violence. The organizers took the city to court arguing that the restrictions on their rally were too stringent, and, hence, violations of the First Amendment. The court agreed with the organizers, and the Giuliani administration had to relax those rules. The event didn't draw as many people as had been predicted, and occurred without violence.

Libel and Invasion of Privacy

As of now, no court case has tested whether prior restraint might be OK in a case dealing with libel or invasion of privacy law.

Symbolic Speech

Symbolic speech is when someone communicates a point of view by using symbols, street theater, short phrases, or other non-verbal methods. This kind of speech became popular in the 1960s during civil rights, anti-Vietnam War protests, women's rights, and other political demonstrations. It was designed to take advantage of the power of TV news to communicate images. Examples of symbolic speech are flag burning, making satirical effigies of political figures, holding up two fingers in a peace sign, bra burning, a group standing silently in front of a military base, or splashing fake blood on the steps of Congress. Symbolic speech is a staple of demonstrations all around the world now. Dozens of cases have been heard by the courts questioning whether the government can censor or prevent symbolic speech. We'll mention just a few of them.

Draft-card burning to protest the Vietnam War was common during the 1960s. A group of young men would gather in a public place and burn their draft cards while the TV and print photographers recorded the event. Many of these protesters were arrested by local police and convicted in local courts. Eventually, the issue made its way to the Supreme Court. In 1968, the Court ruled that burning a draft card was not speech protected by the First Amendment. In effect, the Court said the card was government property since it had been issued by the government, and burning it was destroying government property.

Other kinds of symbolic speech were upheld by the courts as clear indications of political speech that enjoy the highest level of protection under the First Amendment.

In a case out of Iowa, high school students were suspended for wearing black armbands to protest the war. They fought up to the Supreme Court in the case known as *Tinker v. The Des Moines Independent Community School District*. The Court ruled that the students had a right to wear the armbands. The Court said students did not leave their First Amendment rights at the school door, and that wearing the armbands posed no serious risk to disrupting the activities of the school.

Another case involved a young man attempting to enter a courthouse in Los Angeles wearing a coat with the phrase "Fuck The Draft" written on the back.

He was arrested and convicted. The case went to the Supreme Court in 1971, which ruled that the man had the right to wear the coat, including on government property. The Court said this was clearly political speech.

There have been many cases involving the American flag. Flag burning, wearing a flag on the seat of your pants, flying the flag upside down (a symbol of surrender), and using the flag in irreverent ways in art have all been tested in the courts. The Supreme Court has consistently ruled this as protected speech.

This is why some have pushed for an amendment to the U.S. Constitution to prohibit desecration of the flag. That amendment has not passed. One of the problems is defining what desecration is. Is it stepping on a flag or burning it? Or does it include flag symbols on clothing or using the flag for commercial purposes, such as to promote a car dealership?

Hate Speech vs. Action

Many colleges across the U.S. in the past 20 years have passed so-called "anti-hate speech" codes. These codes are designed to prohibit students from insulting other students based on their race, gender, sexual orientation, or political views, which might create a "hostile" environment for those in such groups. A majority of states have also passed some kind of "anti-hate speech" laws. In 1992, the Supreme Court ruled that it is a violation of the First Amendment to pass laws or codes that attempt to censor the content of speech. That is, it's legal to call someone a racist name, denigrate someone's religion, or sexual orientation. The codes and laws were declared to be overly broad and forced a kind of "political correctness" on people who may have minority views.

Hate speech, then, is legal. But what about hate crimes? Hate crimes are those in which a normal crime has been committed, such as assault, vandalism, or murder. If it can be proven that the crime was motivated by some kind of "hate," such as dislike of Jews or gay people, the state may add time to the sentence of the person convicted. There is, in our system, a clear difference between speech and action. It is often said that you have the right to swing your arms any way you want until they come into contact with my face. The point here is that a crime is an action. If someone has desecrated a cemetery, beat up a Muslim person, or painted swastikas on a synagogue—that is a crime. Adding time in jail for these kinds of hate-motivated actions is constitutional. In a case out of Mississippi in 1993, in which several black youths attacked a white boy because he was white, the Court ruled unanimously that the hate crimes laws are within the Constitution. Chief Justice William Rehnquist wrote, in part:

> "… *A physical assault is not by any stretch of the imagination expressive conduct protected by the First Amendment. …*"

KKK and Free Speech

In the 1960s, a Ku Klux Klan member challenged an Ohio law that prohibited organizing people to preach hatred or overthrow the government. He had been arrested at a rally for speaking about hatred of Jews and blacks. He had made comments about taking action to force the government to change its laws. The state also presented evidence that weapons and a Bible were found at the KKK rally. There was no violence. The Supreme Court overturned the conviction of the KKK member in the Supreme Court case *Brandenburg v. Ohio*. The Court said that the state may not forbid advocating force except in circumstances where "such advocacy is directed to inciting or producing **imminent** lawless action and is **likely** to incite or produce such action." (Emphasis added.)

This means that only when and if expression merges with criminal behavior will it be considered outside the protection of the First Amendment. Later rulings in so-called "hate speech" cases, which will be discussed in a subsequent section, are based on the decision in Brandenburg.

In 2003, the Supreme Court ruled on a 50-year-old cross-burning law in Virginia. The Court, in a 5–4 decision, struck down the law that banned cross burning except in cases where prosecutors could prove the intent of the cross burning was racial intimidation. Justice Sandra Day O'Connor, giving the majority opinion, wrote:

> "*We conclude that while a state consistent with the First Amendment may ban cross burning carried out with the intent to intimidate, the provision in the Virginia statute treated any cross burning as prima facie evidence of intent to intimidate renders the statute unconstitutional.*"

In a dissent, Justice Clarence Thomas, the only black member of the Court, wrote that all cross burning was meant to intimidate and could never represent freedom of expression. He wrote:

> "*This statute prohibits only conduct, not expression. Just as one cannot burn down someone's house to make a political point and then seek refuge in the First Amendment, those who hate cannot terrorize and intimidate to make their point.*"

Several states and the District of Columbia have passed statutes that prohibit cross burning.

Private Prior Restraint

One issue that needs to be clarified, at this point, is that government censorship and private censorship are different things. If Wal-Mart decides not to sell a CD because it doesn't like the content of the songs or the cover art, it is within its rights. When 7-Eleven stores decide not to sell *Penthouse* or *Playgirl* magazines, that's not illegal. These are examples of private censorship, and they often please or anger many Americans. But it is within the First Amendment rights of companies to decide what they sell. The law is mostly concerned with attempts by government to limit speech.

There are several other situations where certain kinds of speech might be subject to possible government control. For instance, there's a whole body of law that deals with commercial speech. You may not advertise a claim for a product or service that is clearly false. Congress passed a law in the 1960s that prohibits cigarette advertising in broadcasting. TV stations must provide at least three hours a week of educational programming for children. Broadcast political commercials may not be censored by the station. There are other examples, but remember, the First Amendment deals with government intrusion into free expression, not private individuals or companies.

Exercises

1. Which entity has the legal responsibility to insure a fair trial under the Sixth Amendment, the press or the state?
2. Intelligence agents may not speak or write without permission from their agency. The Supreme Court said this is not a First Amendment issue. What kind of issue is it?
3. What are some of the requirements for determining whether something is legally obscene?
4. Define symbolic speech.
5. May a private business censor the material it sells without a First Amendment problem?

For Critical Discussion or Writing

1. Would it serve democracy better if former intelligence agents were able to speak freely about what they did in service to the United States?
2. Would you ban hate speech on radio and television? If you say yes, who would decide what speech is considered hate speech?
3. Does your college have a "speech" or "values" code? Do you think it's constitutional?
4. What do you think about the TV shows that discuss high-profile criminal cases where the host and guests claim someone is guilty or innocent before there has been a trial?

CHAPTER 9

Public's Perception of Journalists

We've just examined government restrictions on the press as well as the role of the press in society. Looking at the past as well as the present, you will notice an interesting phenomenon. Whether it was New York Colonial Governor William Cosby going after John Peter Zenger for allowing his opponents to criticize him, or the public questioning why journalists would want access to public records that include crime scene photos at the massacre in Newtown, Connecticut, the press has always been the target of criticism with calls for restraint by government and citizens alike.

It has always been popular to criticize the news media. Its members are said to be pushy, disrespectful, and willing to do anything to sell newspapers, or in the case of TV or radio, airtime.

It is somewhat ironic that the public, whom the news media strive to inform and keep knowledgeable, has not regarded journalists or their work highly.

A 2010 Gallup Poll of American adults found that only 43 percent had a fair or great amount of trust and confidence that the news media reported the news fully, accurately, and fairly. Conversely, 57 percent said they either had no trust and confidence or not very much trust and confidence in the news media getting it right.

It marked the fourth consecutive year that the majority of American adults expressed little or no trust or confidence in America's news media.

What does this mean to a nation for whom the press is supposed to provide information if the citizens don't trust the information they receive? Exactly whom does the public trust.

That same 2010 Gallup Poll survey of American adults revealed the following levels of trust in several institutions in American society:

American Institutions	Percent of Americans who Trust a Great Deal
The Military	44
Small Business	30
The Police	26
Church/Organized Religion	25
The Medical System	16
The Presidency	16
The U.S. Supreme Court	15
The Public Schools	14
Television News	**11**
Organized Labor	10
Banks	9
The Criminal Justice System	9
Newspapers	**9**
Health Maintenance Organizations	8
Big Business	7
Congress	4

Source: Gallup (2010)

What is the cause for the low regard for the news media? Certainly among the factors are the following public perceptions of the news media:

News Media Bias

The view that certain TV News stations are liberally skewed (MSNBC) or conservatively skewed (Fox News) is a constant complaint leveled by the public with the notion that the coverage they present is thus inherently biased.

Clearly though, according to the 2010 Gallup Poll, most American adults—48 percent—regard the news media as liberal, 15 percent said they thought they were conservative, while 33 percent said they were about right.

Another kind of perceived bias has to do with advertising. Surveys indicate that some people believe large advertisers influence news stories. For example, if a company spends a lot of money with a news organization, the editors will ignore or downplay negative news about that advertiser. Journalism ethics codes say advertisers should not receive favored treatment, but there are cases where ad money has influenced coverage.

Skewing Facts and Images

There have been criticisms about the news media presenting misleading images. One such example is the Trayvon Martin killing that portrayed a picture of a much younger Martin, and a picture of the shooter, George Zimmerman, in a mug shot from a previous arrest. Some say the news media are virtually trying people in the press, and giving the impression that the accused are guilty in the "courtroom of public opinion."

Insensitivity

Journalists are seen as cold and insensitive, caring only about the story and nothing about the people they may trample in the process. There have been instances when reporters seeking a story have called a gunman holding a hostage. There have been other instances when TV news cut into children's programming to show a standoff that resulted in an on-air suicide. There is also the increasingly graphic, violent nature of regularly scheduled news broadcasts.

Celebrity News

Others say the news media are too involved in reporting news on celebrity scandal and gossip. Who cares about who is seeing whom when there are more important matters in the world going on?

The Public Perception After Disasters and Tragedies

Despite the seeming lack of trust and confidence in the news media, the public turns to this same news media during times of natural or unnatural disasters. Whether it was the attack on September 11, 2001, the power outages along the East Coast following the effects of Hurricane Irene in 2011, or the shooting in Newtown, Connecticut, in December 2012, the public seeks its news via smartphones, laptops, TV, tweets, newspapers, and radio.

Journalists—like Umpires

In essence, gauging the public's sentiment about the news media can be a difficult proposition, shifting with each news story that comes along. It is why journalists can only consider themselves like umpires in a baseball game: They do their best to prepare and practice and make the right call; but they understand that when the game is over, the spectators will not praise them for a job well done, and will sure point fingers and kick and scream if they mess up.

It's part of the job. But is it a job that still requires journalists? With smartphones in the hands of more Americans today than ever before, couldn't people just post their own pictures and descriptions of events? Wouldn't that be enough? Couldn't we count on citizen-driven reporting to keep us informed without journalists?

If There Were No Journalists

News is part of our everyday life; there will always be a need for people to provide us with news and information. But what if there were no journalists to report the news? What if your neighbor, your friend, or anyone who happened to see something did the reporting? Could we count on them to keep us informed about what's going on? What would be the effect of millions of people sending their pictures and commentary on things they saw? Who would pare down the important from the unimportant? Do we really want a word-for-word description of every event? More importantly, could we trust what they put before us?

Of course, there are those who say that you can't trust anything you read or hear from the established news companies right now. So what's the difference?

Let's address this first by looking into our trust of the traditional news organizations. You've seen the polls. Presumably, included in these numbers are those on the political left who don't trust the news coming from the news media of the political right, and those on the political right who don't trust the news coming from the news media of the political left. Still, despite this reality and the low trust in numbers for the news media, the truth is, by and large, we do trust what we see and hear from news media organizations.

When there is a story of an accident or a coming weather event or a crisis in a certain region, there is a tendency to trust and believe it. The same goes for major stories—there is the presumption of truth.

Does that mean there is complete trust in the news media? Hopefully, not. There is always a need for healthy skepticism by all for all, including the news media. The journalists who comprise the news media are not infallible. There are things they could do to improve their performance and certain qualities that could be employed to make them better.

Yet, as imperfect as journalists are, consider what life would be like in this nation if there were no journalists. When we say journalists, we mean those who are trained to determine what is news, as well as select sources, ask questions, interview, report, write, shoot, edit, and broadcast what they have learned to the American people. These are important qualities that distinguish journalists from others who simply write information without attributing it. Attribution is the "he said," "she said," or "according to" part of journalism. Unless it is an opinion piece or an analysis, journalists are supposed to report the events, and keep their personal thoughts and feelings out of the story. They use human sources, meaning other people who have information on the event; or they use physical sources, meaning documents—unless they happen to be an eyewitness to the event themselves.

Journalists are accountable for what they produce. They are accountable to the public as well as their editors. Without the news media, who would be controlling the information? If it is not a free news media, then it is a government or some other entity with some stake in informing you of only what it wants you to know with its own particular spin on it. If that were the case, who would be the watchdog keeping an eye on our elected leaders?

Think about how you come to learn about events that are happening in the world around you. That world could be local, as in your town or campus housing, or another part of the state, region, country, or world. If you are a newspaper or magazine reader, then you might learn about events through the print media. If you listen to the radio, then you hear it from there. Or if you're watching TV or monitoring the Internet through your computer or smartphone, you might hear it from there. But the point is, you are hearing it from people who were there, or who have spoken with and interviewed those who were there.

Still, one common criticism of journalists is that they are not "objective" and they constantly "filter" the news so the public doesn't get the whole story. Let's examine that.

Objectivity vs. Fairness

Though the public uses the term "objective" on a regular basis, many journalists don't like it. As philosophers point out, none of us can be completely objective. We all see the world through the lens of our background and experience. To that extent, since reporters are humans, they can't be "objective." But remember, that is also true of the sources who speak to reporters. We know that even eyewitnesses to crime are often mistaken when they attempt to identify a criminal following the traumatic event. When several people witness something, each views it in different ways. Have you ever played the telephone game where one person starts a message and whispers it to the next until the message goes all the way around a circle? Usually, the message is distorted by the time it gets to the end.

That's the kind of problem the courts must deal with and so, too, must journalists. People are not machines, and with our biases and the simple problems of observing accurately, the process of reporting things clearly is very difficult. So, "objectivity" is a problematic word. Most journalists like to use the phrases "fair and balanced" or "complete and accurate." We mean that we should listen to all sides, observe carefully, and try to report what happened as factually as possible to the public. Fairness and balance can usually be achieved, but it requires reporters of good will, and sources who will try to tell their side of the story accurately.

The issue of filtering needs to be discussed as well. When people criticize journalists for filtering, they often mean not reporting "objectively," as discussed above. But they also mean that journalists don't report the whole story. They, say the critics, pick and choose the facts and angles they want to report, and they show the reporters' biases. That can happen if a reporter is not careful. However, think of filtering in another way, a way that really gets to the center of what journalists do.

If there was a city council meeting last night that went on for three hours, the newspaper could just print a transcript of every word spoken. It would take up several pages in the paper. But would you read that? A rare few might. But most of us would not be that interested in every tiny detail, and we don't have time to read that long a story. What the journalist does is listen, study the issues, talk with the relevant sources and participants, and make choices about what is important and what is not. Journalists prioritize, analyze, condense, and write about the items in the three-hour meeting that are the most important to the most people. That is very much filtering, but without it no one would read a newspaper, follow their "smart phone," or watch TV news. Journalists are filters. That's part of the job description.

It is a job that involves trust. Despite the polls, there is an inherent trust in the news media. When we turn on our smartphone, laptop, iPad, TV, or radio, or when we read through an actual newspaper or magazine, we believe the pictures we see, the voices we hear, the words we read. We trust that the person who is presenting the story has interviewed the necessary sources, and is reporting honestly and fairly.

As imperfect as journalists are, they play a valuable role in keeping the American people informed, and holding both people and institutions accountable.

Exercises

1. True or false. Journalists rank highly among the institutions with whom the public has trust and confidence.
2. What are some of the reasons why the public has a low regard for the news media?
3. What has it often been popular for the public to do with regard to the news media?
4. Describe some of the qualities of a journalist.
5. What is attribution?
6. What are two types of sources journalists use?

For Critical Discussion or Writing

1. What is your view of the news media?
2. Describe why you do or do not trust the news media.
3. Describe how your life would be if there were no news media. Would it be better, worse, or the same?
4. If there were no news media and you had the chance to start a process for gathering and reporting news, how would you go about it?
5. What changes would you make from the present newsgathering process in America?

CHAPTER 10

What is News?

Consider for a moment that you are a member of a cave-dwelling community thousands of years ago. What would be your concerns? They would include food, shelter, controlling the fire, worrying about the weather, and, in short—survival.

One day a scout comes running breathlessly into the village. He runs right to the chief. He tells him that he has seen other humans in the next valley. They were hunting mastodons. They didn't see him, the scout tells the chief. The village is abuzz. Are these other humans dangerous? Will they kill all the food the village needs to survive? The news that the scout has rushed back to the small tribe affects all of them. The chief calls all the village people together to discuss the threat and what to do.

One woman doesn't attend the meeting. She is struggling to help her one-year-old child live. The little girl is gasping for breath. The mother tries to help. At the village council meeting, suddenly, the chief grabs his chest and falls to the ground in agony. Will he live? Will the baby? Which of the two do you think the village people are more worried about?

Suddenly, the bright day begins to turn dark, even though there's not a cloud in the sky. The villagers are frightened. The sun is disappearing. They cry and gasp. As the chief regains his breathing, he is facing almost total darkness. He thinks it must be an extraordinarily bad omen. The gods have sent another tribe to hunt in their territory on the same day they are losing the sun.

Each of the things happening in the cave village is a kind of news. News can be defined as something that affects a substantial number of people as well as something we did not know before. People, or institutions, or countries of prominence, are usually more newsworthy than less powerful ones. That's why people would be more concerned about the chief. Extraordinary events like an eclipse are fascinating to us as well.

News Values

There are other ways to define what some might call news values, but all the definitions are not just invented by journalism scholars in some ivory tower. They are simply part of human nature. Whether it's pleasant to think about or not, we are more interested in famous and powerful people than ordinary ones. Events that impact lots of us are more essential than those that affect only a few. And odd things, from growing an 800-pound pumpkin to flying a balloon solo around the globe, hold our attention.

Here are some other ways to think about what is news. Paul Davis, who was a TV news director at several major stations in the U.S. over a more than 50-year career in journalism, told his reporters and editors to think about several words:

1. Conflict
2. Proximity
3. Prominence
4. Magnitude
5. Personal Impact
6. Oddity

Av Westin Sr., who produced ABC TV Network news shows in the 1970s and 1980s, wanted his reporters and editors to think of several questions. He told the Archive of American Television in a 2011 interview that the questions are:

1. Is my community safe?
2. Is my nation safe?
3. Is my world safe?

Notice that Westin starts with community. We are more concerned about events happening close to us. An accident that ties up traffic on our local highway is more relevant to us than one across the country. This is the same as "proximity" above. Westin added several questions: Is there something that could make me sad, fearful, happy? Is there something I should know about my world tonight?

Some news managers use the three I's—Impact, Interest, Information—to define news.

Melvin Mencher, author of *News Reporting and Writing*, uses TIPPCUC. It means Timeliness, Impact, Prominence, Proximity, Currency, Unusualness, and Conflict.

Notice that all of these definitions are similar to each other, and each of them relates back to the cave village where the inhabitants are concerned about the events shaping their lives.

Of course, these news definitions can be distorted in the marketplace. The best example is prominence. Most tabloid-style celebrity journalism is based on the "prominence" of the stars. There are different kinds of prominence. The president, a general, a chief of police have real power. A starlet cannot veto tax bills, send troops into battle, or arrest anyone. But her affairs with other celebrities, and her clothing (or lack of it) make the tabloid news. For many people that is a trivializing of prominence, but it is obviously a big factor in this country in relation to what is reported in many magazines, newspapers, entertainment TV shows, and websites. It's become a whole industry with magazines, such as *Entertainment Weekly*, *People*, *US*, and TV shows, such as *Access Hollywood*, *Entertainment Tonight*, and the *E* cable network. *TMZ* operates both online and on TV. Celebrity news leaks into mainstream news media as well, often pushing aside news that has a more serious impact on our lives, such as decisions in Congress, health care, or education.

Who Chooses What Will Be News?

How do the events happening in any day end up in the paper, magazine, or on the air as news stories? In several ways. What follows is a rundown of some of the ways journalists sort through all the information available to them and make decisions about what to report to the public.

Every day a flood of mail, e-mail, phone calls, Tweets and texts arrive at the newsrooms of all kinds of news organizations. They include dozens of press releases from a wide range of interest groups. A company is introducing a new product and wants you to do a story about it. A politician is proposing a new bill. The department of transportation is announcing when a section of the interstate will be closed for repairs. A star is coming to the local theater and is available for an interview. A professional athlete will be signing autographs at the local mall. Letters of complaint from the audience, tips on possible news stories, praise for a story well done—all come into newsrooms in a seemingly endless stream. All of the people or institutions sending the material want a story done about their special event or proposal. One journalism job is to sort through all of that material to decide if any of it is newsworthy.

News outlets also subscribe to wire services (Associated Press is the largest) that provide stories and photos all day long. The broadcast stations are connected to networks that send complete stories and sound bites from newsmakers. There are specialized news services that provide stories in such areas as business, medicine, sports, and entertainment news. These wire services and networks provide a huge volume of news to their clients every day. The local newspaper or station can pick and choose among the stories offered.

Local reporters are talking with news sources, going to meetings, doing interviews, and writing fresh stories each day. The job of the reporter is to find interesting and important events, discover trends, sniff out wrongdoing and, of course, report on local crime, accidents, fires, demonstrations, and other events that might occur in any given day.

As journalists choose stories, they are thinking about the definitions we've just discussed. The decisions made will depend on each news outlet. They are thinking about their particular audience. What does that audience want or need? Is this story more or less important than that one? Do we have the staff to do that story well?

Newspapers have been called the "daily miracle." The editors are sorting through reams of stories and deciding, on deadline, what to include. They will consider which photographs to print, how to present the news graphically, and when to get it all to the presses on time to be printed and delivered the next morning. Broadcasters refer to the need to fill airtime with news as "feeding the beast." Especially in large cable TV news operations and all-news radio stations, the volume of news is huge. Of course, the Internet is a major tsunami of news and information every day. The hot story this evening may be old by tomorrow morning. Journalists must operate in this pressure cooker and keep their common sense. It's a difficult, but important and rewarding job.

News Paths

There are predictable ways that an event becomes a news story. Though it can get more complicated than what we are about to describe here, there are basically two kinds of news stories. Journalists give them various titles, but let's call them spot news and feature news.

Spot news stories are those events that occur to which a reporter responds. These events are time-sensitive and must be reported immediately. They include fires, storms, accidents, crimes, Election Day, a government vote on an issue, a trial, a sports game, etc. These are events that happen and the journalist reacts to them. The journalist arrives at the fire, observes, interviews eyewitnesses, victims, and officials, and writes the story. The object is to report, as clearly as possible, what happened.

Feature stories are those events that are not as time sensitive and often require extensive reporting, writing and rewriting, and fact-checking before they are published, posted, or broadcast. In feature stories the journalist is more proactive. This group of stories includes, but is not limited to, government corruption, ongoing wars, white collar crime, celebrity news, reports on charities, covering political campaigns, science, medicine, entertainment reviews, food, education, business, trends and fads in society as well as reviews of books, music, and other items.

There is overlap between spot news and feature stories, but because sources can vary in these kinds of stories, it's useful to think of them as separate categories. Let's take a look.

Spot News

At the scene of a spot news story, a journalist will talk with a variety of sources. Let's say it's a fire. She will find the firefighter in charge and, if he is not busy at the moment, ask him for an overview. How serious is the fire? Will it spread? Is anyone hurt? Do you know yet how it started? She will then speak with any eyewitnesses. What did you see? Did you know the people who live there? How many live there? If there are uninjured people at the scene, she will ask them the typical reporter's questions: What happened? Who was inside the house? Why did the fire start? Where did it start? When did it start? How did it happen? As she takes notes or records answers, she is assembling facts and opinions. Notice that each of the people she speaks with has a unique perspective. Each knows part of the story. Each filters the answers to the reporter's questions through his or her own experience of the event. The reporter is trying to piece together a story, as complete as possible, from this mosaic. It's like a puzzle, but the pieces don't necessarily fit together neatly. This process happens every day as reporters go about their duties. When the story is published, the basic facts are seldom wrong. A building burned. One person was killed. The firefighters put it out. Eyewitnesses say they think it was arson, but the fire department isn't sure and will continue its investigation. But if several reporters cover the same story, there will be differences. Each reporter spoke with the same officials, but different witnesses or victims.

Usually the basic facts are used in both stories, but depending on the reporters' writing ability, the sources they used, and variables like when the reporter arrived on the scene, the stories will be different in nuance and substance. Each reporter will choose to include or omit things that other reporters will think important. This is an example of the filters involved in getting a story as accurately as possible.

After the reporter writes her story, an editor will then look at it, often several editors. They will change some of the writing. They will ask the reporter questions about things they don't think are clear. If it's a broadcast story, someone will edit the tape, and someone else will decide where it will run in the TV newscast. Then, when the audience members see or read it, they will filter it through their own knowledge and experience.

Spot News

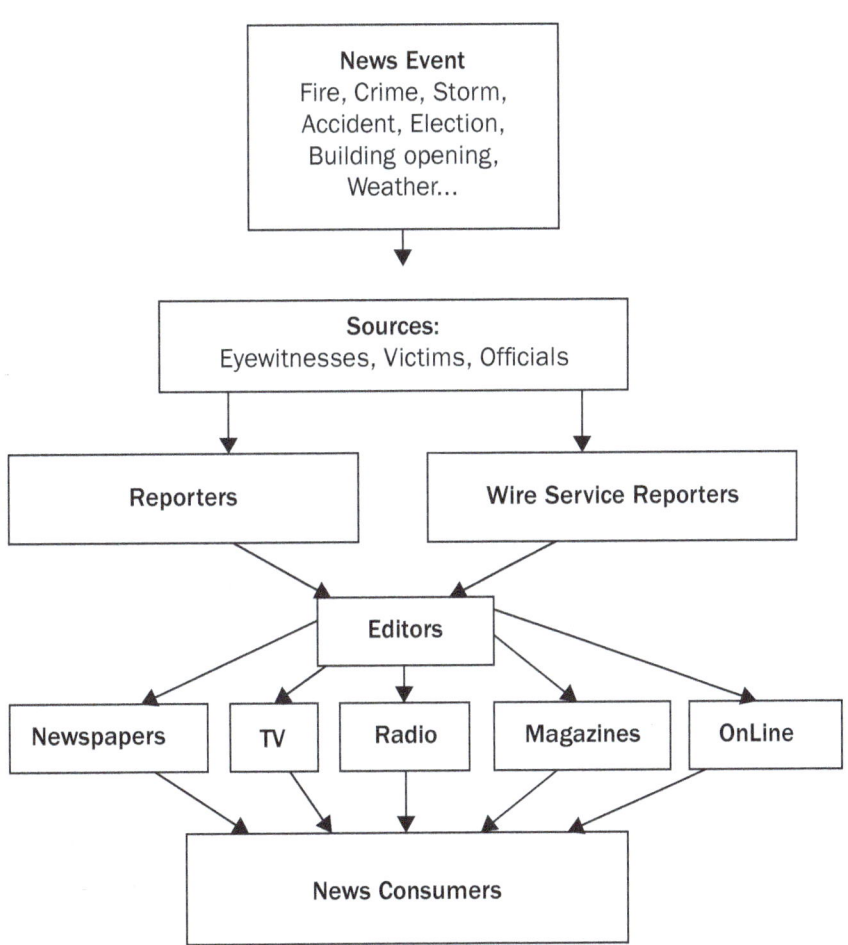

Breaking spot news, especially large and chaotic events like a mass shooting or bombing, are sometimes problems for reporters. They like to be first with important news, but pressure to be first can lead to errors. This has become especially true, as the Internet has developed into a greater news source. Tweets, Facebook postings, and other digital methods of transmitting news have increased the speed at which we can get information. In the early hours following the shootings of school children and teachers at Sandy Hook Elementary School in Newtown, Connecticut, some sources reported the shooter was not Adam Lanza, but his brother. In the Boston Marathon bombings, at least two news outlets online said the bomber was a missing student from Brown University. Those stories were wrong. They were corrected eventually, but not before misinformation was sent to the audience. Being first is nice, but good journalists must always attempt to be accurate. If not, they lose respect with the public.

The chart below shows some typical filters along the path of getting from a news event to a story that's published or broadcast.

Feature News

Feature stories go through a different, but similar process. Let's say a reporter gets a tip that a politician is taking bribes to vote a particular way. He starts calling his sources to find out if there's any truth to the accusation. Before he publishes anything, the ethics committee in the legislature opens an investigation into the case, making it public for the first time. The reporter lost his "scoop" (getting the story first), but it's still important news. He calls members of the ethics committee to find out the charges and any evidence they will share with the public. They refer him to the public relations spokesperson for the committee. He calls the legislator who refuses to talk to the press. Instead, the legislator releases a statement through his spokesperson. The spokesperson says the legislator has done nothing wrong and will defend himself vigorously. The reporter calls the company alleged to have paid the bribes. The company's public relations spokesperson issues a statement saying the charges are false. The head of the company will not comment to the press. The company says to call its lawyers. The reporter begins to try to find any documents that might prove or disprove the allegations.

Notice some of the differences between the spot news story just described (above) and this kind of story below:

This story will be ongoing and the deadline will not be tonight. (The initial announcement by the ethics committee will be covered as spot news, but the continuing developments will be feature stories.) The story might be reported over several days, weeks, or months.

The reporter is forced to talk with public relations people or lawyers instead of the actual people charged with wrongdoing or those investigating it.

This is a relatively modern fact of life in journalism. In the 1970s, it was common to speak with the actual sources. Today, in almost all kinds of feature and investigative stories, sources are protected by a public relations department, whose job is to make its client look good. This is true of entertainment and sports stars, politicians, business people, and most institutions, including colleges, hospitals, and nonprofit organizations. Journalists prefer to talk with the actual people involved, but they are often forced to talk with PR spokespersons, who filter the material to try to ensure that their clients are seen in the best possible light. This process makes it more difficult to find the "truth" and report it to the public. Obviously, from the point of view of those under press scrutiny, it's important to try to control the message the press will report to the public.

The path feature news stories usually take is shown in the chart below:

Feature News

```
                    ┌─────────────────────────┐
                    │       News Event        │
                    │   White Collar Crime,    │
                    │  Government Corruption,   │
                    │    Sports, Charities,     │
                    │   Entertainment News...   │
                    └─────────────────────────┘
                                 │
                                 ▼
                    ┌─────────────────────────────┐
                    │          Sources            │
                    │  Public Relations People    │
                    │       Official Sources      │
                    │ Documents, Witnesses, Friends, Co-workers, │
                    │      Relatives, Enemies...   │
                    └─────────────────────────────┘
                       │                      │
                       ▼                      ▼
            ┌──────────────────┐   ┌──────────────────────┐
            │    Reporters     │   │ Wire Service Reporters │
            └──────────────────┘   └──────────────────────┘
                       │                      │
                        ▼          ▼
                    ┌──────────────┐
                    │   Editors    │
                    └──────────────┘
          ┌──────────┬────┬────────┬─────────┬─────────┐
          ▼          ▼    ▼        ▼         ▼
    ┌──────────┐ ┌──────┐┌──────┐┌──────────┐┌────────┐
    │Newspapers│ │  TV  ││Radio ││Magazines ││ OnLine │
    └──────────┘ └──────┘└──────┘└──────────┘└────────┘
          │        │      │        │          │
          ▼        ▼      ▼        ▼          ▼
    ┌─────────────────────────────────────────────┐
    │              News Consumers                  │
    └─────────────────────────────────────────────┘
```

Possible news events go through these paths every day. At each stage, with each interview or observation, the story will be filtered. Each stage will add clarity or make a story more confusing. Informed news consumers should understand this process. Much of the time, the end result is a pretty good snapshot of the "truth" about the event or individual. But, like most human endeavors, it is not perfect and never will be.

Who's Responsible for How the Story Is Played in Print or Broadcast?

If it's a newspaper or magazine story, an editor will choose a headline, decide on pictures or graphic design, decide where to place it, and how much space to give it. The reporter has no control over these things.

If the story is produced for TV, many people will be involved in the process as well. A photographer will work with the reporter in the field, and, though the reporter will write the story, it will be edited by a video editor. A producer will refine the script and decide how long it will be and where it will be placed in the newscast. An anchor will introduce it. TV news is very much a team effort and it's the whole team that makes decisions about what to cover and how to cover it. Online journalism varies. Some websites are highly professional with safeguards like those in more traditional news media. Others will post almost anything, including rumors and clear untruths. Choosing the most reliable news sources is, of course, the responsibility of each individual.

Good journalists strive to be fair and balanced in their reporting, and work hard to report as accurately as possible.

Good news consumers, as active citizens in a democracy, should use several news sources to be as well informed as possible.

Exercises

1. Define news.
2. Name and describe six or seven news values that determine whether something merits coverage.
3. Why are newspapers sometimes called "daily miracles"?
4. Why don't many journalists like the word "objective"?
5. Describe spot news and feature news.

For Critical Discussion or Writing

1. What is your view of the American news media?
2. What was the most important news story of the past year? Why?
3. Given what you've learned about how journalists define news, are there stories you think should NOT be reported?
4. What do you think reporters could do to be better at their jobs?
5. Do you think it's good that spokespeople often speak for powerful people to the press now?

CHAPTER 11

Who Owns American Media?

The ownership of media in the United States is, at the same time, extraordi-narily broad and remarkably concentrated. There are thousands of magazines, daily and weekly newspapers, radio stations, TV operations, movie companies, book publishers, record companies, video producers, newsletters, and websites in this country. There is everything from the mom and pop weekly newspaper with 2,000 readers to the daily *New York Times* or the *Wall Street Journal* with millions. There are tiny radio stations in rural areas and huge radio conglomerates, one of which— iHeartRadio —now owns over 800 radio stations. There are magazines that cater to tiny segments of the public like *Woodshop News*, and those that aim at a mass audience, such as *People* or *Cosmopolitan*. There are political magazines, environmental newsletters, business journals, women's rights monthlies, newspapers for gay activists and gun lovers. There are books and magazines for kids and also for kinky sex fetishes. And of course, there's the Internet with its vast universe of information and opinion. The breadth and depth of American media is, frankly, amazing. There is so much entertainment, news, and information available to us now that no person could understand it all in a lifetime.

But with all this variety, there are also troubling issues of ownership. Who owns the media often dictates what kinds of news and entertainment society will receive. A publisher with a strong political point of view will, in many cases, want to have his or her publication reflect those views. When a huge conglomerate owns many kinds of media, its concern for profit may mean a homogenization of content that is designed to never offend anyone. It's a kind of dumbing-down, one-size-fits-all product without nuance or journalistic courage. Inversely, an owner may attempt to be perverse or titillating in an effort to increase sales.

Who owns the media is a vital question for people concerned about how our democracy works, and, especially, the trust we place in news about the society in which we live. Journalists believe their role is to "seek truth and report it." How does that objective mesh with the issue of ownership in a democratic, but capitalist, profit-oriented system?

Where Does the Money Come From in the News Media?

- Advertising: Media companies sell ads. The more time or space they sell for a higher cost, the more they make.
- Subscriptions: Newspapers, magazines, cable TV, cable radio, and the Internet also make money from sales of individual copies or monthly fees.
- Underwriting: Public television and radio and a few small magazine publishers and websites collect money only from grants or donations.

The more dollars earned, the more media outlets an owner can potentially purchase. Or, owners can elect to improve the depth and quality of its news coverage.

What are the Average Profit Margins in the News Media?

Businesses have to make a profit to survive. One of the major changes in newspapers and broadcast stations in the past couple of decades is the level of profit expected. In the 1970s, newspapers were considered solid if they earned 10 percent to 15 percent annual profit, and broadcasters operated successfully with profit margins from 20 percent to 25 percent. (In this discussion, profit margin refers to the percentage of take-home money owners get at the end of the year after all expenses are paid.) By the mid-1980s, broadcasters were expected to earn at least 40 percent, and many earned 50 percent annually. Newspaper owners came to expect profits of 20 percent to 25 percent each year. The *New Haven Register* in Connecticut earned profits of over 30 percent one year. For perspective, supermarket chains are happy with profits of three to five percent annually. Profits for media companies are now less predictable.

Of course, there are news media outlets that lose money and some go out of business. The development of the Internet for news and commercial purposes has caused older or "traditional" media some serious financial challenges. These issues are not simple, but can be attributed to three basic areas of concern. The first is the slowness of American news media to respond to advertisers moving to the Internet. Classified ads were long a stable part of newspapers' income. The advent of online services like Craig's List cut newspaper revenue significantly and local newspapers didn't figure out how to respond. Next, during the late 1990s and early part of this century, the large conglomerate media owners often borrowed huge amounts of money to buy more outlets. When hard economic times hit, they were not able to pay back the investors, often hedge funds and investment banks who lent them the money. Several newspapers and magazines have gone out of business in the U.S., and others have declared Chapter 11 bankruptcy. Two major chains are examples. The Tribune Company (which owns the *Chicago Tribune, the Los Angeles Times*, other papers and TV and radio stations) and JRC (which owned dozens of papers) went into bankruptcy.

Both are out of bankruptcy now, but they are changed companies. The JRC still owns a number of papers, but is controlled by a new company called Digital First Media. The Tribune Company is looking to sell several of its newspapers, and has begun buying more TV stations around the country. Major portions of both chains are now controlled by large investment banks and hedge funds.

Just 20 or 30 years ago, ownership of media was much more varied than it is today. There were newspaper chains that owned 50 or 60 daily papers. There were broadcast networks of course, and they provided programming, including news, for the entire country. But the national networks were permitted to own no more than seven local TV stations. Other non-network owners could also own only seven TV stations and 42 AM and FM radio stations.

Many chains that owned lots of newspapers or broadcast stations were family businesses, and their fortunes had been made in the media. That is, their business was news or entertainment, but not manufacturing, food, or software. The principle job of media chains just a few years ago was media.

As merger-mania hit the rest of the American economy in the 1980s, it hit the media too. Large conglomerates bought up newspapers and magazines. Today, several chains own more than 100 each of the country's approximately 1,600 daily newspapers. One chain owns over 130 weekly newspapers.

Some publishing companies put out dozens of national magazines. Many large media businesses own all sorts of print media, film companies, record companies, websites, book publishers, and billboard companies. Congress loosened ownership rules in broadcasting and now several companies own more than 150 of the 15,000 radio stations. Disney, Viacom, News Corps, Time Warner, and Comcast are now some of the largest owners of U.S. media. Phone companies own cable networks and vice versa. Companies like Sony own movie companies. The merger mania is still going on.

Where once there were hundreds of individual voices controlling media, now a few dozen own most of the means of mass communication in the United States. Conglomerates that make pudding or iPods also own controlling interests in news media.

In a book first published in the early 1980s called *Media Monopoly*, author Ben Bagdikian noted that about 50 corporations controlled a majority of American media. He updates the book every few years. In his most recent edition, *The New Media Monopoly*, he writes that five companies now control most American media outlets. Says Bagdikian:

> *"These five huge corporations—Time Warner, Disney, Murdoch's News Corporation, Bertelsmann of Germany, and Viacom (formerly CBS)—own most of the newspapers, magazines, books, radio and TV stations, and movie studios of the United States."*

Is this bad or good? Some say that it provides better efficiency; that big, powerful companies can provide better programming and print material more cheaply; and that their power makes them better able to stand up to pressure from society or government.

Critics say these very efficiencies create blandness; that big companies with lots of money to lose will take no chances; that they offer news and programming that is only designed to keep the masses and government regulators happy; and that they are unwilling to challenge the status quo.

Some say big owners won't permit their journalists to act as a watchdog to the government or other powerful forces because they have too much to lose. Others say the companies will be so powerful they will control the government.

Structure of Print News Media

Publisher
This is the person who runs the overall operation at the newspaper or magazine. Remember, with corporate ownership of many news media, the publisher will answer to a corporate office at the company's headquarters.

Circulation
This department makes sure the publication is getting subscriptions and newsstand sales. It also makes sure it's delivered on time each day, week or month.

Production
This department prints the publication. It makes sure the printing presses are working properly and the publication gets produced. The huge printing presses used are expensive pieces of equipment that need to be carefully maintained.

Advertising
This department sells display and classified ads. It often creates ads for smaller advertisers. It also ensures ads placed in the publication are what the advertisers have paid for. Classifieds are usually handled by telephone or internet. Display ads are sold by local, regional and national sales representatives.

Business
This department handles such items as contracts, purchase of supplies, and the money for paychecks.

Editorial:
This is where the editors, reporters, copywriters and photographers are. **Editor-in-Chief** is responsible for all the news that is printed. Below the Editor-in-Chief are a series of supervising editors. Usually there is a **Managing Editor** who oversees the daily operation of the news room. This person may have several assistants known as **Assistant Managing Editors**. Then there are **Section Editors**. Each section of a publication will usually have editors in charge of local news, suburban news, sports, business, entertainment, arts, photos, food, lifestyle, editorials, graphic design and wire services. Depending on the size of the operation, there will be more or few section editors. At small places, the Editor-in-Chief may do all these jobs; at larger operations, there will be many editors. Next, there are **Copy Editors** who read each story for spelling, grammar, and news reporting problems in reporters' copy. Finally, there are **Reporters** who usually work with one section; their "beat" is a town, the courts, police, sports, business. Most **Photographers** and some reporters work on "general assignment," which means they do any story they are asked to do. Most newspapers and magazines will have an **Online Editor** who designs and updates the Web site. At most newspapers and magazines, about 20 percent of the jobs will be in editorial.

Structure of Broadcast News Media

General Manager
This person runs the overall broadcast operation. He or she usually answers to a parent corporation's headquarters.

Sales
This department sells advertising and promostes the stations' programming.

Production
Engineers, Studio Camera people, Directors. They produce local programs, commercials and make sure equipment works.

Programming/ Operations
Program Directors decide what kind of entertainment shows and the format the station will do. Operations Manager handles day-to-day logistics, hires engineers, studio camera people.

Business
Business Manager, Clerks, Office Staff make sure checks get paid, budgets handled and vendors get paid.

News
News Director – Decides on the vision of the news department, hires and fires new staff.
Executive Producer or **Assistant News Director** – Often runs the daily news operation.
Chief Photographer – In charge of all photographers.
Line Producers – They are in charge of individual news shows. They write newscasts.
Field Producers – They are reporters in the field who don't go on air. They are responsible for developing stories and sources.
Assignment Desk Editors – They assign reporters and shooters to stories. Research stories.
Reporters – They go out and interview, report, write and go on air with their stories.
Tape Editors – They edit video or audio tape.
Tape Coordinators – They catalog file tape and find video for current stories.
Assistant Producers – These are beginning jobs. they help with everything in the newsroom.
Photographers – Shoot video for news stories.
Anchors – News, Sports, Weather. They write, report and are the on-air faces and voices.
Webmaster – They design and udate the station's website.

At the average TV station about 20 to 25 percent of the total jobs will be in the news department. In radio, it depends on the kind of format at the station. If it's all news, then obviously most of the jobs will be news jobs. At music stations, jobs would be for DJ's, copy writers, commercial producers.

Is media conglomeration a serious problem? Can laws be passed within the Constitution to try to make sure media ownership is diverse?

These are questions without easy answers, but the debate is an important one for American citizens. Let's look at the structure of the print and broadcast media:

Fragmentation of Audiences

In the mid-1970s, a TV mini-series like *Roots*, the saga of a black slave family, could capture the American imagination. When it aired, people were talking about it all over the country. The same was true of big news stories, such as Watergate and the Vietnam War. That same focus on a news event occurred when terrorists struck on September 11, 2001. National TV, radio, and magazines brought the country together. But today, many radio, cable TV, magazines, websites, and even some newspapers are highly specialized. The Internet has permitted millions of people to find their own special interests, or make their own shows. Many kinds of media now aim at a fragment of the country's more than 300 million people. If they capture only one percent, that's three million people. You can make good money if you appeal to the right fragment. Many newspapers and magazines do well financially with audiences in the few thousands.

This means that many people, who a few years ago would know about a big story and its importance, may not know much about it today. They are using news from the niche related to their individual interests and not necessarily paying attention to broader issues that are important to the country or their hometowns. The traditional national TV networks—NBC, ABC and CBS—have a lower percentage of viewers, and the niche cable TV networks have increased viewers. There are all-sports networks, all-entertainment, all-music, and all-comedy currently available. The Internet and video games have siphoned off more consumers. Popular music has fragmented tremendously; now there are radio stations formatted to attract relatively small segments of musical tastes. Modern country music, traditional country, hip-hop, various kinds of rock, jazz, pop, show tunes, and many others all have their own exclusive stations. Tiny media that would have died years ago because of the difficulty of attracting an audience are finding a spot on the Internet. At the same time, huge media companies provide syndicated programming and news to millions of people that are exactly the same all over the country.

Does this specialization and fragmentation of audiences pose a threat to a unified country? Will local news continue to be reduced in scope because big media fill up local papers and stations with the same stories they produce for all their news outlets?

It's important to understand a reality about ownership that complicates matters and frustrates those who seek easy answers. When news media ownership was less concentrated, there were owners of newspapers, TV or radio stations, and small chains who did a terrible job. There were also many who served their communities extraordinarily well. Some big media companies serve the public interest in positive ways and still make money. The New York Times Company owns several newspapers and broadcast stations, and the *New York Times* itself remains one of the best newspapers in the world. The Washington Post Company and the McClatchy newspaper group and National Public Radio do responsible and hard-hitting journalism. There are also big media conglomerates whose performance is questionable at best. These are the outfits that cut news staffs, reduce or eliminate local news, and seldom produce any reporting of high quality. They only worry about profits, and cater to special interests such as businesses that buy lots of advertising.

There is another issue that should be considered. Most media are owned and controlled by whites. Hispanic-owned media outlets are growing, but are still relatively small. Blacks own a smaller portion of American media than their percentage of the total population. The number of minorities—Blacks, Asians, Native Americans, Spanish speakers—working as journalists has increased over the past 20 years, but remains lower than the percentage of the total minority population in the country.

With this analysis in mind, the question remains: Is it acceptable in a democracy to concentrate vast media power in fewer and fewer hands? Is a monopoly on news and entertainment as important as a monopoly in gasoline or computer software? If we have so many media, won't all voices be heard? Or, will many voices be effectively lost because some media companies are so big that they have little interest in presenting diverse viewpoints? These are questions that the American society will continue to confront in the years ahead.

Exercises

1. What profit percentages do newspapers and broadcast stations earn?
2. What does fragmentation of audiences mean?

For Critical Discussion or Writing

1. Is it OK for large companies to control much of the U.S. Media?
2. How important is local news vs. national news?

CHAPTER 12

Journalism Ethics

Are you an ethical person? Do you think most people are ethical? What about professions like doctors or lawyers? Do you think most of them are ethical? What about business people, accountants, or factory workers? Do you believe most police officers have a strong ethics base? What about clergy?

Ethics, or the lack of them, affect us regularly. Getting correct change, trusting the doctor, accepting what a politician says are all examples of this reality.

What are the ethical guidelines for the news media? Are the codes of ethics in journalism similar to the ethical codes of lawyers or doctors? Who enforces journalism codes of ethics? Is there a way, within the First Amendment, to enforce journalism ethics?

These are some of the questions we explore in this section. We will discuss press ethics in the context of the greater society, and offer examples of various ethics codes.

Trust and the News Media

Trust. Here's that word again. Reporting news requires a substantial amount of trust between the reporters and the news consumers. Where does that trust come from? When you read a paper or magazine, listen to broadcast news, or log into an Internet news site, how do you know the news is accurate? If the radio news says there's a traffic backup caused by an accident on the interstate, do you believe it? When the paper reports that a fire has driven a family from its home, is that information credible? Perhaps the most important element in a discussion of journalism ethics is credibility.

If you ask people if they believe the news, most will recall the old saying: "Believe half of what you see, and none of what you hear." As earlier noted, in reality, a majority of people trust the news media to report stories like those above. We believe for several reasons. First, the news media have a history of being right. When the TV station says the storm has knocked out power to a section of the city, it's usually accurate. When news media report on a vote in Congress, it's most often correct information. When you move away from these kinds of easily verifiable stories, the credibility of the journalists comes more into play. Can you trust the report that claims the president is going to ask the cabinet secretary to resign? Will the phone company lay off hundreds of workers next week as the business reporter says? If you pay attention to these issues, you realize the mainstream news media are usually right when they publish such stories.

Good reporters are careful. They report what they can verify. And, they understand that if they are wrong, it's their credibility on the line. Reporters can be fired for making mistakes of a serious nature. One way to understand this is to realize that the most important thing a reporter or a news outlet has to offer is credibility. If news reports can't be trusted by the audience, news consumers will vote with their wallets and not purchase that newspaper or magazine, or listen to that broadcast station, or click on that website again. If clicks, circulation, or ratings decline, there is less money to pay staff, and production costs, and profits will be reduced. The very existence of the news operation may be in jeopardy. If the audience can't trust the news to be reliable and accurate, in a society with many news outlets, it will go elsewhere. There is an economic incentive in the U.S. for the news media to avoid making serious mistakes or doing unethical things.

That doesn't mean reporters or news media outlets are always ethical. They aren't. Journalism, like other industries, has its bad participants. There can be economic incentives to be unethical, such as refusing to do news stories about serious problems with an advertiser's product so that advertiser will continue to advertise.

Why News Media Won't "Do Anything" to Increase Ratings/Sales Pages

There is another criticism of news media in the U.S. that we should mention. It's that news media will do "anything" to increase ratings or improve circulation. It's true that bigger audience numbers mean more money coming in. But, like many things, it's more complicated than that. A newspaper, for instance, sets advertising rates well in advance of any particular story. If a major story breaks and the paper covers it extensively, it will be on the front page and, usually, several pages inside the paper. Because ad rates have already been set, however, the newspaper receives the same amount of revenue it would have recorded had the big story not occurred. Subscription rates change slowly; the paper doesn't get more money because it covered the big story well. The only element that may change when a big story occurs is that the newspaper may sell more newsstand copies. But the price of a paper on the newsstand is only a small fraction of what it costs to produce the paper. In broadcasting, networks and local stations often drop commercials to cover a major news story. They can lose money in the process. Some kinds of media will "do anything for ratings," it seems. But that criticism against the higher quality, mainstream news media is usually inaccurate. Online reports have developed some more difficult problems. The more "clicks" you get, the greater your audience. Some reporters are paid more if more people read or watch their stories. This, obviously, has the potential for websites to offer stories that are "sexy" to increase traffic. There's a lot of attention paid to attracting more readers online. If you've read "reviews" of products or services online you may wonder if the "raves" are real. Some are and some aren't. The federal government investigates some of this activity under false advertising laws. Intelligent news consumers need to be aware of their sources of information and choose credible ones.

Codes for Journalists

There is a history in the U.S. of ethics codes in journalism. The first was written by the American Society of Newspaper Editors in 1926. Over the years, other journalism groups, individual newspapers, magazines, and broadcast stations have adopted their own codes. These codes are guidelines. They are meant to offer journalists a set of suggestions about what SHOULD be done if a journalist wants to maintain credibility.

These codes are not like those of doctors or lawyers. The members of those professions must pass extensive exams and be licensed to practice medicine or law. They can lose their licenses if they are found guilty of malpractice or unethical behavior. Under the First Amendment, with its free speech and press guarantees, the government may not decide who can speak or publish. This means anyone can become a journalist. There are no licenses required. So who enforces journalism ethics? Part of the answer is in the economic incentives previously mentioned.

What about the moral codes and training of individual journalists? Are the reporters and editors ethical people? Do they care about informing the public as accurately as possible? University journalism programs have courses in media law and ethics that require students to think about ethics in the business and understand why ethical behavior is important. Veteran journalists often talk with young reporters about conflicts of interest and other kinds of ethical pitfalls.

Watchdogging the Journalists

Another powerful tool in enforcing journalism ethics is the First Amendment itself. If a publication does something unethical, other publications often report on the issue. When *Time* magazine published a cover picture of O. J. Simpson that darkened his face and made him (according to many observers) look more sinister, other journalists criticized *Time* publicly. *Time* had to apologize. When ABC News used actors to re-create a scene that appeared to show an alleged American spy handing a briefcase to a Soviet spy without telling the audience the scene was not real but dramatized, ABC was severely rebuked by other journalists and had to apologize on the air. Other groups also keep watch over journalists.

When an NBC producer edited the audiotape of George Zimmerman's 911 call that misleadingly made it appear that he described Trayvon Martin's race without being prompted, Newsbusters, a part of the Media Research Center, called it to the nation's attention. The producer was fired.

In Minnesota, a News Council made up of private and public representatives heard cases of alleged journalism ethics violations. It held hearings, listened to all sides, and issued reports. The Council did not have the power to file any criminal or civil charges, but its reports could serve as a powerful tool to embarrass poor behavior on the part of journalists. The concept was to use the Council's First Amendment power to rebuke journalists who have stepped over the ethical line. It served the public for 41 years, ending operations in 2011 due to a drop in the number of complaints and a loss of funding. News councils are rare, and some journalists think they are a bad idea because they might step over the line and infringe on First Amendment freedom of the press.

However, the fact that journalists (and those monitoring the profession) can and do criticize other journalists is a helpful way to curb bad behavior. Public reaction, especially with the extensive use of blogs and "comments" sections online, can also reveal and criticize unethical behavior.

Certainly, like in many fields, there are numerous opportunities for unethical behavior in journalism.

Some Ethical Conflict Scenarios

In the Appendix, you will find ethics codes from two journalism organizations. Your instructor can talk with you about the codes, and offer examples of ethical problems and conflicts that happen all the time in journalism. A few of the kinds of issues that arise are listed below.

- A reporter from a large national paper talks with a source high in the government who reveals the name of a CIA covert agent. The source wishes to remain anonymous and the reporter agrees. But the law says the government official cannot reveal the name of an undercover agent. When an investigation begins to discover who revealed the name, should the reporter testify about who told her the agent's name?

  (Note: Most journalists believe they cannot act as an effective watchdog of government if they don't rely on anonymous sources occasionally. They say many big stories, like the Watergate reports that caused President Richard Nixon to resign, could have never been done without some anonymous sources.)

- A department store chain is a big advertiser in the local newspaper. A reporter at the paper finds out the store is breaking labor laws by forcing employees to work overtime without pay. Will the paper publish a story about the labor law violations, or will it decline the story because it doesn't want to take the chance the store will cancel all its advertising?

- A sports reporter is offered the chance to fly on the team plane for free, the cost of her seat paid for by the team. Should she accept the free travel, or should she and her TV station decline the team's offer?

- A local reporter is asked to join the board of directors of the nonprofit Red Cross chapter in town. The board is unpaid, and it's an honor to be asked to serve. The board meets once a month, and helps decide how to use the chapter's money. It also hires the executive director. Should the reporter join the board?

- A reporter does a feature story on a turkey farm just before Thanksgiving. At the end of the interview with the farmer, he offers the reporter a nice fresh turkey as a small token of his appreciation for the reporter's interest. Should the reporter take the turkey?
- There's a Gay Pride rally happening on the town green. Should the editor send a gay reporter to cover it or a straight one? Does it matter?
- A reporter is working on a hot story about a local political scandal. One very important source agrees to speak to the reporter, but doesn't want his name used in the story. He may be worried about losing his job, or perhaps there might be threats against him if he's identified. Should the reporter agree to keep the source anonymous? Why or why not?
- A radio station airs a story that turns out to have some facts that are wrong. Should it air a correction? Or should it not air a correction because admitting mistakes makes the station seem weak and sloppy which might hurt its image?

Again, these are just a few of the many ethical issues that journalists encounter in the course of their jobs. For a complete understanding of how journalists are expected to respond to these challenges, please review the codes of ethics and conduct of the Society of Professional Journalists and the Radio-Television News Digital Association in the Appendix.

Exercises

1. Why are good ethics considered important in journalism?
2. What do the ethics codes say about plagiarizing?
3. Journalism codes of ethics say advertisers should not influence the news. Why?
4. Are newspaper subscription rates usually affected by a "big" story?
5. What does the SPJ Ethics Code say about truth?

For Critical Discussion or Writing

1. If you were a journalist, would you lie to get a really important story?
2. Do you think it would be a good idea to have government set up a commission to hold hearings and punish journalists who are found to be unethical?
3. What are some of the First Amendment problems around the idea of enforcing journalism codes of ethics the same way lawyers' or doctors' rules are enforced? (Doctors and lawyers can lose their licenses for malpractice.)

CHAPTER 13

Broadcast Regulations

The federal government regulates radio, TV, cable, telephone, and satellite communications in the U.S. How does regulation affect broadcasters' First Amendment rights and the rights of the audience? How are broadcasters different from other media, such as newspapers, magazines, books, video, CDs, or the Internet? Does regulation have an impact on news? Before those questions can be answered, it is important to relate a bit of broadcast history.

Early History

We discussed earlier that the first court cases testing freedom of expression were in the period during and just after World War I. One of the major technological and social changes at the time was the development of radio. The first commercial station, KDKA, went on the air in 1919 in Pittsburgh. Radio rapidly became the craze. Stations were popping up all over the country. Companies like RCA and General Electric (G.E.), which made radio sets, were selling them as fast as they could get them off the assembly line. Fortunes were made just selling the sets. The technology of radio broadcast was not yet sophisticated; stations interfered with each other's signals, they increased power at will, and drifted from one frequency to another. Broadcasters realized that they could make money with advertising, and some of the commercials were less than truthful. There were ads for various elixirs that were guaranteed to cure everything from athlete's foot to cancer. Several stations were selling coupons that promised admission to heaven. There were many religious broadcasts on the air, some filled with hatred for other religions. It was chaotic. The public and the radio station owners themselves started to pressure Congress in the early 1920s to regulate radio. In 1924, Congress passed the first law to set clear radio frequencies and power. In 1927, it passed the Radio Act that declared the airwaves public, and required broadcasters to get federal licenses to broadcast.

There is an important point to understand about broadcast regulation in this country. It was clear to those in power around the world that broadcasting was a remarkably powerful new medium. Most leaders decided that the government should own and operate stations—not just in the new socialist Soviet Union but also in Britain, France, and Japan. Every other government chose to build the stations, hire the staffs, and decide what to program, themselves. There was no independent broadcasting, and, in some countries, such as China and Saudi Arabia, there still isn't. Many European countries did not permit private broadcasting until the 1960s or 1970s. Why did the U.S. go another way?

Remember, in the chaos of the 1920s, socialism was a major fear. The idea of a big federal government, or even state governments, being able to control this new means of communication was frightening to many Americans. Capitalism was a way of life here, and even though American socialists and others were worried about its excesses, the idea of big government control was not acceptable to the majority of Americans or to Congress. To this day, the federal government may not broadcast any regular programming to the U.S. itself. The federal government's Voice of America and several other government-operated radio and television stations may only broadcast to other parts of the world.

Some states developed radio networks, but they were mainly to help get news and educational programming to rural areas not served well by private broadcasters. Many of those stations became the core of the Public Broadcasting System in the 1960s. So what model did the U.S. choose? It's a hybrid. There would be private ownership of the stations, but the government would license and control frequencies, power, technical, and some programming issues.

The 1934 Communications Act

In 1934, Congress and the administration of Franklin Delano Roosevelt passed the Communications Act that created the Federal Communications Commission to regulate broadcasting and interstate telephone and telegraph lines. Eventually they were charged with regulating television, cable, satellites, cell phones, and consumer radio use like CB radios. The FCC is still the agency that regulates telecommunications in the United States.

FCC commissioners are appointed by the president and approved by the Senate. There are now five commissioners, and no more than three can be from the party of the president. They regulate much of the communication we use on a daily basis.

It may be useful to mention that law and regulations are not the same. Congress passes laws. Federal agencies, like the FCC, pass regulations. Those regulations have the force of law but can be overturned by Congress and the president or by the courts. As we discuss electronic communication, understand that some of what we mention is regulation created by the FCC, and some are laws enacted by Congress and the president.

Much of the law established by the 1934 Communications Act is still in place today. The latest major amendments to the Communications Act were passed in 1996. The entire Act is now more than 1,200 pages. Needless to say, we aren't going to try to cover all of it here, but we'll explain some of the basics, especially those elements that affect news and public affairs.

One of the most important elements of the law is the concept that the airwaves belong to the public. The people who get broadcast licenses do not own the airwaves, they just get the right to use them for the period of their license. Those who are granted a license must agree to operate in the "public interest, convenience and necessity."

To Get a Broadcast License in the United States You Must:

1. Be an American citizen of good character. No foreigner may own a controlling interest in a broadcast station. No foreign investor may own more than 24.9 percent of the voting stock in a broadcast station. (You may wonder about Rupert Murdoch, whose News Corporation owns Fox network and other broadcast stations. He's from Australia. To buy into U.S. broadcasting, he became an American citizen in the 1980s.)
2. Prove you can operate the station technically. (You have to be a qualified radio/TV engineer or have hired qualified people.)
3. You must show you are financially stable. (You need enough money to run the station for at least 90 days without any advertising revenue coming in yet.)
4. You must promise the FCC that you will do certain kinds of programming. (Originally, owners were required to air certain amounts of news, education, religion, public affairs about their broadcast area, and agricultural news. This requirement, known as content regulation, was eliminated in the early 1980s by the FCC under the administration of President Ronald Reagan.) Today you have to tell the FCC what you intend to program, and report—when the station's license is up for renewal—whether you did it.

The Business of Broadcasting

There are about 15,000 radio stations and about 2,200 TV stations in the U.S. Radio stations and television station licenses have eight-year terms. After eight years, the stations must go through a renewal process. Broadcasters can lose their licenses if they do not follow the rules. Over the years since 1934, over a hundred radio stations and several television stations have had their licenses taken away by the FCC. The FCC may also fine stations for various infractions of their license responsibilities. For instance, the Howard Stern radio show was fined approximately $4.7 million for broadcasting indecent material. This is one of the reasons Stern signed with Sirius satellite radio, which is not subject to indecency rules.

Passage of the 1996 Telecommunications Act brought numerous changes in broadcast ownership. There used to be strict limits on the number of stations one person or company could own. For instance, before 1996 you could only own 42 radio stations. Now you can own as many as you can buy, except in large markets where there are some limitations. There is a sliding scale for the number of stations you can own in the big cities. For example, in New York City one company can own no more than eight stations. No owner can hold more than 50 percent of the commercial stations in those markets. The changes have meant the creation of huge radio conglomerates like Clear Channel, which owns over 800 radio stations now. Other companies own 100 to 400 stations each.

In TV, one owner may not control local stations that cover more than 39 percent of the total population of the country. This law was passed by Congress in December 2004. That's up from 25 percent before 1996.

Broadcast ownership and conglomeration are serious issues to many people. In 2003, the FCC proposed extending the TV ownership limit to 45 percent. The FCC received over 750,000 comments about the proposed changes, 90 percent of them against the idea. Lawsuits were filed to prevent the regulation from taking effect. In the spring of 2004, a federal court stopped that increase as well as other changes in ownership rules. (As noted above, Congress compromised with the Bush Administration and limited TV ownership to 39 percent.) The FCC had also proposed ending "cross-ownership" rules. That would have permitted companies to own TV and radio stations in the same markets in which they own newspapers. The court stopped that also. The court told the FCC to revisit its proposed ownership changes and come up with a better rationale for increasing the number of TV stations one company could own. In June 2006, the FCC announced that it would officially reconsider the ownership issues. In 2007, it decided to change one ownership rule. It was a long-standing rule that a company could not own a TV station and a daily newspaper in the same city. The FCC voted to permit such ownership in the largest 20 markets in the U.S. We will discuss media conglomeration later in this chapter.

How does broadcast regulation affect the average listener? Do broadcasters have the same First Amendment rights as other forms of media in the U.S.?

Because the airwaves belong to the public and broadcasters are required to serve in the public interest, they are treated differently under the current law.

Here are some examples:

- Congress banned cigarette advertising in broadcasting in the late 1960s. They probably could not legally do that in another medium.
- After a more than 20-year battle by children's rights activists, the government now requires TV stations, to air at least three hours of educational programming for children a week. They could not tell a magazine to publish articles about children.
- Broadcasters may not "cause a panic." This regulation dates from the airing of Orson Welles' adaptation of *War of the Worlds* in 1939. That radio broadcast, which sounded like a real news report about aliens landing in New Jersey, caused people to panic. An adaptation of the same show was broadcast by WPRO in Providence, Rhode Island, in the 1970s. It, too, caused a panic, and the FCC warned the station never to do it again.

Political Campaigns

Broadcasters have some specific responsibilities in relation to political campaigns. Section 315 of the FCC regulations is known as the "Equal Time Rule." This rule is meant to provide a more level playing field for candidates who seek public office. It requires that 45 days before a primary election and 60 days before a general election a station must give or sell equal time to every legal candidate for a particular office. A legal candidate is usually defined as someone who is officially on the ballot. Whether cable TV or satellite broadcasters must also follow the Equal Time Rule is a complicated issue. The FCC has not clarified whether these outlets must always follow the rule.

Here's how it's supposed to work: If a radio station gives Candidate A five minutes of time, let's say, talking with the morning DJ, it must offer five minutes to every other legal candidate in that particular race. If a TV station sells Candidate A 100 commercials, it must offer the same amount of time to every other candidate. Candidates, of course, don't have to buy the time, but the station cannot refuse to sell them time. The station must also charge the candidates what's known as its "lowest unit rate." That's the lowest price it charges its biggest advertisers during the year. A station may elect to permit no candidates on the air at all. But if it permits one, it must obey the Equal Time Rule.

Congress passed a law in 1959 saying that several kinds of programming are exempt from the Equal Time Rule: bona fide newscasts, bona fide news documentaries, and the reporting of on-going news events. The latter category takes into account situations like a sitting president who is running for re-election coming to town to talk about a natural disaster. The station would not have to worry about equal time for other candidates in that kind of case. Though news is basically exempt, stations may be fined for reporting only one side of an election race. The idea is fairness. In recent years, the FCC has granted exemptions from the rule to certain talk shows that occasionally do political "news" interviews. Oprah Winfrey, Jay Leno, Howard Stern, and others have been permitted exemptions when candidates appeared on their shows. This is controversial. Some believe these are entertainment shows, not news shows, and should never be granted exemptions.

There is another important point about campaign commercials: stations may not censor political commercials in any way. No matter what the commercial says, even if it's libelous, gross, or filled with hatred, it may not be censored. Stations may not be sued for airing offensive political commercials.

The Equal Time Rule has been challenged in the courts. An example of the "no censorship" rule comes out of a Supreme Court decision in a Georgia case. A member of the KKK, J. B. Stoner, was running for Congress; WSB Radio in Atlanta refused to air one of his campaign commercials, which was filled with verbal attacks on blacks, because it said it would inflame the community. Stoner took them to court. The Supreme Court ruled that political commercials may not be censored or refused by a station.

Obscenity and Indecency

You need to understand at this point a difference between over-the-air broadcast, satellite, and cable. Over-the-air broadcast, such as your favorite radio station or the TV station you receive without cable or dish, is free. When you dial in a frequency, you hear or see whatever the station is airing at that moment.

You have to make a conscious, voluntary effort to purchase cable or satellite programming, the same way you would buy a magazine or a video. And, if you want premium channels like HBO or one of the X-rated channels, you must pay extra. You choose which kinds of programming you want. This distinction is important in the law.

Obscenity: If material can be proven obscene, like other media, it is not permitted in broadcast.

Indecency: The FCC has regulations against indecency. Congress has passed a law prohibiting it. But what does "indecent" mean?

The legal definition is the broadcast of "material or language that depicts or describes, in terms patently offensive as measured by contemporary community standards for the broadcast medium, sexual or excretory activities or organs."

Indecency doctrine is like a Ping-Pong game. It's hard to keep your eye on where the law is at any given time. It's been the subject of many challenges, court cases, and law revisions in recent years. Is the law an infringement on broadcasters' First Amendment rights? Or, is it a legal exception to those rights, and a good idea to insist on "tasteful" speech in the public arena.

The Supreme Court case that set the First Amendment precedent for indecency was the so-called "Seven Dirty Words" case decided in 1978. A New York City radio station, WBAI, owned by Pacifica, aired comedian George Carlin's monologue that used the words "you can't say on TV." The words are "Shit," "Piss," "Fuck," "Cunt," "Cocksucker," "Motherfucker," and "Tits." The Carlin comedy monologue was broadcast at 2 p.m. A father driving across town with his fifteen-year-old son in the car tuned in to the broadcast and was offended. He complained to the FCC, and the FCC ruled against the radio station. The station appealed and the case ended up in the Supreme Court.

The Court ruled that the broadcast was indecent. It said that the words might be OK in another place, but not on the air, generally, and not during an afternoon broadcast when children were likely to be listening. The Court said that the place and time were inappropriate, "like a pig in the parlor, instead of the barnyard." The Court ruled that the FCC has the right, under its regulatory power, to say "the pig has entered the parlor, and it's not necessary to prove the pig is obscene."

Indecency law is controversial. It is not practical here to mention all of the debates, changes, and counter-changes that have occurred since it was first enacted in 1934. One of the realities of our society is that the definition of what is tasteful changes. In the 1960s, a broadcaster who accidentally said "hell" or "damn" on the air would be in trouble. Listeners would write and call the station to complain. Now, it's common to hear those words—and many other words considered more offensive—on the air without complaint from the audience. For instance, it is common now to hear "pissed off," meaning angry, on the air. But it is still considered legally indecent to say "piss" on the air. Currently, the FCC permits the broadcast of more "adult" material during the period from 10 p.m. to 6 a.m. This is referred to as the "Safe Harbor" time, when it is assumed that most minors are in bed.

Indecency in broadcast has been a hotter issue since the Justin Timberlake/Janet Jackson Super Bowl performance in 2004 where her "costume malfunction" caused a brief baring of her breast. The FCC received thousands of complaints.

Though the FCC had not cracked down on indecency seriously for several years before the Super Bowl, the outcry over Jackson's breast brought increased attention from the agency.

The FCC and Congress increased indecency fines by tenfold to $325,000 per incident in 2006. The FCC had fined the stations carrying the Howard Stern show millions of dollars over the years for indecency. The increased fines led Clear Channel, which aired Stern on six stations, to fire him from those stations. Stern moved to satellite radio in 2006. (The indecency rules do not apply to satellite, although Congress has considered a law to have them apply to both satellite and cable.)

It fined a station in Florida for what it ruled were indecent comments from the DJ, "Bubba the Love Sponge." It reversed its ruling on comments by Bono when he accepted a Golden Globe award on live TV and said, "fucking brilliant." First the FCC said the phrase was "fleeting" and the "F" word used as an adjective. After the Super Bowl, the FCC changed its mind and fined the stations that aired Bono's words.

To give you an idea of the recent back-and-forth between the FCC, the appeals courts, and the Supreme Court, note the following cases:

In 2007 the Second Circuit Court of Appeals overturned the FCC's ruling on "fleeting expletives" in broadcast. The court said that the FCC had changed its enforcement policy about brief words (like those said by Bono and others on live broadcasts) and that the policy was "arbitrary and capricious." They ordered the FCC to rewrite the regulations.

The FCC appealed that ruling to the Supreme Court.

In 2009, the Supreme Court ruled in favor of the FCC and said the stations must pay the fines levied against them. This 5–4 decision said that the FCC had the legal right to enforce indecency laws in broadcast. Justice Antonin Scalia, writing for the majority, said the FCC "could reasonably conclude that the pervasiveness of foul language and the coarsening of public entertainment in other media such as cable, justify more stringent regulation of broadcast programs so as to give conscientious parents a relatively safe haven for their children." This ruling avoided comment on the First Amendment issues.

The Third Circuit Court of Appeals in 2008 threw out the fines against CBS for the baring of Janet Jackson's breast in the Super Bowl.

The FCC also appealed that case to the Supreme Court.

The Supreme Court told the Third Circuit court to re-think the case in light of the high court's 2009 decision in favor of the FCC in the "fleeting expletives" case mentioned above.

Are you dizzy yet? You see what we meant about the law being like a Ping-Pong game?

In 2011 the Supreme Court said it would take yet another look at indecency. It decided to hear a case brought by the Fox network on nudity, expletives, and other indecent content. ABC was also part of this case. The Supreme Court said it would review the FCC's "indecency enforcement regime" to see whether it violates the First Amendment or the due process clause in the Constitution.

The Court announced its decision in 2012. It was a split ruling. It ordered that Fox and ABC pay no fines. The ruling said that broadcasters had not been given fair notice of the change in policy on nudity and profane language. (This is the "due process" part.)

But the Supreme Court did not delve into the First Amendment issue. Justice Anthony Kennedy wrote: "This opinion leaves the Commission (FCC) free to modify its current policy in light of its determination of the public interest and applicable legal requirements. And it leaves the courts free to review the current policy or any modified policy in light of its content and application."

Only one of the justices, Ruth Bader Ginsburg, was willing to take another look at the 1978 opinion in the Carlin "Seven Dirty Words" (Pacifica) case. She wrote: "It was wrong when it was issued. Time and technological advances, and the commission's untenable rulings in cases now before the court show why Pacifica bears reconsideration."

What does this mean? The FCC is ordered to rewrite the indecency rules so they are clear, in advance of any enforcement, to all broadcasters.

Stay tuned. Clearly, indecency doctrine will be back in the courts before too long.

Why do you see and hear so much explicit language and sex on cable or satellite? Because of the difference, outlined above, between those delivery systems and free over-the-air broadcasts. You must voluntarily opt to get cable, or buy premium channels, so it's treated in the law the same way as an X-rated magazine or video. Adults may make the choice to buy this material, but in broadcast radio and TV, children or offended adults may not choose. When you tune in the station, you get whatever it is sending. You could change the station, but the courts have said that's like running after the first blow of an assault. You've still been assaulted.

Multiple attempts by Congress to apply the indecency rule to cable and satellite TV and radio have not passed.

A Note About Indecency and the Internet

Congress has passed three laws to try to apply the broadcast indecency standard to the Internet. All of these attempts have been struck down by the courts as overly broad, and an infringement of the rights of adults to access whatever they like on the Internet. The exception is in libraries that receive federal funds. Congress passed a law that required such libraries to place filters on computers that minors may use or they would lose the federal money. The courts have upheld that law.

Other Regulations and Rulings

There are many other areas of FCC regulations and court decisions that affect communications in the United States. If you would like to know more, there are dozens of books and websites that speak to the issues.

As for now, the law says broadcasters, because of the public airwaves and public interest standards, must temper their First Amendment rights with those of the listeners and viewers who consume the news, entertainment, and public affairs programs in the United States

Exercises

1. Why can broadcast be constitutionally regulated?
2. What is the F.C.C.?
3. What are the rules concerning getting a broadcast license in the United States?
4. What is indecency in broadcast?

For Critical Discussion or Writing

1. Should the airwaves be considered public?
2. Do you agree with the rules against obscenity and indecency?
3. Should companies be able to own as many broadcast stations as they want, or should there be limits?

CHAPTER 14

The Internet

BY JODIE GIL

We've described two very different modes of government regulation when it comes to print and to broadcast media.

Cases like *Miami Herald v. Tornillo* helped solidify the rights of publishers to print without government interference. But in *FCC v. Pacifica*, the Supreme Court decided that not all media types are the same—and broadcast can be subject to government regulation.

So where does the Internet fall? Should the Internet face government oversight, as broadcast does, because of its public all-access nature? Or should it be like print, where government intervention has been repeatedly knocked down?

In the 1990s, Congress—and then the U.S. Supreme Court—faced this exact question.

Communications Decency Act

As politicians and civic leaders used the Internet more, they started to fear for the safety of their children. This was the Wild West, after all. There was no control over what was placed online. Someone, for example, bought the domain name www.whitehouse.com and hosted pornography there. No one was safe!

So in 1996, Congress passed the Communications Decency Act. The law had many sections, and one part dealt specifically with indecent material online. Under the law, anyone who used the Internet to transmit indecent, "patently offensive," or obscene material to a minor could face fines or jail time. Remember, indecency standards (as mentioned in the previous chapter) are lower than those for obscenity, and are up to interpretation based on community standards.

The members of Congress had pornography in mind when drafting the law, but it had real implications for a variety of educational and established websites.

An informational website about sexually transmitted diseases could be construed as "patently offensive." Romance novels targeted toward homosexual audiences—legal to be printed and sold in person—might be in violation of the Communications Decency Act, if sold online.

Dozens of groups signed on in two separate lawsuits challenging the law.

One group was headed by the American Civil Liberties Union and included the *Philadelphia Gay News, Salon Magazine,* and American Booksellers Foundation for Free Expression. The other was headed by the American Library Association and included popular Internet providers, such as AOL.

Let's step back a second and put the time period into perspective.

This was before Google. The *New York Times* had only just started publishing online. Companies were only just starting to get e-mail.

And these disparate groups had to seek understanding and support from the U.S. Supreme Court, which had an average age of 63 in 1997, when the case was heard.

The case—*Reno v. ACLU*—became a mission to educate about the Internet as well as convince the Justices that this new medium deserved all the same protections as the printing press.

The effort was successful. In June 1997, the Supreme Court ruled 9–0 in favor of the free-speech advocates. The Supreme Court decided that the Internet was more like print than broadcast and should therefore be free from content regulations.

"Unlike communications received by radio or television, 'the receipt of information on the Internet requires a series of affirmative steps more deliberate and directed than merely turning a dial,'" the court wrote in its decision.

The court struck down portions of the Communications Decency Act, saying they violated the First Amendment because the wording was essentially a "content-based" restriction on speech in a medium that should receive full First Amendment protection. The court took into account that in trying to protect children, the Communications Decency Act also prevented adults from participating in free speech online. Justices borrowed wording from a previous ruling, saying Congress was trying to "burn down the house in order to roast the pig."

"Although the Government has an interest in protecting children from potentially harmful materials …" the decision stated, "the CDA pursues that interest by suppressing a large amount of speech that adults have a constitutional right to send and receive."

Ethical and Practical Considerations

While the U.S. Supreme Court has ruled in favor of free speech on the Internet, the medium continues to evolve—and so could the legal interpretations of its First Amendment protections.

One of the most challenging—and to some, exciting—features of the Internet is that it throws professional journalists in a ring with everybody else.

As the consumer video camera did earlier in the century and the smartphone in recent years, the Internet opened up more freedom to the average person to communicate to the masses. And it took away some of the control big media companies hold over information.

Crowd Sourcing (User-Submitted Content)

An example of this in play is the real-time coverage of breaking news events. The Internet does much more than allow journalists to update readers minute by minute. Combined with cheaper mobile phones containing quality cameras, the Internet opens up an avenue for citizens to participate in the coverage.

Take, for example, the tornado that swept through Bridgeport, Connecticut, in June 2010. The EF1 tornado touched down in the afternoon of June 24 and cut through roadways, cars, and buildings in the area of East Main, Nichols, and Cedar streets.

That's close to the *Connecticut Post* headquarters, and the newspaper quickly sent several reporters and photographers to the scene. But what they found was a fleet of "citizen reporters" already sharing pictures and updates about the damage. Residents who were near the tornado as it happened started posting pictures and videos to Facebook and Twitter immediately, as reporters were still heading over to the scene.

The citizen contributions gave the *Connecticut Post* a depth of coverage. Not only did the paper have its professional photographs posted online but it created a photo gallery with dozens of reader photos and videos of the storm.

This act of using the power of the community to report on a single event is called crowdsourcing.

CNN has been using crowdsourcing in a major way since 2006, when it launched iReport. A blog post introducing iReport hinted at what was then a revolutionary idea. The blog said:

> *"Don't kid yourselves. This content is not pre-vetted or pre-read by CNN. This is your platform. In some journalistic circles, this is considered disruptive, even controversial. But we know the news universe is changing. We know that even here, at CNN, we can't be everywhere, all the time, following all the stories you care about."*

Problems

In a perfect world, this cross-coverage by journalists and the audience would be a blessing. But this is not a perfect world, and we must remember that the average citizen does not adhere to the same ethical guidelines as journalists do.

The use of reader-reports mixed in with journalistic endeavors raises several questions. First, there's the concern about journalism jobs being outsourced to the crowd. For example, CNN laid off almost a dozen photojournalists in 2011, citing the growth of citizen journalism as one of the reasons.

Another major concern is accuracy. While journalists spend their time checking facts and making sure they only distribute accurate information, readers may or may not have the same intentions. Citizens without the same ethical standards as journalists can easily spread false information to the masses. Consider the misidentification of a Boston Marathon bombing suspect in April 2013. Readers on the online message board Reddit inaccurately identified the Boston Marathon bombing suspect as a missing Brown University student after the FBI released blurry images of the two suspects. The readers did so after listening to police scanners online. Someone, somewhere along the way, misunderstood what police officers said about the suspects, and started identifying the missing student.

The rumor circulated on the message board, and moved over to Twitter, where several news reporters, including ones from Connecticut's WFSB, Politico, and *Newsweek* re-tweeted the inaccurate information.

This misinformation from citizens can also be malicious.

For example, in October 2012, a Twitter user with the handle @ComfortablySmug (later identified as hedge-fund analyst and GOP operative Shashank Tripathi, posted several false updates during Hurricane Sandy in New York City. "BREAKING: Governor Cuomo is trapped in Manhattan. He has been taken to a secure shelter," one false Tweet read. "BREAKING: Con Edison has begun shutting down ALL power in Manhattan," read another. His false tweets about flooding at the New York Stock Exchange building were picked up by some news outlets. News analyses of @ComfortablySmug's false tweets indicated he did it in an effort to pick up more followers.

Celebrity death hoaxes are common on social networks. Among the celebrities who have "died," according to hundreds of false tweets: Jim Carrey, Johnny Depp, Justin Bieber, and Morgan Freeman.

As a result, journalists must be careful to verify information they find on social networks.

Journalistic Errors

It's not just average citizens posting inaccurate information on social networks. Journalists, in their rush to get stories online first, have also made several major errors when covering breaking news in real time online.

In January 2011, several reputable news sources—including NPR, CNN, and Fox News—tweeted that U.S. Representative Gabrielle Giffords was killed in a shooting at a constituent meeting at an Arizona supermarket. In reality, Giffords had been shot, but survived the attack. Craig Silverman, who writes a media accuracy column *Regret the Error* for Poynter.org, says the mistakes were the results of a new, messy type of news coverage. Reporters used to have several hours to sort out the facts before presenting a clean version to publish. Now, readers see the path journalists take in searching for the truth because it is often chronicled in the public, social media sphere.

"Yes, the sausage was being made in front of our eyes with all the messiness that analogy implies," Silverman wrote in one column on the Giffords mistake.

The news media did not learn from the Giffords faux pas. In December 2012, major news outlets misidentified the shooter in the Newtown Sandy Hook Elementary School shooting based on inaccurate information given by sources. In a slower news cycle, that information would have been corrected before news reporters had time to publish it.

Several news organizations have reviewed their breaking news policies after the mistakes of the Newtown coverage, only to repeat the mistakes with the Boston Marathon coverage four months later.

Access Theory and Internet Comments

Remember that decision from *Miami Herald v. Tornillo*? The ruling stated that the government can't force a newspaper to print a response, basically killing Access Theory in print.

The Internet gives Access Theory a new breath of life.

The *New York Times* won't print your response to an article? Post it in the comment section. The comment gets deleted? Start your own website with your point of view. While you might not get the same readership of a powerhouse like the *New York Times*, you have the potential to reach millions of people if your comment picks up steam.

News organizations have long struggled with Internet comments. Spend some time in an anonymous, unmediated forum and you'll see why. People post vicious, often racist, sexist, and homophobic comments without identifying themselves. It's like slapping someone in the dark.

Much of the content in the comment sections of news websites is libelous. That is, it's false and damaging to someone. So why do we see it so often? It's due to another section of the Communications Decency Act—one that wasn't overturned by the Supreme Court in 1997.

Section 230 of the Communication Decency Act states:

> *"No provider or user of an interactive computer service shall be treated as the publisher or speaker of any information provided by another information content provider."*

That basically means that if you host a news website, and someone posts a libelous comment on that site, you aren't responsible for that comment. Most news organizations, bloggers, and other content publishers have interpreted the law to mean that they must leave the comments alone in order to receive this protection. So if a news site edits a comment to take out an insult, the news site now becomes responsible for that comment. That's why so many hateful comments get left alone online—it leaves the publisher legally safer than if the publisher started cleaning up the comments.

Section 230 is great for free speech, notes the Electronic Frontier Foundation. It allows sites like Facebook, YouTube, and Twitter to exist, because the owners of those sites don't have to worry about what content users are posting. "Rather than face potential liability for their users' actions, most would likely not host any user content at all, or would need to protect themselves by being actively engaged in censoring what we say, what we see, and what we do online," the EFF writes on its website explaining Section 230.

But the unmediated comment sections have left many readers with a bad taste in their mouths. Several news organizations have responded by hiring an editor to moderate comments, requiring registration and full names to comment, or shutting down comments altogether.

Jodie Gil is an assistant professor of journalism at Southern Connecticut State University.

Exercises

1. Why was the 1996 Communications Decency Act challenged?
2. In *Reno v. ACLU*, what did the Supreme Court rule in terms of Internet regulation?
3. What is crowdsourcing?
4. Name some examples of the news media reporting inaccurate information in its quest to get information out in real time as breaking news was unfolding.
5. Describe Section 230 of the Communications Decency Act and how it relates to Internet comments.

For Critical Discussion or Writing

1. Should the government protect children from indecent material on the Internet?
2. What are some of the dangers of news organizations using user-submitted content, such as posts on social networks or photos sent to newsrooms?
3. Would it be a violation of the First Amendment to arrest someone like the person tweeting as @ ComfortablySmug? Why or why not? Would his tweets be the same as shouting "fire" in a crowded theater?
4. Should news websites allow anonymous comments? What are the pros and cons?

CHAPTER 15

Politics and the Media

BY MICHAEL C. BINGHAM

To a degree that the Founding Fathers could scarcely have imagined, American politics has become a form of show business. Politicians rely on the mass media to craft narrow and simplistic images of themselves to "sell" to the electorate. This comes at the expense of encouraging debate about complex, substantive issues that actually impact Americans.

One key factor in this transformation is the rise of the career politician whose career goal is to get elected to office and then keep getting re-elected ad infinitum. This is far from what the framers of the Constitution had in mind when they devised "representative" government, a system under which regular, everyday people—farmers, lawyers, merchants—would give up two to six years of their lives, often at some financial or professional cost to themselves, to go to Washington and *represent* their neighbors and friends in Congress.

That was then, this is now. Today our state capitols and Washington, D.C. are populated by a class of people who view politics as a career—potentially a lucrative career when one considers how people who are elected or appointed to higher offices can, after they're out of office, get lobbying jobs, consulting contracts, and even become media "talking heads" themselves, as exemplified by former U.S. Representative Joe Scarborough of MSNBC.

As a result, what Washington is filled with today are people who are *not* like you and me, but are career professional politicians.

If they are to become successful political professionals, candidates for office must become skilled at manipulating the voting public through the mass media. They do this by carefully crafting selective images of themselves to be transmitted through the media, and by cultivating members of the media itself to portray them in favorable terms.

Entire industries have grown up around helping manage candidates for office. Virtually every representative above dogcatcher employs public-relations professionals, press secretaries, and "image consultants" who manage the candidates' appearance and demeanor, from their carefully coiffed hair to their expensive wingtip shoes.

Television Comes of Age

The first U.S. President to grasp how television could transform the political landscape was John F. Kennedy, whose good looks, charisma, and breezy manner with the media contrasted sharply with his opponent in the 1960 presidential campaign, the studied and stiff Vice President Richard M. Nixon.

Throughout much of the campaign, the more experienced Nixon held a slim lead over the Massachusetts Democrat. The tipping point came in a series of four "Great Debates" broadcast on television and radio between September 26 and October 21, 1960. These afforded voters their first real opportunity to see the candidates head-to-head, and the visual contrast was striking.

In August of that year, Nixon had spent two weeks in the hospital recovering from an injury. By the time of the first debate, he was underweight and pale. He refused make-up to improve his color and lighten his heavy "five-o'clock shadow." By contrast, Kennedy, who secretly suffered from a chronic and, at times, debilitating back injury, appeared tan, confident, and well rested.

According to contemporary polls, those who heard the first debate on the radio pronounced Nixon the winner. But the 70 million who watched television were much impressed with the contrast between Kennedy's smooth delivery and the vice president's evident discomfort. Focusing on what they saw, not what they heard, TV viewers pronounced Kennedy the winner of the debates by a significant margin.

More recently, two U.S. presidents have been particularly skillful at using the medium of television to sell themselves to voters. While the notion of a Hollywood actor becoming president might have seemed the stuff of fiction, Ronald Reagan was a good enough actor to convince voters to let him play the role of president for two terms—in large part due to his masterful on-camera performances and practiced poise with the media.

A dozen years after Reagan's election, another good-looking candidate with great hair and boundless charm won an upset victory over an incumbent in a splintered three-way race. Bill Clinton's mastery of the television medium was rewarded with two terms, and although his credibility was compromised by the Lewinsky affair, he remains enormously popular with many Americans.

The politics of Reagan and Clinton had next to nothing in common. What they shared, however, was the ability to sell themselves and their policies to the rest of us using the medium of television.

By contrast, George W. Bush, whose approval ratings plummeted during his second term, in large part due to public fatigue with the war in Iraq, was visibly ill at ease when the cameras went on, and lacked the glibness of Clinton and Reagan.

Other media play key roles in the nation's political dialogue. Talk-radio formats emerged as a major genre in AM radio in the 1980s after most music formats migrated to the higher-fidelity FM band. Many "talkers" have huge followings—Rush Limbaugh was syndicated to 660 stations at his peak of popularity.

For reasons that are hotly debated, much of contemporary talk radio leans to the right end of the political spectrum, including figures such as Sean Hannity, whose show is carried on about 400 ABC stations. But not exclusively: in 2004, former *Saturday Night Live* skit-writer Al Franken became the lead host on the Republican-bashing talk network Air America.

Probably the liveliest political dialogue is found on the Internet. Harking back to the earliest days of American journalism, much of the political content on the blogosphere is wildly partisan. Liberal views are well represented on popular sites such as MoveOn.org and DailyKos.com, while other news aggregators, such as DrudgeReport.com, whose founder, Matt Drudge, "broke" the Monica Lewinsky scandal, give online political commentary a more conservative hue. It should be noted that few blogs perform primary reporting.

The uncensored and unfiltered nature of the Internet lends itself to extreme points of view—after all, it's easier to get attention by saying something outrageous. But many believe that the overall influence of blogs on the nation's political dialogue is, at once, coarsening and polarizing.

However, those types of media are, to a greater or lesser extent, "niche" media compared to the universal reach of television. As politicians understand, perhaps better than anyone else in America, *everyone* watches television.

Key Issues

1. If you are running for public office above the level of dogcatcher, you can't get elected unless voters know who you are. It's not enough for them to hate your opponent, they have to feel as though they know *you*. If they hate your opponent but don't know you, they often will not vote.

2. Indeed, one of the greatest threats to our democracy is declining voter participation among Americans of voting age. It's a decline that began in the 1960s. Given the rise of 24-hour cable news and the ceaseless chatting of the blogosphere, it comes, ironically, at a time of more intense media spotlight on political campaigns than ever before.

3. Candidates can't get known without using the media. There are simply too many potential voters to meet face-to-face. The medium of choice for political campaigns at the state level and up is television, because, as noted, everyone watches TV.

4. Television advertising is breathtakingly expensive. To pay for it, candidates are forced to spend more time begging fat cats for money, and, in many cases, promising them favors once elected, than working on solutions to public policy problems. And, because the economic stakes are so high, many potentially worthy candidates are unwilling to make the sacrifice, thus discouraging many true "citizen-representatives" from becoming involved.

5. In recent years, especially since 2000, political campaigning has become so negative in the media that it taints virtually all candidates—which further serves to turn voters off from participating in the political process.

6. Speaking of negative, many reporters treat important political campaigns as games of cat-and-mouse, with the reporter in the role of the cat. Where personal indiscretions on the part of candidates were once treated with a knowing wink by reporters, today, virtually no area of a candidate's

private life is off-limits to media scrutiny. This game of "gotcha'" reached its apotheosis in the 1988 presidential primary campaign when U.S. Senator Gary Hart, of Colorado, confronted by reporters with rumors about marital infidelity, dared the media to "put a tail" on him to prove it. It didn't take long for a photograph to surface of Hart lounging on the deck of a boat called *Monkey Business*. Seated on his lap was an attractive blonde not named Mrs. Hart. The senator, who before the incident had led his closest Democratic primary rival by 20 percentage points, did not go on to become President of the United States.

7.   Another anti-democratic element is that the predominant role of TV favors telegenic candidates and short sound bites over more thoughtful, but, perhaps, dull candidates, or those whose ideas can't easily be distilled into snappy sound bites. Few Americans at the time of his presidency realized that Franklin D. Roosevelt was, for all practical purposes, wheelchair-bound. One imagines what the likelihood is that a person confined to a wheelchair would be elected president today.

8.   Candidates so fear the media glare they become afraid to say *anything* knowing that any stand they take will immediately make them enemies. Instead of encouraging healthy debate about important issues, this, in fact, discourages or even punishes it. Hillary Clinton, who kicked off her inaugural U.S. Senate campaign by traveling New York State on a "listening tour," and former Connecticut Governor M. Jodi Rell were recent avatars of the speak-no-evil school of campaigning.

9.   Another anti-democratic element is the "bandwagon" effect, by which the media bestows "front-runner" status on a candidate. In the early days of the 2008 presidential primary campaign, Hillary Clinton desperately wanted the media to portray her nomination as inevitable, but rival Barack Obama's surprising fundraising success burst that bubble.

10.   Campaigns are so driven by week-to-week polling that candidates become followers, not leaders, of every momentary whim of the electorate. Thus, candidates are often reduced to telling voters what they want to hear instead of what they *need* to hear.

The Role of Polls

Certainly, the rise of polling has changed the way candidates for office approach political campaigns. Political polls date back at least to the 1824 presidential race between Andrew Jackson and John Quincy Adams. But scientific sampling of electorates first came of age in 1936, when a young statistician named George Gallup accurately predicted that, despite the deepening privations of the Great Depression, Americans would re-elect Franklin D. Roosevelt to a second term.

A popular magazine of the time, *Literary Digest*, had predicted that Republican Alf Landon would win in a landslide. But the magazine's poll contained a fatal sampling flaw: The poll sent postcards to people contained in telephone directories, magazine subscriptions, and automobile registration lists. Thus, the sample was biased toward Republican-leaning voters, a wealthier-than-average population who could afford telephones, magazines, and automobiles during the Depression.

Gallup, instead, employed a method that came to be known as quota sampling, whereby a representative sample of all prospective voters—Republicans and Democrats, Easterners and Westerners, Christians and Jews—was surveyed.

Roosevelt was re-elected with 62 percent of the popular vote.

Gallup himself put it this way: "When a housewife wants to test the quality of the soup she is making, she tastes only a teaspoonful or two. She knows that if the soup is thoroughly stirred, one teaspoonful is enough to tell her whether she has the right mixture of ingredients."

If polling changes political candidates' behavior, it has also changed how the media cover political campaigns. Rather than hold politicians' feet to the fire and force them to take stands on important issues, media outlets, instead, cover political campaigns like sporting events, focusing on who's ahead at any given moment, who's surging, and who's fading.

In reality, a snapshot of voter preferences for one particular candidate over another say, 12 months from the general election, is irrelevant. The only "poll" that really matters is the one that occurs in voting booths the first Tuesday of each November.

Many think the media's focus on horse-race polling turns off, or, at least, burns out, the electorate. And as campaigns for national offices grow ever longer and ever more negative, voters easily grow disgusted with just about all the candidates and their shameless mudslinging.

A Turning Point

For much of the 20th century, most mass news media adopted a non-partisan approach to covering political campaigns. While it is true that such media as daily newspapers endorse candidates for office, most of them, nevertheless, worked to maintain at least the appearance of even-handedness.

It wasn't always like that. From the early years of the Republic until the dawn of the 20th century, many newspapers (the sole mass medium of the time except for books) were highly partisan. In many cases, they functioned as virtual mouthpieces for individual political parties and/or interest groups. As the famous (some would say infamous) editor William Cobbett (a/k/a Peter Porcupine, founder of the violently Federalist newspaper *Porcupine's Gazette and United States Advertiser*) put it, an editor who did not take sides was "a passive fool, and not an editor."

This began to change in 1833, and in the years following, as a new generation of daily newspapers, such as Benjamin Day's *The Sun* (motto: "It Shines for All") sought to build circulation by emphasizing news at the expense of ideology and opinion. This trend continued into the "Yellow" period, when titans, such as Joseph Pulitzer and William Randolph Hearst, stopped at nothing to build circulation numbers to heights never before seen. They understood that if their newspapers were viewed as organs of either the Republican or Democratic parties, they would be anathema to the other half of the electorate. Indeed, it was Pulitzer himself who pioneered the newspaper editorial page in his *New York World*, explicitly walling off opinion from the news pages to burnish the appearance of non-partisanship.

The Last Two Presidential Campaigns

2008: Obama vs. McCain

It was in the media's coverage of the highly charged 2008 presidential election that some observers saw the beginning of a return to a more partisan press. The campaign pitted Barack Obama, a young, attractive, and well-spoken Democratic U.S. Senator from Illinois, against longtime GOP U.S. Senate veteran John McCain, who at 72 was the oldest major-party nominee for president.

The 2008 campaign came at a time of deep polarization among voters, many of whom had never accepted the legitimacy of two-term incumbent George W. Bush (whose own razor-thin margin of victory in 2000 had to be certified by a 5–4 vote of the Supreme Court). Many Americans were, likewise, burned out on two seemingly interminable wars, and the precipitous decline in financial markets in the second half of 2008 created a deepening sense of alarm and, even, panic.

In this highly charged landscape, many elements within the media dropped all pretense of impartiality. Cable TV talking heads like MSNBC's Keith Olbermann and *Fox News'* Sean Hannity made no secret of their presidential preferences (for Obama and McCain, respectively). Meanwhile, talk radio resounded with the bluster of right-wing voices like Rush Limbaugh and Mark Levin thundering about the "socialist" menace obscured by the polished sheen of Obama.

Since the election, many observers have accepted that—irrespective of the fact that different individual media outlets exhibited different biases to different degrees—in the aggregate, news media coverage of the Democratic nominee was more positive than that of his opponent. (Obama's popular-vote margin of victory was 53–46.)

The non-partisan Pew Research Center's Project for Excellence in Journalism surveyed media coverage of the 2008 campaign from the primary election to the November 5 general election. It characterized individual news stories as "favorable," "unfavorable," or "neutral" to the candidate who was the subject of the story.

Pew's conclusion: "Unfavorable stories about McCain outweighed favorable ones by a factor of more than three to one—the most unfavorable of all four candidates" for president and vice president.

"For Obama during this period, just over a third of the stories were clearly positive in tone (36 percent), while a similar number (35 percent) were neutral or mixed. A smaller number (29 percent) were negative," the Pew study continued.

"For McCain, by comparison, nearly six in 10 of the stories studied were decidedly negative in nature (57 percent), while fewer than two in 10 (14 percent) were positive," it concluded.

This is less surprising in light of *another* Pew survey, this one taken in 2004, which found that five times as many journalists described their own personal politics as "liberal" rather than "conservative." But what, perhaps, was shifting just four years later was the propensity of journalists of every ideological stripe to allow their personal political views to seep into their reporting.

2012: Obama vs. Romney

The 2012 presidential campaign pitted Obama, now a known quantity with a three-year track record, against Republican Mitt Romney, a former Massachusetts governor who had earned millions as a successful venture capitalist.

On the surface, Romney's business background may have seemed an ideal tonic for a U.S. economy that stubbornly refused to improve following the financial meltdown of 2007–08. Yet his own track record in public office contained a fatal competitive flaw.

The incumbent's signature legislative accomplishment, the controversial Affordable Care Act of 2010 (a/k/a "Obamacare"), was highly unpopular with large segments of the electorate, in no small part, because it had been ramrodded through the then-Democrat-controlled House and Senate without a single Republican vote in favor.

A campaign centered on repealing Obamacare would have seemed a no-brainer for any Republican challenger—any except Mitt Romney, that is. As Massachusetts governor, he had drafted legislation that would become the prototype for Obamacare, a 2006 law that mandated that every resident of the Bay State purchase health insurance. So Romney's ability to run against Obamacare was fatally compromised from the outset of the campaign.

In terms of message, the Obama campaign reaped measurable success portraying Romney as a "vulture capitalist" out of touch with the concerns of middle-class Americans (based on the latter's track record with mergers-and-acquisitions firm Bain Capital). By contrast, Romney, much like McCain four years earlier, foreswore personal attacks on Obama, and had difficulty achieving traction with criticism of the administration's record on issues, such as the economy.

Whereas many Americans were surprised at the newly partisan tone of media coverage of the 2008 presidential campaign, four years later such coverage had become a widely accepted reality of the journalistic landscape. Few expected Fox News, for example, to overlook stories critical of the administration, or the *New York Times* to cut the Romney campaign much slack. When conservatives argued ex post facto that the "mainstream" media deck was stacked against their candidate, they cited coverage of two stories in particular to bolster their claim.

In September, *Mother Jones* magazine released a secretly recorded video of Romney talking to donors about the 47 percent of Americans who don't pay income taxes. Much of the media went ballistic over the utterance. Over the next three days, the broadcast network morning and evening shows churned out 42 stories on the tape, nearly 90 minutes of coverage, according to the Media Research Center. ABC's *Good Morning America* called it a "bombshell rocking the Mitt Romney campaign," while ABC *World News* anchor Diane Sawyer characterized it as a "political earthquake."

At about the same time, a September 11 attack on the U.S. Embassy in Benghazi, Libya, left four Americans dead, including the U.S. ambassador to that North African country. In late September, news broke only that the Obama team had known within 24 hours that the attack was likely the result of terrorism.

That contradicted claims from White House Press Secretary Jay Carney, U.N. Ambassador Susan Rice, Secretary of State Hillary Clinton, and the President himself that the attack was a "spontaneous" reaction to an anti-Muslim video posted on YouTube. Yet ABC took nearly two days to bring this story to viewers, while CBS and NBC held off for three days. Even following Obama's re-election, much of the media seemed uninterested in getting to the bottom of the Benghazi story, and conservatives cite that selective indifference as symptomatic of media bias.

On the critical advertising battlefront, the Obama campaign was significantly more efficient than the challenger in targeting swing voters. Team Obama's young tech whizzes employed social media to isolate some 15 million potential swing voters and learn what TV shows they watched through, for example, Facebook "likes." So while the Romney advertising decision-makers favored the traditional approach of high-cost six o'clock news and prime time TV ad buys, Obama's advertising buyers went for niche cable buys (e.g., one a.m. repeats of *The Insider* and afternoon episodes of *Judge Joe Brown*) and non-news programs (which cost significantly less than prime-time broadcast network advertising).

While the Republicans—at $605 million—actually spent more on television advertising than the Obama campaign's reported $452 million, they yielded less "bang for the buck" because they were paying to reach a large pool of voters that included millions of enrolled Republicans and Democrats whose votes were never in play. Ironically, notwithstanding the unprecedented level of spending, about two-thirds of the country's solidly red and blue states—saw virtually no campaign ads.

Even after the election, the Romney team seemed not to grasp this fundamental reality. "We were still trying to inform likely voters who Mitt Romney was," GOP strategist Stuart Stevens told the *New York Times Magazine.* "And until you get those voters, you're insane to go off and say, 'We're going to try to win this with left-handed Lithuanians.'"

But as November 6, 2012, proved, the Obama campaign was more successful than the Republicans at influencing voters in key swing states, such as Ohio, Florida, and Pennsylvania, and because of it, reclaimed the White House.

For Sale: High Office?

Because the cost of buying television advertising drives national level political campaigns, the question is raised: can candidates buy their way into higher office?

The incontrovertible answer is: maybe. Examples abound on both sides. Business-media mogul Mike Bloomberg proved there is one way, and only one way, for a Republican to become mayor of New York City—by spending mountains of cash. (Bloomberg later changed his party affiliation to Independent.)

On the opposite side of the ledger is the 1992 presidential race won by the candidate who came in *third* in raising money. Bill Clinton spent $32 million during the campaign, nearly 25 percent less than incumbent George H. W. Bush's $42 million, and 20 percent less than the $40 million (most of it his own money) spent by eccentric billionaire H. Ross Perot, who ran as an Independent.

Just over a decade later, those dollar figures seemed positively quaint: in 2004 George W. Bush spent $306 million to Democratic challenger John F. Kerry's $241 million, and was rewarded with a 51–48 popular-vote victory.

And the dialing-for-dollars arms race continues to escalate apace: In the watershed 2008 primary and general election campaigns, candidates more than doubled spending from just four years before, to

$1.7 billion. The first major-party nominee to reject federal funding for the general election campaign, Obama raised more than $740 million, according to *Bloomberg Business News*, vastly eclipsing the $228 million McCain was able to muster. Significantly, between September 1 and November 24, according to the Federal Elections Commission, the Democrat outspent his rival by a 4–1 margin.

(An entire chapter could be written here about the vast financial windfall this represents to the media—most dramatically, to broadcast media in small but key early-primary markets like Des Moines, Iowa, and Manchester, New Hampshire.)

On January 20, 2010, the U.S. Supreme Court ruled by a 5–4 vote to lift a ban (imposed by a 2002 law popularly known as McCain-Feingold) on the broadcast, cable, or satellite transmission of "electioneering communications" paid for by corporations or labor unions in the weeks leading up to primary and general elections.

Writing for the majority, Justice Anthony M. Kennedy asserted: "If the First Amendment has any force, it prohibits Congress from fining or jailing citizens, or associations of citizens, for simply engaging in political speech." In other words, corporations are entitled to free speech, just like individual citizens.

But opponents of the ruling, including President Obama himself, warned that allowing corporate money to flood the political marketplace would corrupt democracy.

No thinking person doubts that money has had a corrupting influence on American politics since the 18th century. But many thinking people disagree about possible ways to reform the system—and even if the system can, indeed, be reformed.

There are those who believe candidates would be freed from spending most of their time "dialing for dollars" if campaigns were 100-percent publicly financed. But there are two problems:

1. Because the "public" is *us*, that means taxes would have to be raised to generate the hundreds of millions of dollars that national campaigns consume.
2. Because the current system favors incumbents, who begin every election cycle with the advantage in name-recognition and fundraising ability over any and all challengers, no incumbent is likely to vote for this sort of reform, since it would level the playing field to their disadvantage.

What if the media gave free time to all candidates? Then no one would have to pay the vast sums national campaigns now consume. But why would the media do that—and forego the embarrassment of riches political campaigns spend to advertise with them? And who would make the media give advertising away? Not the government, of course, which can't tell the press what to do without repealing the First Amendment.

Michael C. Bingham is an adjunct professor of journalism at Southern Connecticut State University.

Exercises

1. What is the "bandwagon" effect in media coverage of political campaigns?
2. Why did television viewers and radio listeners reach different conclusions about who "won" the 1960 Kennedy-Nixon debates?
3. What method did George Gallup use to create a more accurate forecast of the 1936 presidential election results than had been attainable previously?
4. Do the candidates able to raise (or spend) the most money on their campaigns always win?

For Critical Discussion or Writing

1. Why is mass media coverage of U.S. political campaigns so superficial? Wouldn't voters be better served by more in-depth examination of important issues?
2. The predominant role of television in political campaigns favors physically attractive or "telegenic" candidates. Could a physically unattractive man or woman be elected president today? How about a candidate confined to a wheelchair?
3. Does "anything goes" coverage of candidates' personal lives and peccadilloes discourage otherwise qualified potential candidates from running for office because they fear every "bad" thing they ever did will be revealed?

PART V
Assembly

Chapter 16: The Right to Peaceably Assemble

March on Washington

The Right to Peaceably Assemble

When Citizens Restrict Other Citizens' Right to Assemble

We have spoken a great deal about government attempts to restrict the First Amendment, only touching on the fact that citizens themselves are often the restrictors of others' First Amendment rights. It occurs when one group does not want to hear what another group says or tolerate what it stands for. It occurs when government officials look the other way, or give active or tacit approval when one group seeks to trample another's right to assemble. This has been particularly true in the right to peaceably assemble. This right means individuals can legally gather with others to express themselves. The key word is "peaceably." The First Amendment does not protect those who assemble and behave violently.

Yet, too often throughout America's history, those who object to a certain cause have assembled to violently suppress those who have assembled peaceably. When that happens, free expression is restricted, if not snuffed out altogether. Why? Because the right to assemble is so interwoven with the four other rights in this Amendment that with its loss, so go the others.

Think about it. Suppose you have the right to free speech, a free press, the right to petition, and the right to worship (or not)—but you aren't allowed to meet with like-minded individuals to discuss your beliefs, views, feelings, thoughts, strategies, and teachings?

Following are some of the many examples when Americans have tried to exercise this right and faced stiff opposition from both citizens and government.

The Abolitionist Movement

Abolitionists were those in the mid-1800s who opposed slavery. This preceding sentence, however, does not do justice to the degree of fervent animosity the Abolitionist Movement generated among people throughout the country, both North and South. The movement would eventually grow and prove to be on the right side of history. But before it reached that place, its members were subjected to verbal and physical abuse from all walks of society.

The November 22, 1834, edition of *The Liberator*, the abolitionist newspaper of William Lloyd Garrison, contained the following article; it originally appeared in the *Ohio Observer* regarding mobs breaking up abolitionist meetings:

> *"The increasing disposition to prevent free discussion and decide all questions by brute force rather than reason and argument is one of the most appalling signs of the times and symptoms of speedy ruin to our country. When once it becomes general to substitute mobs for law, our liberties are gone, we are a ruined nation."*

Less than three years later, the *Pittsburgh Gazette* of March 22, 1837, published a *Buffalo Commercial Advertiser* article that presented an unflinching update of the social climate:

Figure 16-1. William Lloyd Garrison

> *"It is certainly strange that the subject of slavery cannot be touched by a public speaker, even in the gentlest of manner, without running the risk of exciting a mob. Subjects which must vitally affect the interests of the North, can be discussed calmly, and men can disagree peaceably, but an attempt to influence the public mind upon slavery, is almost sure to be attended by acts of lawless violence."*

The violence was not figurative; it was literal. Eight months after *The Gazette* published these words, a pro-slavery mob killed newspaper editor and abolitionist Elijah Lovejoy in Alton, Illinois.

The newspapers of the time provide numerous accounts of peaceably assembled abolitionists having their meetings and other public gatherings violently disrupted and its attendees attacked. No one was spared, as noted in the August 24, 1849, edition of *The Liberator* that described how Garrison himself was "flying bare-headed for his life" before a mob that was infuriated by his views. He had good reason to flee; the Georgia State Legislature reportedly put a $5,000 bounty on his head to "incite someone to take his life."

For most white Americans, the notion of freeing blacks was unfathomable. Blacks were not regarded as human beings. The June 21, 1850, edition of *The Liberator* captured some sense of this feeling when citing the words of the editor of the *Merchant's Day-Book*: "The feelings of the slave is nothing, his interests are nothing, he is a slave, he is property, his manhood is another's."

Such sentiment was particularly prevalent in the South, but was common in the North as well, and prompted the violence. In the support of slavery's end, there were abolitionist citizens who also assembled to violently stop slavery, such as when masters or their agents came North to try to reclaim runaway slaves under the Fugitive Slave Act.

Remember that the right to assemble applies to peaceable assemblies. How does one define peaceable? Does one group have a right to loudly protest another group's meeting? Are they outside the First Amendment only if the group becomes violent?

The right to assembly was only as good as the law enforcement people gathered to enforce it. For this period, it was seldom good. The mob ruled.

Suffragists and the Picket

Picketing is another form of assembly. It involves a group (but could also be one person alone) standing outside a place of work or other venue to protest something, usually bearing signs. Such was the case with one group of suffragists who, after getting nowhere with President Woodrow Wilson in its demand for women's right to vote, took to picketing at the White House—as noted in the January 10, 1917, *Washington Herald*:

Figure 16-2. Suffragists Picketing White House

"Twelve suffragettes, who will be known as 'silent sentinels,' will go on guard duty at the White House this morning at 9 o'clock, so that hereafter President Wilson will not be able to leave the executive mansion without being reminded of the demand of women for political liberty.

"These guards will carry banners with such inscriptions as: 'Mr. President, how long must women wait.'

"Squads will be stationed about the White House daily … This is generally regarded as the most militant move ever made by the suffragists of this country …"

They stood for eight hours that day. The president initially ignored them. Then he began tipping his hat. There was outrage, interestingly, by other women who dubbed themselves anti-suffragists. Many considered their picketing disrespectful and unladylike. Still, the pickets were peaceful until America entered World War I and two suffragists, Lucy Burns and Mrs. Lawrence Lewis (as she was identified in the paper), members of the National Women's Party, carried a banner to greet the Russian envoy in June 1917. The banner said: "We the women of America, tell you that America is not a democracy. Twenty million women are denied the right to vote … Tell our government that it must liberate its people before it can claim free Russia as an ally."

It was lunch hour, with scores of people passing by. As men and women gathered to read the banners, cries of "Traitor!" and "Treason!" arose. They were called enemies of America because they also criticized the president, calling him deceitful. Before long, a crowd of 250 people pounced upon their banners and tore them down. The June 20, 1917, *Washington Times* headline read: "ENRAGED MOB IN FRONT OF WHITE HOUSE TEARS DOWN SUFFRAGISTS' BANNER WHICH ATTACKED THE PRESIDENT." Police made no arrests of the attackers. However, shortly after, the picketers were arrested for obstructing the sidewalk.

Scores would be arrested and jailed.

Carrie Chapman Catt, head of the National Woman Suffrage Association, disapproved of the picketing and called it an unnecessary embarrassment to the President. Her way of moving women's rights forward was to give speeches, gather signatures, and send petitions, (See The Right to Petition chapter.)

Ultimately the President signed the bill granting women the right to vote. It came after pressure—the pickets, the arrests of picketers, one woman going on hunger strike and being force-fed. Could the movement's goals have been achieved without the pickets?

Could the pickets have garnered results without the petition and political work of Chapman Catt? Though parties on each side may disagree with the other's methods, sometimes the different approaches work together.

"Reds"

America's opposition to anarchists, socialists, communists, and other radical groups has been cited in previous chapters covering restrictions on speech and publications. It was government, by restrictive laws such as the Espionage and Sedition Acts, as well as citizens, through mob rule, that helped restrict their right to peaceably assemble. The press also had a role in its position against their gathering,

Figure 16-3. Socialists in New York City's Union Square

Bain News Service / Copyright in the Public Domain.

though it seemed their words simply mirrored much of the mood of the country. This was reflected in the May 2, 1919, *New York Tribune* headline describing the May Day riots: "May Day Demonstrations Broken Up by Mounted Police and Soldiers, Who Ride Down Mobs," and the article that followed:

> "(In Cleveland) Socialist headquarters was totally wrecked by angry civilians bent on putting an end to the demonstration. Socialists and sympathizers in East Ninth Street and at Public Square were ridden down by mounted policemen and by soldiers in army tanks and trucks ...

> "In Boston, attempts to halt a parade in the Roxbury district resulted in street fighting, in which four policemen were shot, many persons hurt and scores arrested.

> "In Homer City, Penn., Indiana, Penn., and other towns of that state with large foreign populations, state police charged "Red" parades and broke them up ... Other cities, from the Atlantic to the Pacific, were the scene of minor disturbances."

Later that year, the *Philadelphia Evening Ledger* of Nov 24, 1919, would report on the arrest of three Philadelphia men who were planning to take part in a radical rally. Leaping ahead to the 1940 Smith Act and McCarthyism of the 1950s, there would be a range of laws and practices designed to restrict assemblies of those with radical beliefs.

Unions

In the early half of the 20th Century, workers who wanted to unionize clashed often with the owners of companies or the owners' hired security guards. Not just one industry was affected. There were strikes at mines, steel mills, auto plants, textile manufacturers, and many other employers, large and small. Dock workers, rubber company employees, and truck drivers all tried to organize into unions to increase wages and improve workplace safety. In many cases, the attempts included picketing in front of places of employment. It was not rare for whole families to attend these rallies. Often, local police, and even the National Guard in several states, broke up pro-union demonstrations. Across the country, a number of these confrontations ended in violence, with many people killed or injured. The estimates of the number of deaths over the first 35 years of the 20th century vary, but it's clear that thousands of people were killed or injured when they assembled to create unions. Many national or local unions were forged during this period.

Figure 16-4. The "Silent Parade" in New York City

In the 1960s and '70s, migrant farm workers, under the leadership of Cesar Chavez, organized into the United Farm Workers Union. They demonstrated, called for boycotts of farmers' crops like lettuce, and petitioned the government for better labor laws to protect workers in the fields. The efforts were often met with firings and violence. The UFW was effective, however, in getting improved wages and conditions for its workers through negotiations with farm owners.

The Civil Rights Movement

A prime example of the right to peaceably assemble and the laws and violent opposition that rose up against it was the Civil Rights Movement in America. Though the Civil Rights Movement is typically said to have begun with the Montgomery Bus Boycott in 1955, one of the first massive black protests occurred decades earlier with the "Silent Parade" of July 28, 1917. On that day, anywhere from 8,000 to 10,000 blacks marched silently down New York's Fifth Avenue to protest the race riots in East St. Louis, and lynchings in general.

"Negro children from Sunday and public schools in the city led the parade, followed by the women garbed in white, with the men bringing up the rear," said the *Indianapolis News* of July 28, 1917.

Contributing Editor James Weldon Johnson (who years earlier wrote the *Negro National Anthem*, and authored the acclaimed novel *The Autobiography of an Ex-Colored Man*) described the parade in the *New York Age* of August 2, 1917:

> "No written word can convey to those who did not see it the solemn impressiveness of the whole affair. The effect could be plainly seen on the faces of the thousands of spectators that crowded along the line of the march. There were no jeers, no jests, not even were there indulgent smiles; the faces of the onlookers betrayed emotions from sympathetic interest to absolute pain. Many persons of the opposite race (white) were seen to brush a tear from their eyes ... The power of the parade consisted in its being not a mere argument in words, but a demonstration to the sight ..."

The 1960s brought peaceful assemblies with the Freedom Riders, young blacks and whites boarding buses to test the new federal law banning segregation on buses and at bus stations during interstate travel. They faced mobs and violence, with scores of the Freedom Riders jailed.

There were sit-ins in North Carolina where blacks were arrested for sitting at "Whites Only" lunch counters. In Birmingham in 1963, town officials turned fire hoses and police dogs on black demonstrators, many of them children. As the nation and the world saw these images, public opinion turned against what was regarded as an abuse of power, along with a violation of the First Amendment right to assemble peaceably. Throughout the Sixties, people assembled to protest across the land, including the memorable 1963 March on Washington.

These assemblies influenced other movements ranging from women's rights, gay and lesbian rights, and the anti-war movement.

Figure 16-5. Female Protester Offers Flower

Albert R. Simpson / U.S. Army / Copyright in the Public Domain.

Vietnam Anti-War Protesters

For anyone around during the Vietnam War, few could imagine a more tumultuous time. Of course, you know from a previous chapter that World War I was said to be more tumultuous. There were, however, similarities. The fight against communism spurred many on, just as the fight against the Kaiser was the rallying cry in the First World War.

Vietnam, however, was a longer war with no end in sight. The mood shifted. The big difference, too, was the news media's coverage. With TV, Vietnam became the first living-room war. That is, war coverage was featured daily, and families eating dinner would see it on the evening news. Gradually the mood changed. People began to object to the war. Some burned draft cards. Songs of protest hit the radio waves. Mass protests sprang up in college campuses around the country. High school students also protested. Those who protested against the war were said to be un-American, just as in previous wars. The country became divided between "hawks" and "doves."

Demonstrators and police tangled, with violence breaking out. At the 1968 Democratic Convention in Chicago, police tear-gassed and beat protesters in what was later called a police riot. At Kent State in 1970, Ohio National Guardsmen fired upon students protesting the U.S. invasion of Cambodia, killing four, and wounding nine; it widened the war and brought more mass protests.

These protests ultimately played a major role in America pulling out of Vietnam.

Westboro Baptist Church

The anti-gay, Westboro Baptist Church has mounted small protests in many parts of the country over several years. They have protested at military funerals with signs that say, "God Hates Fags." Though their message is hateful to most people, the courts have ruled the church members have the right to assemble because they followed the local laws in relation to the time, place, and manner they demonstrated. Government may not legally stop such speech because the majority doesn't like it.

The Tea Party Movement

Another example of the impact of assembly has been the emergence of the "Tea Party" Movement in U.S. politics. These conservative Americans organized themselves against "big government" and other fiscal and social policies of the administration of President Barack Obama. They publicly rallied and demonstrated loudly for their point of view. They were effective. They had enough influence to win the House of Representatives for the Republicans in 2010 and hold a majority in 2012. Its members have been able to move the center of the Republican Party significantly to the right in the years since they first organized.

Black Lives Matter

Sparked by the police killings of Eric Garner in July 2014 (caught on video being choked to death by a New York Police officer—"I can't breathe"), and the police shooting of Michael Brown in Ferguson, Missouri, in August 2014, protests sprang up in cities across America under the banner of Black Lives Matter.

These protests led to people of all races exercising their right to assemble in ways ranging from marching with signs, to laying their bodies in the streets, to stopping traffic and other First Amendment protests.

Figure 16-6. Protester holds signs during Black Lives Matter demonstration in New York City in November 2014.

A Right for All

Today, it is generally recognized that people have the right to protest and are allowed to do so with fewer restrictions than before. The right to peaceably assemble is an integral part of the First Amendment.

The attempts to restrict it have worked at some points in history, but the attempts have galvanized others into making sure that their voices are heard. The right to peaceably assemble covers the popular and unpopular. Just as there have been civil rights marches and freedom marches, there were Ku Klux Klan rallies and Nazi Party demonstrations, including one in Skokie, Illinois, in the late 1970s. In that instance, town officials attempted to spare its residents, many of them concentration camp survivors, from the specter of Nazi protesters. The court, however, overruled them and granted the Nazis the right to march in Skokie.

The Law of Peaceable Assembly

Government has attempted to control assembly in many ways by passing various kinds of laws. Police have arrested people for walking on the sidewalk with a protest sign, broken up protests in parks, required people showing anti-presidential feelings at a political rally to be held in areas far from the politician, and in many other situations. Over the years, the Supreme Court has established several ways to consider whether laws that restrict the right to assemble are constitutional. These are often referred to as "time, place and manner" rules. It means that the government, federal, state or local, can write laws that, for instance, require those wishing to hold a parade get a permit first. The governments can set times and routes for the parade. There is a First Amendment right to hold the parade, but not at times and in ways that cause undue inconvenience or stress to other citizens. Blocking traffic at rush hour is usually not a popular idea. There must be a balance between the right to expression and the right of others to go about their lives.

The Supreme Court has ruled that local authorities cannot prevent religious groups from going door-to-door to promote their faith. Various states have passed laws requiring that anti-abortion protestors not block access to health clinics for women.

The Supreme Courts has created a four-part test for such laws:

1. *Are the laws "content neutral"? That means the law may not discriminate against a particular kind of speech.*
2. *Are the laws "narrowly drawn"? The courts have ruled that a very broad law that prevents many kinds of assembly would be unconstitutional.*
3. *Does such a law serve a "significant government interest"? There must be a real and important reason for governments to create the law.*
4. *Does the law leave open "other means of communication" for the group who wishes to assemble? To be within the Constitution, the law must not close off all means of presenting an individual's or group's ideas.*

Some examples of laws that are permitted under the court's test are those limiting the volume of loud-speakers at protests. The idea is: If it's too loud, it interrupts the rights of others nearby to work or go to sleep. Another might be preventing assembly on a beach that is environmentally endangered. Protestors may not trespass on private property or legally "sit-in" in government offices. When the "Occupy Wall Street" protests occurred around the country, police broke up many of them using laws that say you may not stay in a public park for more than a certain period of time. In New Haven, Connecticut, the "Occupy" protestors set up tents on the historic Green, a public area in the center of the town. They stayed there for several months. Eventually, the police tore down the tents and moved the protestors off the Green based on issues of sanitation, damage to the Green, and an increase in minor crime.

Another aspect of the law is that where you assemble makes a difference. The courts have established "traditional public forums," "limited public forums," and "non-public forums." Parks, streets, town squares, among other normally public spaces, are considered traditional public forums. The government may create minimal restrictions in these places, as noted above, but assembly can't be prevented overall. Limited public forums are public parts of places, such as the statehouse grounds, public colleges, and parts of a courthouse, among others. In these spaces, more government restriction is permitted. It would not be permissible to protest loudly during a trial in a courtroom, but would probably be acceptable on the courthouse steps. Non-public forums are parts of public buildings, such as individual's offices, jails, airports, private property, and other areas, where public speech or assembly would not normally occur. In these areas, laws may be much more restrictive. You would be arrested for trying to assemble within the walls of a prison.

Many court cases have dealt with various kinds of assembly over the life of the United States. Because assembly protests are intentionally public and anger some people, there will be others. But, within the limits outlined above, citizens, particularly those with little access to other means of communication, still have significant rights to peaceably assemble under the First Amendment.

Exercises

1. What do "time, place and manner" restrictions mean?
2. Does the Constitution protect the right to assembly even when the message of the minority is very unpopular?
3. Is it legal to block traffic during rush hour to make a political point?
4. What were some of the groups in our history who have used the power of assembly to cause changes to laws?
5. Name some examples of cases where the right to assemble was met with violence from other citizens?

For Critical Discussion or Writing

1. Do you think authorities around the country should have been permitted to close down "Occupy Wall Street" protests despite the First Amendment's clause on freedom of assembly?
2. How do you think the public should respond to groups like the KKK or the Westboro Baptist Church when they protest in public?
3. Have the courts given the government too much leeway to control assembly, or is the balance about right?

PART VI
Petition

Chapter 17: The Right to Demand Government Change

BLOG   PHOTOS & VIDEO   BRIEFING ROOM   ISSUES   the ADMINISTRATION

WE the PEOPLE
YOUR VOICE IN OUR GOVERNMENT

CREATE A PETITION   OPEN PETITIONS   RESPONSES   HOW & WHY

WE PETITION THE OBAMA ADMINISTRATION TO:

Restore Net Neutrality By Directing the FCC to Classify Internet Providers as "Common Carriers".

On January 14, 2013, the U.S. Court of Appeals for the District of Columbia Circuit that struck down the Federal Communications Commission's open Internet rules, commonly known as "Net Neutrality" because ISPs are not classified as "common carriers". This ruling allows ISPs to charge companies for access to its users and charge users for access to certain services. Fewer companies will be able to afford access for innovative ideas and products.

We urge the President to direct the FCC to classify ISPs as "common carriers" so that the words of the FCC chairman may be fulfilled: "I am committed to maintaining our networks as engines for economic growth, test beds for innovative services and products, and channels for all forms of speech protected by the First Amendment."

Created: Jan 15, 2014

Issues: Consumer Protections, Innovation, Technology and Telecommunications

Learn about Petition Thresholds

SIGNATURES NEEDED BY FEBRUARY 14, 2014 TO REACH GOAL OF 100,000	0	TOTAL SIGNATURES ON THIS PETITION	100,706

Online petition for net neutrality

The Right to Demand Government Change

Are you angry about a decision made by your city council? Do you have a great idea about something you think the state legislature should do? Under the First Amendment you have the right to create a petition, convince others to sign it, and present it to the government without fear of legal reprisal. This right seems ingrained in most U.S. citizens; it's something we take for granted. But it's a right that does not exist in many parts of the world where you might be arrested, or worse, for petitioning the government for a "redress of grievances."

The Roots of Petitions

The idea that citizens should be able to complain to the government is often traced to the creation of the Magna Carta in England in 1215. The English barons under King John were very unhappy with his rule. They organized and created this "great charter" that granted them various rights and forced King John to sign it. In effect, they petitioned the government for a redress of their grievances. The "Declaration of Rights" was passed by the English Parliament in 1689 and said, clearly, that citizens could not be prosecuted for petitioning the King. The right to petition rulers became part of English common law. Several American colonies had recognized the petitioning right before the Revolution. The Declaration of Independence is an example of the right to tell the ruling powers you don't accept what they are doing.

When the founders of the U.S. Constitution wrote the First Amendment, they included petition along with religion, speech, press, and assembly. Perhaps because of its common law roots, the right to petition has not seen the number of court challenges as have other parts of the First Amendment. Legal scholars say petition is also considered by the courts to be connected to free speech and assembly. That is, when there have been issues that seemed to be about the right to petition, many of the cases have been argued as free speech or assembly cases.

The Freedom Forum defines petition this way:

> *"To petition the government for a redress of grievances means that citizens can ask for changes in the government. They can do this by collecting signatures and sending them to their elected representatives; they can write, call or e-mail their elected representatives; they can support groups that lobby the government."*

The First Amendment Center uses these words:

> *"Historically, a petition was a written request stating a grievance and requesting relief from a ruling authority, such as a king. In modern America, petitioning embraces a range of expressive activities designed to influence public officials through legal, nonviolent means."*

Slaves' Petition for Freedom

In 1788, three years before the First Amendment was ratified, black slaves in New Haven petitioned the state for the abolition of slavery in Connecticut. The petition describes how they were dragged from their native lands, leaving their mothers, fathers, sisters, and brothers, and asking if this was humane, before asking for "liberation."

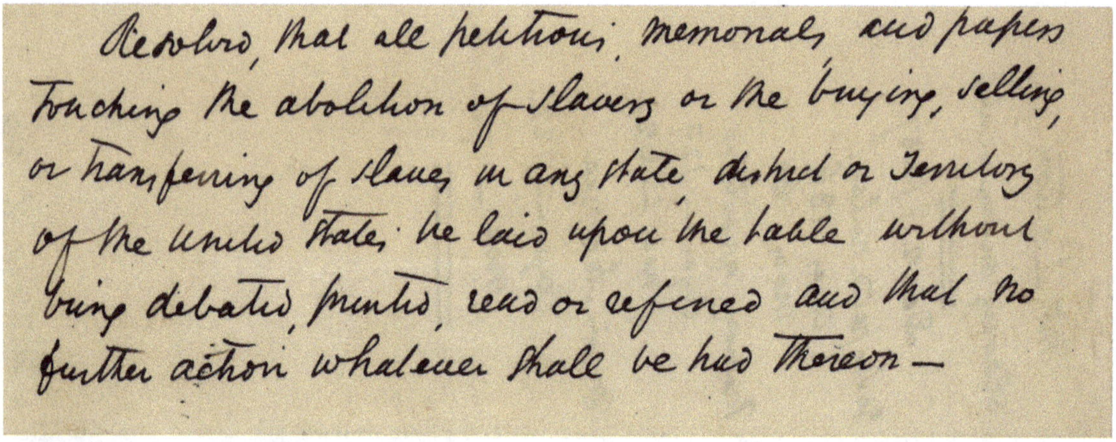
Resolved, that all petitions, memorials and papers touching the abolition of slavery or the buying, selling, or transferring of slaves in any state, district or Territory of the United States be laid upon the table without being debated, printed, read or referred and that no further action whatever shall be had thereon—

This handwritten note in May 1836 formed the basis for the House resolution gag rule on all petitions relating to slavery. It reads: "Resolved, that all petitions, memorials and papers touching the abolition of slavery or the buying, selling or transferring of slaves in any state, district or territory of the United States be laid upon the table without being debated, printed, read or referred and that no further action whatever shall be had thereon–"

Figure 17-1. Gag Rule

The petition was not acted upon. That, however, did not stem the petitions that followed. In the 1830s, those who wished to end slavery sent thousands of petitions to Congress demanding abolition.

There was one period when the U.S. House of Representatives took away the right to petition. In the spring of 1836, Southern members of Congress, and some of their allies in the North, passed a rule in the House that all petitions on the issue of slavery be "laid upon the table." That meant there would be no action taken, and the rule said these petitions would not even be read. Former President John Quincy Adams, who was then a member of the House of Representatives, argued this was a "gag" rule. He said that it ran counter to the Constitution's protection of petition rights in the First Amendment. Adams fought the rule for several years. As the anti-slavery movement gathered supporters in the North, it put more pressure on elected representatives to change the rule. In 1844, Adams was able to convince members of the House to overturn the rule and restore the right to petition.

Petitions were also used to secure buildings for use, such as a July 12, 1849, petition from nearly 40 Chicagoans to the mayor and city council seeking use of City Hall for a speech by "well known and successful advocates of African freedom and human rights, Frederick Douglass and Charles Remond."

Women's Suffrage

On April 10, 1917, Carrie Chapman Catt, head of the National American Woman Suffrage Association, petitioned the Speaker of the House to establish a committee for women's suffrage. She leveraged this by pointing out that the countries of England, France, and Russia "have promised women suffrage in the near future."

The Right to Petition

The right to petition in the U.S. Constitution has been used over the centuries for many causes. Candidates can petition their way onto a ballot. Many states have the right to referendum, in which people can force various kinds of legislative or constitutional change by gathering signatures on petitions to permit a vote on an issue. These referenda have meant tax cuts, tax increases, changed laws on marriage, and many other citizen concerns.

The right to petition is broad. It includes all levels of government and all branches: executive, legislative, and judicial. It includes filing a lawsuit against a particular government program. It gives lobbyists the right to request that the government do something, or change something. (Lobbyists, the courts have said, however, have no more First Amendment freedom under the Constitution than any other citizen.) It gives citizens the right to ask a place of business to take some action, as in the petition by New Haven, Connecticut, residents in 2013 seeking the owner of Toad's Place (a renowned venue for concerts) to cancel a scheduled appearance by rocker Ted Nugent because of racial comments he made about Trayvon Martin, as well as previous comments. A petition may not include libelous statements or other expressions that the courts have ruled to be outside the protections granted by the First Amendment, such as obscenity or national security.

Governments—local, state and federal—must provide some method of accepting petitions. It is important to know that a governmental body has no obligation to do anything after it receives a petition. It is free to ignore it. The city council, legislature, court, or president can choose to do nothing about a grievance petition. Of course, that leaves citizens the right to show up at the polls and vote those who refused to "redress their grievances" out of office. It is important to note that the Internet has made it easier for citizens to file a petition on any issue they feel strongly about. A number of sites provide online petitions. It remains up to citizens to make their voices heard through this provision of the First Amendment.

Exercises

1. What does petition mean?
2. What document in 13th century England is said to have begun the idea of petitioning the government?
3. Give some examples of petitioning the government for redress of grievances.

For Critical Discussion or Writing

1. If you wanted to petition the government, what grievance would you address and why?
2. Do you think the laws should be changed to require that government officials formally reply to a petition?

PART VII

Putting Freedom of Expression to Use

CHAPTER 18

Speak!

We have covered the five freedoms of the First Amendment ranging from assembly to religion to the press to the petition and, of course, speech.

Having a voice to express yourself is a powerful thing.

But having the freedom to speak does not mean you can do it well.

The ability to speak effectively in public requires study and practice. This skill is not limited to those who are TV personalities, radio hosts, or politicians. Consider the many jobs and situations where being able to speak articulately is important.

Teachers must face the public (their classes) every day and attempt to communicate effectively with students using the spoken word. Nurses and doctors need to make sure patients understand what they are saying. Sales people must explain their product or service well so a prospect understands it and will buy. Scientists often are required to deliver the news of their discoveries to their peers in a public presentation. Members of the clergy, business people, lawyers, computer trainers—all must be able to communicate verbally. Most jobs require that you speak clearly.

When the president delivers the State of the Union address you can bet it's been written and re-written many times. The president and his staff go over every word to make sure it says what they want it to say. This is also true of broadcast news anchors. Unless they are reporting live, TV and radio news people write everything they say on the air in advance.

Most of us can become competent at public speaking. Some people have a natural knack for it. Some people have a real fear of it. The fear can make them freeze or try to avoid speaking altogether. These concerns can usually be overcome with practice and knowledge.

Do your homework and be prepared. The more you know about your subject, the more confident you will be presenting it. Understand that the audience is not normally the "enemy." It is most often made up of people who are there to hear what you have to say and want you to succeed. There are other tactics, such as regulating your breathing or looking over the heads of the audience members, that can help reduce fear.

Remember, when you are speaking in public, people are listening to you, not reading your words. You must write for the ear. The words you decide to use should depend on the audience you are trying to reach. We would use different language when speaking to a third grade class than we would to a group of adult scientists. Here are some tips on writing for the ear.

I. Choosing a Topic

The first recommended speaking topic is the First Amendment itself. Everyone should memorize it and know it inside out. For topics that follow, you have a wealth of material from the different sections on this book, both past and present. You can also role-play. For instance, you can be John Peter Zenger and lament why you were thrown in jail. Or be one of the suffragists who picketed President Wilson's White House when some nasty folks tore up your sign. Or you can take a position on whether you think the First Amendment needs changes. Or why news media should be regulated. The topics are endless. But choose something that interests you, and make yourself the expert on it.

The most important first step is choosing a topic. Make it good.

II. Time and Length

It is imperative that you plan how long your speech will be. It will determine how many words to write. We suggest a speech of 2-1/2 to 3 minutes. The corresponding length of the written speech should be no more than 250 to 350 words.

III. Know Your Audience

You must know your audience. You will present differently to grade school children than you would before a distinguished group of elderly citizens or your peers. Adjust your words accordingly. Recognize your audience and determine your angle of appeal: personal, economic, social, political, ethical, moral, etc.

IV. The Five-Point Outline

The following five-point formula is an excellent way to frame your presentation so you cover the most important parts of your speech. (See the Oral Presentation Speech Outline section in the Appendix.)

1. **<u>Grab them with a "Grabber"</u>:** This is the most important part of your presentation. Your first words or sentence(s) should quickly grab their attention and interest. It could be as follows:
   - A direct challenge
   - A paraphrased quotation or saying
   - A question
   - A description of a scene
   - An anecdotal story

2. **Explicitly tell them why this is important/why they should care:** Following your grabber, explicitly state why this is important or why they should care. Example: "This is important because …" or "You should care about this because …" The goal here is to answer the question of how your topic affects them personally.

3. **Explicitly tell them your objective:** Clearly and explicitly state what you will prove or achieve through this presentation. Example: "Through this presentation, I will show you why …" or "My objective is to inform you about …" or "Through this presentation, you will learn …"

4. **"Show" them examples to support your point:** Your "word" and opinion alone are not enough. Provide two or three attributed examples to support your position. Facts, statistics, quotations, analogies, or personal examples are ideal. Example: "According to a 2014 Gallup Poll, 55 percent of Americans said …" Be sure to choose the examples that will best flow with your presentation and move your presentation forward. But don't overdo it.

5. **Tell them what you want them to do/summarize:** This is the second most important part of your presentation. Ideally, you want to have your audience take some form of action, such as calling or writing. But sometimes, an informative presentation may focus on changing one's way of thinking or one's position. Thus, it may not have a strong bid for action. In such cases, a summation will do. However you choose to conclude your presentation, do it memorably. Do not fizzle. Write strong words to end strong.

V. Writing the Speech

From your outline, write your speech by filling in the information. Keep the following in mind: (See the Speech Format section in the Appendix.)

1. **<u>Use words easily understood by the audience:</u>** That doesn't mean you are talking down. It means you are trying to communicate effectively. They don't have a dictionary with them to look up words while you speak. If you must use a complicated word, explain it. Carcinogenic means a substance or agent that causes cancer, but well over 50 percent of the public don't understand the word.

2. **<u>Use short sentences:</u>** Long sentences filled with clauses are hard to follow. Short sentences are easier: "John hit Bill." "The president says he'll veto the bill." "The river is polluted." If you find yourself writing a long sentence, break it into two or three sentences.

3. **<u>Attribute first:</u>** Attribution usually comes first in speeches. We need to know who is speaking *before* you paraphrase or quote.

4. **Write conversationally:** One way to help do that quickly is to use contractions. For example: "I *won't*" instead of "I *will not*." "They *can't*" instead of "They *cannot*." Most of us talk with contractions. It's a simple step to begin writing the way most of us speak.

   Use your ears. Hear the way people speak. How do you speak? Most humans don't say, "Ann *states* that the First Amendment should be changed." *States* is a formal verb. Use *says* because it's less formal and more conversational.

   If not overdone, you can use vernacular speech. (Benjamin Gitlow said "he was havin' none of that." The mayor said, "You don't criticize the mayor.")

5. **Write tight:** Remember most speeches are relatively short. How can you cram enough info into such a short time? First, know the topic. If you don't understand it, how can you expect anyone else to? Kenn Venit, a TV news consultant, suggests that as you sit down to write, try to think of three or four things a person needs to know to understand the topic. If you try to put much more in a short speech, you will simply confuse the audience.

6. **Use active verbs:** Avoid the passive voice. When possible, use single syllable verbs. Keep the subject and verb together. "Assembly moves people." The Absolutist Theory flew the coop long ago."

VI. Practice, Practice, Practice

After you have written it, print it out, then stand up and practice it by reading it out loud. Which words flow from your lips? Which ones are tongue twisters? Because words on paper sound differently when they are read versus when they are spoken, it is important to read and re-read it to hear how it flows. Have your pen in hand to make necessary changes. You will find while doing this that more thoughts and words will come. That's OK. Make the adjustments. Don't feel you are glued to the exact words in your outline. It was a guide to get you going. But do maintain those five-point areas. After you have fine-tuned your speech, print it out or save it on your phone, and practice, practice, practice.

VII. Delivery

There are three ways to deliver or present your speech:

1. **Reading it:** In academic circles, when graduate students and professors present a scholarly paper at a conference, they will often read it verbatim. This is the accepted mode of presentation, but unless the presenter applies inflection and spirit into the delivery, it is the least inspiring way to present information. Why? The voice is usually monotonous, there is little to no eye contact, and there are little to no hand gestures. It is also usually delivered sitting down.

2. **Memorizing it:** Knowing your speech word-for-word is an asset. For one, it demonstrates commitment. Obviously you cared enough to take time to learn your speech. It also projects confidence.

It frees you to apply eye contact to the audience watching you. It also frees your hands so you can use gestures at appropriate points. Lastly, it gives you a full range of opportunities to vary your voice and put feeling into what you are saying. This last point is important. If you apply rote memorization so that you are just saying the words with no indication of understanding or feeling of what you are saying, it is little better than reading it. So be sure you internalize your speech. That is, you know it, feel it, and believe in the words you are saying.

3. **A Blend:** This is a combination of reading and memorizing. You learn and know the material by memorizing most of it—the key passages. You read short passages from either the speech or note cards, but you do it with the same inflection and spirit as if you were not reading it. Think of the reading part as the short bridge to your main road of memorized passages. So, your eyes look down to read for a brief stretch before you look up and out at your audience for your memorized passages. Done effectively, you will have the same freshness and spontaneity as a memorized speech.

Note: It is important to be able to adjust to the variables of life. If something interesting, funny, or just plain out of the ordinary occurs before or during your presentation, be flexible enough to incorporate it into your speech. That includes something a speaker may have said or done before you.

VIII. Voice

It's not just what you say; it's how you say it. This is particularly true when delivering a speech. If you sound bored, listless, and unenthusiastic, your audience will be bored, listless, and unenthusiastic. If you speak with enthusiasm, conviction, and variety in your voice, your audience members will share your enthusiasm and be eager to hear more. They will also applaud you for making their time well spent. Here are some tools to prepare your voice, using as an example, the following line:

Through the Internet and smartphone, everyone has a voice in the marketplace of ideas.

1. **Volume:** Speak loud enough so everyone can hear. That does not mean shout. Present in a strong, controlled voice.

   Example: *Through the Internet and smartphone, everyone has a voice in the marketplace of ideas.*

2. **Inflection/Emphasis:** Emphasize key words and ideas. Some words will command more emphasis than others.

   Example: *Through the Internet and smartphone, <u>everyone has a voice</u> in the marketplace of ideas.*

3. **Pauses/Silence:** Planned pauses and silence can work wonders in dramatically making your point.

   Example: *Through the Internet and smartphone (Pause), everyone has a voice (Pause) in the marketplace (Pause) of ideas.*

4. **Pace:** Changing the pace or speed of your delivery will keep the audience following every word and avoid monotony.

   Example: *(Fast) Through the Internet and smartphone, (Slow) everyone has a voice in (Slower) the marketplace (Slowest) of ideas.*

5. **All together:** Putting these all together will give you a lively speech. Do be sure to enunciate clearly.

IX. Eyes, Hands, Feet

Given in order of importance, these three items do matter.

1. **Eyes:** We can't emphasize enough the importance of eye contact when delivering your speech. If you look down at the floor or up at the ceiling, you will not connect with your audience. If you focus on one side of the room only, you will have others feeling left out. Look at your audience. Sweep your eyes from one side to the next. You can look away or to the side on occasion, as if you are gathering your thoughts or about to present a significant point. But be sure you establish consistent eye contact.
2. **Hands:** Some wonder what to do with their hands. Here's what not to do: Don't keep them in your pocket, twist your hair, or tug your clothes. Do use them to make gestures to emphasize a point. Using the hands actually enables you to draw your speech out of you in a dramatic, feeling way. Just don't overdo it. And be sure it is both natural as well as rehearsed in conjunction with the other parts of your speech.
3. **Feet:** First, do you stand or sit? While there are times when a presentation may allow you to sit, you should usually deliver your presentation while on your feet. Your delivery and whole demeanor changes when you are standing rather than sitting. Aside from this aspect, when you are presenting, be sure you don't lean on anything (chair, wall) or stand stiff as a statue. Instead, move around from side to side when presenting, stopping at times to make a point, then moving again. You can move forward and backward. Be careful not to intrude on personal space.

X. Visual Aids

While these can be handy, the object here is for you to present using just your words rather than, say, a Power Point presentation or a handout. Regarding the latter, any written material should be handed out after your presentation. If you hand it out before, your audience will end up reading it rather than watching and listening to you.

This is not to say that some visual aids cannot be used. Just keep it simple. For instance, if you are speaking about a whistleblower, bring a whistle. If you are talking about unlocking the voice of freedom, bring a lock with a key. Visual aids like these are clever, to the point, and add to your presentation. Lastly, keep them out of sight until you are ready to use them.

XI. Appearance

Looks do matter. By that we mean you want to ensure you are neat and appropriately attired. If your presentation is before a formal audience, dress to the occasion. Regardless of whether it is formal or informal, there are a few things you don't want to do.

- Don't wear clothing with words or pictures (unless it is part of your visual aid). They distract from you and your message.
- Don't wear a T-shirt or any clothing that shows your hairy chest or too much cleavage.
- Don't chew gum or place anything else in your mouth. Not only does it impede your voice but it looks unprofessional.
- Don't wear shorts, hats, or sandals.
- Don't wear sunglasses.

There are, of course, a number of "don'ts" that we might have missed. Not listing them does not mean they are "do's." Use good judgment.

XII. Spirit

It's another word for enthusiasm. It is contagious. If you are excited, then your audience will be excited. Deliver your presentation with good spirit, energy, and enthusiasm.

XIII. Video Oral Presentation

For video oral presentations for an online course, most of the above applies, plus you will need to ensure you have solid lighting, clear audio, a neutral background (no pictures, posters, children running around), and no sound distractions.

XIV. Overcoming

As noted earlier, there are those who are truly terrified of public speaking. It could be a fear rooted in an anxiety disorder, speech impediment, English as a second language, or some other challenge. While it can be tempting to wish to opt out of speaking altogether, we believe what we have presented here should give you the tools to overcome your fears. Do note that you are not alone. There have been a number of students who have faced similar challenges. Some overcame them; some did not. Ultimately it is up to you. If it helps, you should know that when you're up there speaking, the audience is rooting for you. With that in mind, we offer the column that one of the authors wrote about a former student who overcame her fear and inspired her classmates. (See the Students Speech, Free Expression section in the Appendix.)

PART VIII

End Note

This book has taken you through some of the triumphs of free expression in the U.S. It has also related some of the defeats where the freedom of citizens to criticize their government or speak out on a serious social issue was seriously curtailed. Where are we today? The international journalism organization, Reporters Without Borders, conducts an annual survey of the level of press freedom around the world. In 2014, it dropped the ranking of the United States to 46th among 180 countries studied. Here is a portion what they wrote about the survey results:

> *"Countries that pride themselves on being democracies and respecting the rule of law have not set an example, far from it. Freedom of information is too often sacrificed to an overly broad and abusive interpretation of national security needs, marking a disturbing retreat from democratic practices ... The trial and conviction of Private Bradley Manning and the pursuit of NSA analyst Edward Snowden were warnings to all those thinking of assisting in the disclosure of sensitive information that would clearly be in the public interest. U.S. journalists were stunned by the Department of Justice's seizure of Associated Press phone records without warning in order to identify the source of a CIA leak ..."* (The full survey is at www.rsf.org)

This is, of course, only one study of press freedom, and it's written from the perspective of journalists who want as much freedom as possible to report on a society. Clearly, the U.S. has not shut down websites, closed news outlets, or killed reporters, as has been the case in several other countries. But the freedoms we enjoy are always fragile. Only with vigilance by citizens, and with their active participation in democracy, can the U.S. protect the First Amendment and the rights it grants us. Remember, these are not privileges granted by some beneficent monarch, but rights to which each of us is entitled. Without the freedoms permitted by the Constitution, citizens would know much less about medical advances, science, music, art, social movements, politics, and much more. The freedom to express yourself and organize others around a cause you believe in, can be eroded, as has occurred in the past. Taking it for granted is a poor strategy. We have outlined your rights in "The Power of Free Expression in America." It is up to you to protect them for today and generations to come.

PART IX

Appendices

The Declaration of Independence

IN CONGRESS, July 4, 1776.

The Unanimous Declaration of the Thirteen United States of America

When in the Course of human events, it becomes necessary for one people to dissolve the political bands which have connected them with another, and to assume among the powers of the earth, the separate and equal station to which the Laws of Nature and of Nature's God entitle them, a decent respect to the opinions of mankind requires that they should declare the causes which impel them to the separation.

We hold these truths to be self-evident, that all men are created equal, that they are endowed by their Creator with certain unalienable Rights, that among these are Life, Liberty and the pursuit of Happiness.—That to secure these rights, Governments are instituted among Men, deriving their just powers from the consent of the governed,—That whenever any Form of Government becomes destructive of these ends, it is the Right of the People to alter or to abolish it, and to institute new Government, laying its foundation on such principles and organizing its powers in such form, as to them shall seem most likely to effect their Safety and Happiness. Prudence, indeed, will dictate that Governments long established should not be changed for light and transient causes; and accordingly all experience hath shewn, that mankind are more disposed to suffer, while evils are sufferable, than to right themselves by abolishing the forms to which they are accustomed. But when a long train of abuses and usurpations, pursuing invariably the same Object evinces a design to reduce them under absolute Despotism, it is their right, it is their duty, to throw off such Government, and to provide new Guards for their future security.—Such has been the patient sufferance of these Colonies; and such is now the necessity which constrains them to alter their former Systems of Government. The history of the present King of Great Britain is a history of repeated injuries and usurpations, all having in direct object the establishment of an absolute Tyranny over these States. To prove this, let Facts be submitted to a candid world.

He has refused his Assent to Laws, the most wholesome and necessary for the public good.

He has forbidden his Governors to pass Laws of immediate and pressing importance, unless suspended in their operation till his Assent should be obtained; and when so suspended, he has utterly neglected to attend to them.

He has refused to pass other Laws for the accommodation of large districts of people, unless those people would relinquish the right of Representation in the Legislature, a right inestimable to them and formidable to tyrants only.

He has called together legislative bodies at places unusual, uncomfortable, and distant from the depository of their public Records, for the sole purpose of fatiguing them into compliance with his measures.

He has dissolved Representative Houses repeatedly, for opposing with manly firmness his invasions on the rights of the people.

He has refused for a long time, after such dissolutions, to cause others to be elected; whereby the Legislative powers, incapable of Annihilation, have returned to the People at large for their exercise; the State remaining in the mean time exposed to all the dangers of invasion from without, and convulsions within.

He has endeavoured to prevent the population of these States; for that purpose obstructing the Laws for Naturalization of Foreigners; refusing to pass others to encourage their migrations hither, and raising the conditions of new Appropriations of Lands.

He has obstructed the Administration of Justice, by refusing his Assent to Laws for establishing Judiciary powers.

He has made Judges dependent on his Will alone, for the tenure of their offices, and the amount and payment of their salaries.

He has erected a multitude of New Offices, and sent hither swarms of Officers to harass our people, and eat out their substance.

He has kept among us, in times of peace, Standing Armies without the Consent of our legislatures.

He has affected to render the Military independent of and superior to the Civil power.

He has combined with others to subject us to a jurisdiction foreign to our constitution, and unacknowledged by our laws; giving his Assent to their Acts of pretended Legislation:

For Quartering large bodies of armed troops among us:

For protecting them, by a mock Trial, from punishment for any Murders which they should commit on the Inhabitants of these States:

For cutting off our Trade with all parts of the world:

For imposing Taxes on us without our Consent:

For depriving us in many cases, of the benefits of Trial by Jury:

For transporting us beyond Seas to be tried for pretended offences

For abolishing the free System of English Laws in a neighbouring Province, establishing therein an Arbitrary government, and enlarging its Boundaries so as to render it at once an example and fit instrument for introducing the same absolute rule into these Colonies:

For taking away our Charters, abolishing our most valuable Laws, and altering fundamentally the Forms of our Governments:

For suspending our own Legislatures, and declaring themselves invested with power to legislate for us in all cases whatsoever.

He has abdicated Government here, by declaring us out of his Protection and waging War against us.

He has plundered our seas, ravaged our Coasts, burnt our towns, and destroyed the lives of our people.

He is at this time transporting large Armies of foreign Mercenaries to compleat the works of death, desolation and tyranny, already begun with circumstances of Cruelty & perfidy scarcely paralleled in the most barbarous ages, and totally unworthy the Head of a civilized nation.

He has constrained our fellow Citizens taken Captive on the high Seas to bear Arms against their Country, to become the executioners of their friends and Brethren, or to fall themselves by their Hands.

He has excited domestic insurrections amongst us, and has endeavoured to bring on the inhabitants of our frontiers, the merciless Indian Savages, whose known rule of warfare, is an undistinguished destruction of all ages, sexes and conditions.

In every stage of these Oppressions We have Petitioned for Redress in the most humble terms: Our repeated Petitions have been answered only by repeated injury. A Prince whose character is thus marked by every act which may define a Tyrant, is unfit to be the ruler of a free people.

Nor have We been wanting in attentions to our British brethren. We have warned them from time to time of attempts by their legislature to extend an unwarrantable jurisdiction over us. We have reminded them of the circumstances of our emigration and settlement here. We have appealed to their native justice and magnanimity, and we have conjured them by the ties of our common kindred to disavow these usurpations, which would inevitably interrupt our connections and correspondence. They too have been deaf to the voice of justice and of consanguinity. We must, therefore, acquiesce in the necessity, which denounces our Separation, and hold them, as we hold the rest of mankind, Enemies in War, in Peace Friends.

We, therefore, the Representatives of the united States of America, in General Congress, Assembled, appealing to the Supreme Judge of the world for the rectitude of our intentions, do, in the Name, and by Authority of the good People of these Colonies, solemnly publish and declare, That these United Colonies are, and of Right ought to be Free and Independent States; that they are Absolved from all Allegiance to the British Crown, and that all political connection between them and the State of Great Britain, is and ought to be totally dissolved; and that as Free and Independent States, they have full Power to levy War, conclude Peace, contract Alliances, establish Commerce, and to do all other Acts and Things which Independent States may of right do. And for the support of this Declaration, with a firm reliance on the protection of divine Providence, we mutually pledge to each other our Lives, our Fortunes and our sacred Honor.

There were 56 signatures on the Declaration.

The First Amendment of the U.S. Constitution

Congress shall make no law respecting an establishment of religion, or prohibiting the free exercise thereof; or abridging the freedom of speech, or of the press; or the right of the people peaceably to assemble, and to petition the government for a redress of grievances.

The Alien Act: An Act Respecting Alien Enemies—1798

SECTION 1. Be it enacted by the Senate and House of Representatives of the United States of America in Congress assembled,

That whenever there shall be a declared war between the United States and any foreign nation or government, or any invasion or predatory incursion shall be perpetrated, attempted, or threatened against the territory of the United States, by any foreign nation or government, and the President of the United States shall make public proclamation of the event, all natives, citizens, denizens, or subjects of the hostile nation or government, being males of the age of fourteen years and upwards, who shall be within the United States, and not actually naturalized, shall be liable to be apprehended, restrained, secured and removed, as alien enemies. And the President of the United States shall be, and he is hereby authorized, in any event, as aforesaid, by his proclamation thereof, or other public act, to direct the conduct to be observed, on the part of the United States, towards the aliens who shall become liable, as aforesaid; the manner and degree of the restraint to which they shall be subject, and in what cases, and upon what security their residence shall be permitted, and to provide for the removal of those, who, not being permitted to reside within the United States, shall refuse or neglect to depart therefrom; and to establish any other regulations which shall be found necessary in the premises and for the public safety: Provided, that aliens resident within the United States, who shall become liable as enemies, in the manner aforesaid, and who shall not be chargeable with actual hostility, or other crime against the public safety, shall be allowed, for the recovery, disposal, and removal of their goods and effects, and for their departure, the full time which is, or shall be stipulated by any treaty, where any shall have been between the United States, and the hostile nation or government, of which they shall be natives, citizens, denizens or subjects: and where no such treaty shall have existed, the President of the United States may ascertain and declare such reasonable time as may be consistent with the public safety, and according to the dictates of humanity and national hospitality.

SECTION. 2. And be it further enacted,

That after any proclamation shall be made as aforesaid, it shall be the duty of the several courts of the United States, and of each state, having criminal jurisdiction, and of the several judges and justices of the courts of the United States, and they shall be, and are hereby respectively, authorized upon complaint, against any alien or alien enemies, as aforesaid, who shall be resident and at large within such jurisdiction or district, to the danger of the public peace or safety, and contrary to the tenor or intent of such proclamation, or other regulations which the President of the United States shall and may establish in the premises, to cause such alien or aliens to be duly apprehended and convened before such court, judge or justice; and after a full examination and hearing on such complaint, and sufficient cause therefor appearing, shall and may order such alien or aliens to be removed out of the territory of the United States, or to give sureties of their good behaviour, or to be otherwise restrained, conformably to the proclamation or regulations which shall and may be established as aforesaid, and may imprison, or otherwise secure such alien or aliens, until the order which shall and may be made, as aforesaid, shall be performed.

SECTION. 3. And be it further enacted,

That it shall be the duty of the marshal of the district in which any alien enemy shall be apprehended, who by the President of the United States, or by order of any court, judge or justice, as aforesaid, shall be required to depart, and to be removed, as aforesaid, to provide therefor, and to execute such order, by himself or his deputy, or other discreet person or persons to be employed by him, by causing a removal of such alien out of the territory of the United States; and for such removal the marshal shall have the warrant of the President of the United States, or of the court, judge or justice ordering the same, as the case may be.

APPROVED, July 6, 1798.

The Sedition Act: An Act in Addition to the Act, Entitled "An Act for the Punishment of Certain Crimes Against the United States"

SECTION 1. Be it enacted by the Senate and House of Representatives of the United States of America, in Congress assembled,

That if any persons shall unlawfully combine or conspire together, with intent to oppose any measure or measures of the government of the United States, which are or shall be directed by proper authority, or to impede the operation of any law of the United States, or to intimidate or prevent any person holding a place or office in or under the government of the United States, from undertaking, performing or executing his trust or duty, and if any person or persons, with intent as aforesaid, shall counsel, advise or attempt to procure any insurrection, riot, unlawful assembly, or combination, whether such conspiracy, threatening, counsel, advice, or attempt shall have the proposed effect or not, he or they shall be deemed guilty of a high misdemeanor, and on conviction, before any court of the United States having jurisdiction thereof, shall be punished by a fine not exceeding five thousand dollars, and by imprisonment during a term not less than six months nor exceeding five years; and further, at the discretion of the court may be ho]den to find sureties for his good behaviour in such sum, and for such time, as the said court may direct.

SECTION. 2. And be it farther enacted,

That if any person shall write, print, utter or publish, or shall cause or procure to be written, printed, uttered or published, or shall knowingly and willingly assist or aid in writing, printing, uttering or publishing any false, scandalous and malicious writing or writings against the government of the United States, or either house of the Congress of the United States, or the President of the United States, with intent to defame the said government, or either house of the said Congress, or the said President, or to bring them, or either of them, into contempt or disrepute; or to excite against them, or either or any of them, the hatred of the good people of the United States, or to stir up sedition within the United States, or to excite any unlawful combinations therein, for opposing or resisting any law of the United States, or any act of the President of the United States, done in pursuance of any such law, or of the powers in him vested by the Constitution of the United States, or to resist, oppose, or defeat any such law or act, or to aid, encourage or abet any hostile designs of any foreign nation against United States, their people or government, then such person, being thereof convicted before any court of the United States having jurisdiction thereof, shall be punished by a fine not exceeding two thousand dollars, and by imprisonment not exceeding two years.

SECTION. 3. And be it further enacted and declared,

That if any person shall be prosecuted under this act, for the writing or publishing any libel aforesaid, it shall be lawful for the defendant, upon the trial of the cause, to give in evidence in his defence, the truth of the matter contained in Republication charged as a libel. And the jury who shall try the cause, shall have a right to determine the law and the fact, under the direction of the court, as in other cases.

SECTION. 4. And be it further enacted,

That this act shall continue and be in force until the third day of March, one thousand eight hundred and one, and no longer: Provided, that the expiration of the act shall not prevent or defeat a prosecution and punishment of any offence against the law, during the time it shall be in force.
APPROVED, July 14, 1798.

The Espionage Act—June 15, 1917

SIXTY-FIFTH CONGRESS. Sess. I. Ch. 30 1917.

Be it enacted by the Senate and House of Representatives of the United States of America in Congress assembled:

Title I. ESPIONAGE.

Section 1.
That (a) whoever, for the purpose of obtaining information respecting the national defense with intent or reason to believe that the information to be obtained is to be used to the injury of the United States, or to the advantage of any foreign nation, goes upon, enters, flies over, or otherwise obtains information, concerning any vessel, aircraft, work of defense, navy yard, naval station, submarine base, coaling station, fort, battery, torpedo station, dockyard, canal, railroad, arsenal, camp, factory, mine, telegraph, telephone, wireless, or signal station, building, office, or other place connected with the national defense, owned or constructed, or in progress of construction by the United States or under the control or the United States, or of any of its officers or agents, or within the exclusive jurisdiction of the United States, or any place in which any vessel, aircraft, arms, munitions, or other materials or instruments for use in time of war are being made, prepared, repaired, or stored, under any contract or agreement with the United States, or with any person on behalf of the United States, or otherwise on behalf of the United States, or any prohibited place within the meaning of section six of this title; or (b) whoever for the purpose aforesaid, and with like intent or reason to believe, copies, takes, makes, or obtains, or attempts, or induces or aids another to copy, take, make, or obtain, any sketch, photograph, photographic negative, blue print, plan, map, model, instrument, appliance, document, writing or note of anything connected with the national defense; or (c) whoever, for the purpose aforesaid, receives or obtains or agrees

or attempts or induces or aids another to receive or obtain from any other person, or from any source whatever, any document, writing, code book, signal book, sketch, photograph, photographic negative, blue print, plan, map, model, instrument, appliance, or note, of anything connected with the national defense, knowing or having reason to believe, at the time he receives or obtains, or agrees or attempts or induces or aids another to receive or obtain it, that it has been or will be obtained, taken, made or disposed of by any person contrary to the provisions of this title; or (d) whoever, lawfully or unlawfully having possession of, access to, control over, or being entrusted with any document, writing, code book, signal book, sketch, photograph, photographic negative, blue print, plan, map, model, instrument, appliance, or note relating to the national defense, willfully communicates or transmits or attempts to communicate or transmit the same and fails to deliver it on demand to the officer or employee of the United States entitled to receive it; or (e) whoever, being entrusted with or having lawful possession or control of any document, writing, code book, signal book, sketch, photograph, photographic negative, blue print, plan, map, model, note, or information, relating to the national defense, through gross negligence permits the same to be removed from its proper place of custody or delivered to anyone in violation of his trust, or to be list, stolen, abstracted, or destroyed, shall be punished by a fine of not more than $10,000, or by imprisonment for not more than two years, or both.

Section 2.

(a) Whoever, with intent or reason to believe that it is to be used to the injury or the United States or to the advantage of a foreign nation, communicated, delivers, or transmits, or attempts to, or aids, or induces another to, communicate, deliver or transmit, to any foreign government, or to any faction or party or military or naval force within a foreign country, whether recognized or unrecognized by the United States, or to any representative, officer, agent, employee, subject, or citizen thereof, either directly or indirectly and document, writing, code book, signal book, sketch, photograph, photographic negative, blue print, plan, map, model, note, instrument, appliance, or information relating to the national defense, shall be punished by imprisonment for not more than twenty years: *Provided,* That whoever shall violate the provisions of subsection (a) of this section in time of war shall be punished by death or by imprisonment for not more than thirty years; and (b) whoever, in time of war, with intent that the same shall be communicated to the enemy, shall collect, record, publish or communicate, or attempt to elicit any information with respect to the movement, numbers, description, condition, or disposition of any of the armed forces, ships, aircraft, or war materials of the United States, or with respect to the plans or conduct, or supposed plans or conduct of any naval of military operations, or with respect to any works or measures undertaken for or connected with, or intended for the fortification of any place, or any other information relating to the public defense, which might be useful to the enemy, shall be punished by death or by imprisonment for not more than thirty years.

Section 3.

Whoever, when the United States is at war, shall willfully make or convey false reports or false statements with intent to interfere with the operation or success of the military or naval forces of the United States or to promote the success of its enemies and whoever when the United States is at war, shall willfully cause or attempt to cause insubordination, disloyalty, mutiny, refusal of duty, in the military or naval forces of the United States, or shall willfully obstruct the recruiting or enlistment service of the United States, to the injury of the service or of the United States, shall be punished by a fine of not more than $10,000 or imprisonment for not more than twenty years, or both.

Section 4.

If two or more persons conspire to violate the provisions of section two or three of this title, and one or more of such persons does any act to effect the object of the conspiracy, each of the parties to such conspiracy shall be punished as in said sections provided in the case of the doing of the act the accomplishment of which is the object of such conspiracy. Except as above provided conspiracies to commit offenses under this title shall be punished as provided by section thirty-seven of the Act to codify, revise, and amend the penal laws of the United States approved March fourth, nineteen hundred and nine.

Section 5.

Whoever harbors or conceals any person who he knows, or has reasonable grounds to believe or suspect, has committed, or is about to commit, an offense under this title shall be punished by a fine of not more than $10,000 or by imprisonment for not more than two years, or both.

Section 6.

The President in time of war or in case of national emergency may by proclamation designate any place other than those set forth in subsection (a) of section one hereof in which anything for the use of the Army or Navy is being prepared or constructed or stored as a prohibited place for the purpose of this title: *Provided,* That he shall determine that information with respect thereto would be prejudicial to the national defense.

Section 7.

Nothing contained in this title shall be deemed to limit the jurisdiction of the general courts-martial, military commissions, or naval courts-martial under sections thirteen hundred and forty-two, thirteen hundred and forty-three, and sixteen hundred and twenty-four of the Revised Statutes as amended.

Section 8.

The provisions of this title shall extend to all Territories, possessions, and places subject to the jurisdiction of the United States whether or not contiguous thereto, and offenses under this title, when committed upon the high seas or elsewhere within the admiralty and maritime jurisdiction of the United States and outside the territorial limits thereof shall be punishable hereunder.

Section 9.

The Act entitles "An Act to prevent the disclosure of national defense secrets," approved March third, nineteen hundred and eleven, is hereby repealed.

Title II. VESSELS IN PORTS OF THE UNITED STATES.

Section 1.

Whenever the President by proclamation or Executive order declares a national emergency to exist by reason of actual or threatened war, insurrection, or invasion, or disturbance or threatened disturbance of the international relations of the United States, the Secretary of the Treasury may make, subject to the approval of the President, rules and regulations governing the anchorage and movement of any vessel, foreign or domestic, in the territorial waters of the United States, may inspect such vessel at any time, place guards thereon, and, if necessary in his opinion in order to secure such vessels from damage, or injury to any harbor or waters of the United States, or to secure the observance of the rights and obligations of the United States, may take, by and with the consent of the President, for such purposes, full possession and control of such vessel and remove therefrom the officers and crew thereof and all other persons not specially authorized by him to go or remain on board thereof. Within the territory and waters of the Canal Zone the Governor of the Panama Canal, with the approval of the President, shall exercise all the powers conferred by this section on the Secretary of the Treasury.

Section 2.

If any owner, agent, master, officer, or person in charge, or any member of the crew of any such vessel fails to comply with any regulation of rule issued or order given by the Secretary of the Treasury or the Governor of the Panama Canal under the provisions of this title, or obstructs or interferes with the exercise or any power conferred by this title, the vessel, together with her tackle, apparel, furniture, and equipment, shall be subject to seizure and forfeiture to the United States in the same manner as merchandise is forfeited for violation of the customs revenue laws; and the person guilty of such failure, obstruction, or interference shall be fined not more than $10,000, or imprisoned not more that two years, or both.

Section 3.

It shall be unlawful for the owner or master or any other person in charge or command of any private vessel, foreign or domestic, or for any member of the crew or other person, within the territorial waters of the United States, willfully to cause or permit the destruction or injury of such vessel or knowingly to permit said vessel to be used as a place of resort for any person conspiring with another or preparing to commit any offense against the United States, or in violation of the treaties of the Unites States or of the obligations of the United States under the law of nations, or to defraud the United States, or knowingly to permit such vessels to be used in violation of the rights and obliga-tions of the United States under the law of nations; and in case such vessel shall be so used, with the knowledge of the owner or master or other person in charge or command thereof, the vessel, together with her tackle, apparel, furniture, and equipment, shall be subject to seizure and forfeiture to the United States in the same manner as merchandise is forfeited for violation of the customs revenue laws; and whoever violates this section shall be fined not more than $10,000, or imprisoned not more that two years, or both.

Section 4.

The President may employ such part of the land or naval forces of the United States as he may deem necessary to carry out the purpose of this title.

Title III. INJURING VESSELS ENGAGED IN FOREIGN COMMERCE.

Section 1.

Whoever shall set fire to any vessel or foreign registry, or any vessel of American registry entitled to engage in commerce with foreign nations, or to any vessel of the United States as defined in section three hundred and ten of the Act of March fourth, nineteen hundred and nine, entitled "An Act to codify, revise, and amend the penal laws of the United States," or to the cargo of the same, or shall tamper with the motive power or instrumentalities of navigation or such vessel, or shall place bombs or explosives in or upon such vessel, or shall do any other act to or upon such vessel while within the jurisdiction of the United States, or, if such vessel is of American registry, while she is on the high seas, with intent to injure or endanger the safety of the vessel or of her cargo, of persons on board, whether the injury or danger is so intended to take place within the jurisdiction of the United States, or after the vessel shall have departed therefrom; or whoever shall attempt or conspire to do any such acts with such intent, shall be fined not more than $10,000 or imprisoned not more than twenty years, or both.

Title IV. INTERFERENCE WITH FOREIGN COMMERCE BY VIOLENT MEANS.

Section 1.

Whoever, with intent to prevent, interfere with, or obstruct or attempt to prevent, interfere with, or obstruct the exportation to foreign countries of articles from the United States shall injure or destroy, by fire or explosives, such articles or the places where they may be while in such foreign commerce, shall be fined not more than $10,000, or imprisoned no more than ten years, or both.

Title V. ENFORCEMENT OF NEUTRALITY.

Section 1.

During a war in which the United States is a neutral nation, the President, or any person thereunto authorized by him, may withhold clearance from or to any vessel, domestic or foreign, which is required by law to secure clearance before departing, to forbid its departure from port or from the jurisdiction of the United States, whenever there is reasonable cause to believe that any such vessel, domestic or foreign, whether requiring clearance or not, is about to carry fuel, arms, ammunition, men supplies, dispatches, or information to any warship, tender, or supply ship or a foreign belligerent nation in violation of the laws, treaties or obligations of the United States under the law of nations; and it shall thereupon be unlawful for such vessel to depart.

Section 2.

During a war in which the United States is a neutral nation, the President, or any person thereunto authorized by him, may detain any armed vessel owned wholly or in part by American citizens, or any vessel, domestic or foreign (other than one which has entered the ports of the United States as a public vessel), which is manifestly built for warlike purposes or has been converted or adapted from a private vessel to one suitable for warlike use, until the owner or master, or person having charge of such vessel, shall furnish proof satisfactory to the President, or to the person duly authorized by him, that the vessel will not be employed by the said owners, or master, or person having charge thereof, to cruise against or commit or attempt to commit hostilities upon the subjects, citizens, or property of any foreign prince or state, or of any colony, district, or people with which the United States is at peace, and that the said vessel will not be sold or delivered to any belligerent nation, or to an agent, officer, or citizen of such nation, by them or any of them, within the jurisdiction of the United States, or, having left that jurisdiction, upon the high seas.

Section 3.

During a war in which the United States is a neutral nation, it shall be unlawful to send out of the jurisdiction of the United States any vessel built, armed, or equipped as a vessel of war, or converted from a private vessel into a vessel of war, with any intent or under any agreement or contract, written or oral, that such vessel shall be delivered to a belligerent nation, or to an agent, officer, or citizen of such nation, or with reasonable cause to believe that the said vessel shall or will be employed in the service of any such belligerent nation after its departure from the jurisdiction of the United States.

Section 4.

During a war in which the United States is a neutral nation, in addition to the facts required by sections forty-one hundred and ninety-seven, forty-one hundred and ninety-eight, and, forty-two hundred of the Revised Statutes to be set out in the masters' and shippers' manifests before clearance will be issued to vessels bound to foreign ports, each of which sections of the Revised Statutes is hereby declared to be and is continued in full force and effect, every master or person having charge or command of any vessel, domestic or foreign, whether requiring clearance or not, before departure of such vessel from port shall deliver to the collector of customs for the district wherein such vessel is then located a statement duly verified by oath, that the cargo or any part of the cargo is or is not to be delivered to other vessels in port or to be transshipped, on the high seas and, if it is to be so delivered or transshipped, stating the kind and quantities and the value of the total quantity of each kind of article so to be delivered or transshipped, and the name of the person, corporation, vessel, or government, to whom the delivery or transshipment is to be made; and the owners, shippers, or consignors of the cargo or such vessel shall in the same manner and under the same conditions deliver to the collector like statements under oath as to the cargo or the parts thereof laden or shipped by them, respectively.

Section 5.

Whenever it appears that the vessel is not entitled to clearance or whenever there is reasonable cause to believe that the additional statements under oath required in the foregoing section are false, the collector of customs for the district in which the vessel is located, may, subject to review by the Secretary of Commerce, refuse clearance to any vessel, domestic or foreign, and by formal notice served upon the owners, master, or person or persons in command or charge of any domestic vessel for which clearance is not required by law, forbid the departure of the vessel from the port or from the jurisdiction of the United States; and it shall thereupon be unlawful for the vessel to depart.

Section 6.

Whoever in violation of any of the provisions of this title, shall take, or attempt or conspire to take, or authorize the taking of any such vessel, out of port or from the jurisdiction of the United States, shall be fined not more than $10,000 or imprisoned not more than five years, or both; and in addition, such vessel, her tackle, apparel, furniture, equipment, and her cargo shall be forfeited to the United States.

Section 7.

Whoever, being a person belonging to the armed land or naval forces of a belligerent nation or belligerent faction of any nation and being interned in the United States, in accordance with the law of nations, shall leave or attempt to leave said jurisdiction, or shall leave or attempt to leave the limits of internment in which freedom of movement has been allowed, without permission from the proper official of the United States in charge, or shall willfully overstay a leave of absence granted by such official shall be subject to arrest by any marshal or deputy marshal of the United States, or by the military or naval authorities thereof, and shall be returned to the place of internment and there confined and safely kept for such period of time as the official of the United States in charge shall direct; and whoever, within the jurisdiction of the United States and subject thereto, shall aid or entice any interned person to escape or attempt to escape from the jurisdiction of the United States, or from the limits of internment prescribed, shall be fined not more than $1000 or imprisoned not more than one year, or both …

Sedition Act of 1918

Section 3.

Whoever, when the United States is at war, shall willfully make or convey false reports or false statements with intent to interfere with the operation or success of the military or naval forces of the United States, or to promote the success of its enemies, or shall willfully make or convey false reports or false statements, or say or do anything except by way of bona fide and not disloyal advice to an investor or investors, with intent to obstruct the sale by the United States of bonds or other securities of the United States or the making of loans by or to the United States, and whoever when the United States is at war, shall willfully cause or attempt to cause, or incite or attempt to incite, insubordination, disloyalty, mutiny, or refusal of duty, in the military or naval forces of the United States, or shall willfully obstruct or attempt to obstruct the recruiting or enlistment services of the United States, and whoever, when the United States is at war, shall willfully utter, print, write or publish any disloyal, profane, scurrilous, or abusive language about the form of government of the United States or the Constitution of the United States, or the military or naval forces of the United States, or the flag of the United States, or the uniform of the Army or Navy of the United States into contempt, scorn, contumely, or disrepute, or shall willfully utter, print, write, or publish any language intended to incite, provoke, or encourage resistance to the United States, or to promote the cause of its enemies, or shall willfully display the flag of any foreign enemy, or shall willfully by utterance, writing, printing, publication, or language spoken, urge, incite, or advocate any curtailment of production in this country of any thing or things, product or products, necessary or essential to the prosecution of the war in which the United States may be engaged, with intent by such curtailment to cripple or hinder the United States in the prosecution of war, and whoever shall willfully advocate, teach, defend, or suggest the doing of any of the acts or things in this section enumerated, and whoever shall by word or act support or favor the cause of any country with which the United

States is at war or by word or act oppose the cause of the United States therein, shall be punished by a fine of not more than $10,000 or the imprisonment for not more than twenty years, or both: *Provided*, That any employee or official of the United States Government who commits any disloyal act or utters any unpatriotic or disloyal language, or who, in an abusive and violent manner criticizes the Army or Navy or the flag of the United States shall be at once dismissed from the service. …

Section 4.

When the United States is at war, the Postmaster General may, upon evidence satisfactory to him that any person or concern is using the mails in violation of any of the provisions of this Act, instruct the postmaster at any post office at which mail is received addressed to such person or concern to return to the postmaster at the office at which they were originally mailed all letters or other matter so addressed, with the words 'Mail to this address undeliverable under Espionage Act' plainly written or stamped upon the outside thereof, and all such letters or other matter so returned to such postmasters shall be by them returned to the senders thereof under such regulations as the Postmaster General may prescribe.

APPROVED, May 16, 1918.

Smith Act of 1940

The Alien Registration Act of 1940, usually called the Smith Act because the antisedition section was authored by Representative Howard W. Smith of Virginia, was adopted at 54 *Statutes at Large* 670–671 (1940). The Act has been amended several times and can now be found at 18 *U.S. Code* § 2385 (2000).

§ 2385. Advocating Overthrow of Government.

Whoever knowingly or willfully advocates, abets, advises, or teaches the duty, necessity, desirability, or propriety of overthrowing or destroying the government of the United States or the government of any State, Territory, District or Possession thereof, or the government of any political subdivision therein, by force or violence, or by the assassination of any officer of any such government; or

Whoever, with intent to cause the overthrow or destruction of any such government, prints, publishes, edits, issues, circulates, sells, distributes, or publicly displays any written or printed matter advocating, advising, or teaching the duty, necessity, desirability, or propriety of overthrowing or destroying any government in the United States by force or violence, or attempts to do so; or

Whoever organizes or helps or attempts to organize any society, group, or assembly of persons who teach, advocate, or encourage the overthrow or destruction of any such government by force or violence; or becomes or is a member of, or affiliates with, any such society, group, or assembly of persons, knowing the purposes thereof—

Shall be fined under this title or imprisoned not more than twenty years, or both, and shall be ineligible for employment by the United States or any department or agency thereof, for the five years next following his conviction.

If two or more persons conspire to commit any offense named in this section, each shall be fined under this title or imprisoned not more than twenty years, or both, and shall be ineligible for employment by the United States or any department or agency thereof, for the five years next following his conviction.

As used in this section, the terms "organizes" and "organize," with respect to any society, group, or assembly of persons, include the recruiting of new members, the forming of new units, and the regrouping or expansion of existing clubs, classes, and other units of such society, group, or assembly of persons.

Attorney General John Ashcroft, Prepared Remarks, Senate Committee on the Judiciary, September 25, 2001

Chairman Leahy, Senator Hatch, Senators: thank you for the opportunity to discuss the Administration's proposed changes in the law to give law enforcement the tools we need to fight terrorism.

In his address to Congress and the nation last Thursday, President Bush declared war on terrorism. As Attorney General, it is my duty to respond to this call to action by ensuring the capacity of United States law enforcement to perform two related critical tasks: First, prevent more terrorism, and second, to bring terrorists to justice.

The American people do not have the luxury of unlimited time in erecting the necessary defenses to future terrorist acts. The danger that darkened the United States of America and the civilized world on September 11 did not pass with the atrocities committed that day. Terrorism is a clear and present danger to Americans today.

Intelligence information available to the FBI indicates a potential for additional terrorist incidents. I testified before the House Judiciary Committee yesterday regarding the possibility of attacks using crop dusting aircraft.

Today I can report to you that our investigation has uncovered several individuals, including individuals who may have links to the hijackers, who fraudulently have obtained, or attempted to obtain, hazardous material transportation licenses.

Given the current threat environment, the FBI has advised all law enforcement agencies to remain alert to this threat.

And, I urge Americans to notify immediately the FBI of any suspicious circumstances that may come to your attention regarding hazardous materials, crop dusting aircraft or any other possible terrorist threat. The FBI website is (or rather) our toll-free telephone number is 866-483-5137. Again, the toll-free number is 866-483-5137.

This new terrorist threat to Americans on our soil is a turning point in America's history. It is a new challenge for law enforcement. Our fight against terrorism is not merely or primarily a criminal justice endeavor—it is defense of our nation and its citizens. We cannot wait for terrorists to strike to begin investigations and make arrests. The death tolls are too high, the consequences too great. We must prevent first, prosecute second.

I can assure the Committee and the American people we are conducting this effort with a total commitment to protect the rights and privacy of all Americans and the Constitutional protections we hold dear.

In the past, when American law enforcement confronted challenges to our safety and security from espionage, drug trafficking and organized crime, we met those challenges in ways that preserved our fundamental freedoms and civil liberties.

Today we seek to meet the challenge of terrorism with the same careful regard for the Constitutional rights of Americans and respect for all human beings. Just as American rights and freedoms have been preserved throughout previous law enforcement campaigns, they must be preserved throughout this war on terrorism.

This Justice Department will never waiver in our defense of the Constitution nor relent our defense of civil rights.

As the members of this Committee understand, the deficiencies of our current laws on terrorism reflect two facts:

First, our laws fail to make defeating terrorism a national priority. Indeed, we have tougher laws against organized crime and drug trafficking than terrorism.

Second, technology has dramatically outpaced our statutes. Law enforcement tools created decades ago were crafted for rotary telephones—not email, the Internet, mobile communications and voice mail.

Every day that passes with outdated statutes and the old rules of engagement is a day that terrorists have a competitive advantage. Until Congress makes these changes, we are fighting an unnecessarily uphill battle. Members of the Committee, I regret to inform you that we are today sending our troops into the modern field of battle with antique weapons.

The anti-terrorism proposals that have been submitted by the Administration represent careful, balanced, and long overdue improvements to our capacity to combat terrorism. It is not a wish list: It is a modest set of essentials, focusing on five broad objectives, which I will briefly summarize.

First, law enforcement needs a strengthened and streamlined ability for our intelligence gathering agencies to gather the information necessary to disrupt, weaken and eliminate the infrastructure of terrorist organizations. Critically, we also need the authority for law enforcement to share vital information with our national security agencies in order to prevent future terrorist attacks.

Terrorist organizations have increasingly used technology to facilitate their criminal acts and hide their communications from law enforcement. Intelligence gathering laws that were written for the era of landline telephone communications are ill-adapted for use in communications over multiple cell phones and computer networks.

Our proposal creates a more efficient, technology-neutral standard for intelligence gathering, ensuring law enforcement's ability to trace the communications of terrorists over cell-phones, computer networks and new technologies that may be developed in the coming years.

These changes would streamline intelligence gathering procedures only. We do not seek changes in the underlying protections in the law for the privacy of law-abiding citizens. The information captured by the proposed technology-neutral standard would be limited to the kind of information you might find in a phone bill. The content of these communications would remain off-limits to monitoring by intelligence authorities, except for under current legal standards.

Our proposal would allow a federal court to issue a single order that would apply to all providers in a communications chain, including those outside the region where the court is located. We need speed in identifying and tracking down terrorists. Time is of the essence. The ability of law enforcement to trace communications into different jurisdictions without obtaining an additional court order can be the difference between life and death for American citizens.

Second, we must make fighting terrorism a national priority in our criminal justice system.

Our current laws make it easier to prosecute members of organized crime than to crack down on terrorists who can kill thousands of Americans in a single day. The same is true of drug traffickers and individuals involved in espionage—our laws treat these criminals and those who aid and abet them more severely than terrorists.

We would make harboring a terrorist a crime. Currently, for instance, harboring persons engaged in espionage is a criminal offense, but harboring terrorists is not.

Third, we seek to enhance the authority of the Immigration and Naturalization Service to detain or remove suspected alien terrorists from within our borders.

The ability of terrorists to move freely across borders and operate within the United States is critical to their capacity to inflict damage on the citizens and facilities in the United States. Under current law, the existing grounds for removal of aliens for terrorism are limited to direct material support of an individual terrorist. We propose to expand these grounds for removal to include material support to terrorist organizations.

Fourth, law enforcement must be able to "follow the money" in order to identify and neutralize terrorist networks.

We need the capacity for more than a freeze. We must be able to seize. Consistent with the President's action yesterday, our proposal gives law enforcement the ability to seize their terrorist assets.

Finally, we seek the ability for the President and the Department of Justice to provide swift emergency relief to the victims of terrorism and their families.

Mr. Chairman, I also want to report to you on the status of the DOJ's activities regarding protecting the civil rights of all Americans. Since September 11, the Civil Rights Division, working closely with the United States Attorneys and the FBI, has opened over 60 investigations into acts involving force or threats of force committed in retaliation for the events of September 11. All of these acts include killings, assaults, the destruction or attempted destruction of businesses, attacks on mosques and worshipers and death threats.

The Department of Justice is firmly committed to pursuing these misguided wrongdoers vigorously. The Civil Rights Division and FBI officials have met with leaders of the Arab American, Muslim and Sikh communities and we have established in the Civil Rights Division an initiative to combat post-terrorism discrimination to ensure that all allegations of violence or discrimination are addressed promptly and effectively.

Let there be no mistake: the Department of Justice will not tolerate acts of violence or discrimination against people in this country based on their race, national origin or religion.

Among the high honors of my life has been the opportunity I have had over the past days and weeks to be in the company of these heroes, these friends of freedom; to meet with and work side-by-side with men and women who have exerted themselves beyond fatigue, who have set aside their own personal agendas and their personal safety to answer our nation's call. The nation has found new leaders—and new role models—in these brave Americans.

Now it falls to us, in the name of freedom and those who cherish it, to ensure our nation's capacity to defend ourselves from terrorists. Today I call upon Congress to act to strengthen our ability to fight this evil wherever it exists, and to ensure that the line between the civil and the savage, so brightly drawn on September 11, is never crossed again.

Uniting and Strengthening America by Providing Appropriate Tools Required to Intercept and Obstruct Terrorism (USA Patriot Act) Act of 2001

PUBLIC LAW 107–56—OCT. 26, 2001

107th CONGRESS
1st Session

H. R. 3162
IN THE SENATE OF THE UNITED STATES

Oct. 24, 2001

AN ACT

To deter and punish terrorist acts in the United States and around the world, to enhance law enforcement investigatory tools, and for other purposes. *Be it enacted by the Senate and House of Representatives of the United States of America in Congress assembled,*

SECTION 1. SHORT TITLE AND TABLE OF CONTENTS.

(a) SHORT TITLE—This Act may be cited as the 'Uniting and Strengthening America by Providing Appropriate Tools Required to Intercept and Obstruct Terrorism (USA PATRIOT ACT) Act of 2001.'
(b) TABLE OF CONTENTS- The table of contents for this Act is as follows:

TITLE I—ENHANCING DOMESTIC SECURITY AGAINST TERRORISM

Sec. 101. Counterterrorism fund.
Sec. 102. Sense of Congress condemning discrimination against Arab and Muslim Americans.
Sec. 103. Increased funding for the technical support center at the Federal Bureau of Investigation.
Sec. 104. Requests for military assistance to enforce prohibition in certain emergencies.
Sec. 105. Expansion of National Electronic Crime Task Force Initiative.
Sec. 106. Presidential authority.

TITLE II—ENHANCED SURVEILLANCE PROCEDURES

Sec. 201. Authority to intercept wire, oral, and electronic communications relating to terrorism.
Sec. 202. Authority to intercept wire, oral, and electronic communications relating to computer fraud and abuse offenses.
Sec. 203. Authority to share criminal investigative information.
Sec. 204. Clarification of intelligence exceptions from limitations on interception and disclosure of wire, oral, and electronic communications.
Sec. 205. Employment of translators by the Federal Bureau of Investigation.
Sec. 206. Roving surveillance authority under the Foreign Intelligence Surveillance Act of 1978.
Sec. 207. Duration of FISA surveillance of non-United States persons who are agents of a foreign power.
Sec. 208. Designation of judges.
Sec. 209. Seizure of voice-mail messages pursuant to warrants.
Sec. 210. Scope of subpoenas for records of electronic communications.
Sec. 211. Clarification of scope.
Sec. 212. Emergency disclosure of electronic communications to protect life and limb.
Sec. 213. Authority for delaying notice of the execution of a warrant.
Sec. 214. Pen register and trap and trace authority under FISA.
Sec. 215. Access to records and other items under the Foreign Intelligence Surveillance Act.
Sec. 216. Modification of authorities relating to use of pen registers and trap and trace devices.
Sec. 217. Interception of computer trespasser communications.
Sec. 218. Foreign intelligence information.
Sec. 219. Single-jurisdiction search warrants for terrorism.

This is an abbreviated version. The official document is accessible online.

Remarks by the President at Signing of the Patriot Act, Anti-Terrorism Legislation, 9:49 a.m. EDT, October 26, 2001

For Immediate Release
Office of the Press Secretary
October 26, 2001

President Signs Anti-Terrorism Bill
Remarks by the President at Signing of the Patriot Act,
Anti-Terrorism Legislation
The East Room
9:49 a.m. EDT

THE PRESIDENT: Good morning and welcome to the White House. Today, we take an essential step in defeating terrorism, while protecting the constitutional rights of all Americans. With my signature, this law will give intelligence and law enforcement officials important new tools to fight a present danger.

I commend the House and Senate for the hard work they put into this legislation. Members of Congress and their staffs spent long nights and weekends to get this important bill to my desk. I appreciate their efforts, and bipartisanship, in passing this new law ...

The changes, effective today, will help counter a threat like no other our nation has ever faced. We've seen the enemy, and the murder of thousands of innocent, unsuspecting people. They recognize no barrier of morality. They have no conscience. The terrorists cannot be reasoned with. Witness the recent anthrax attacks through our Postal Service.

Our country is grateful for the courage the Postal Service has shown during these difficult times. We mourn the loss of the lives of Thomas Morris and Joseph Curseen, postal workers who died in the line of duty. And our prayers go to their loved ones.

I want to assure postal workers that our government is testing more than 200 postal facilities along the entire Eastern corridor that may have been impacted. And we will move quickly to treat and protect workers where positive exposures are found.

But one thing is for certain: These terrorists must be pursued, they must be defeated, and they must be brought to justice. (Applause.) And that is the purpose of this legislation. Since the 11th of September, the men and women of our intelligence and law enforcement agencies have been relentless in their response to new and sudden challenges.

We have seen the horrors terrorists can inflict. We may never know what horrors our country was spared by the diligent and determined work of our police forces, the FBI, ATF agents, federal marshals, Custom officers, Secret Service, intelligence professionals and local law enforcement officials, under the most trying conditions. They are serving this country with excellence, and often with bravery.

They deserve our full support and every means of help that we can provide. We're dealing with terrorists who operate by highly sophisticated methods and technologies, some of which were not even available when our existing laws were written. The bill before me takes account of the new realities and dangers posed by modern terrorists. It will help law enforcement to identify, to dismantle, to disrupt, and to punish terrorists before they strike.

For example, this legislation gives law enforcement officials better tools to put an end to financial counterfeiting, smuggling and money laundering. Secondly, it gives intelligence operations and criminal operations the chance to operate not on separate tracks, but to share vital information so necessary to disrupt a terrorist attack before it occurs.

As of today, we're changing the laws governing information-sharing. And as importantly, we're changing the culture of our various agencies that fight terrorism. Countering and investigating terrorist activity is the number one priority for both law enforcement and intelligence agencies.

Surveillance of communications is another essential tool to pursue and stop terrorists. The existing law was written in the era of rotary telephones. This new law that I sign today will allow surveillance of all communications used by terrorists, including e-mails, the Internet, and cell phones.

As of today, we'll be able to better meet the technological challenges posed by this proliferation of communications technology. Investigations are often slowed by limit on the reach of federal search warrants.

Law enforcement agencies have to get a new warrant for each new district they investigate, even when they're after the same suspect. Under this new law, warrants are valid across all districts and across all states. And, finally, the new legislation greatly enhances the penalties that will fall on terrorists or anyone who helps them.

Current statutes deal more severely with drug-traffickers than with terrorists. That changes today. We are enacting new and harsh penalties for possession of biological weapons. We're making it easier to seize the assets of groups and individuals involved in terrorism. The government will have wider latitude in deporting known terrorists and their supporters. The statute of limitations on terrorist acts will be lengthened, as will prison sentences for terrorists.

This bill was carefully drafted and considered. Led by the members of Congress on this stage, and those seated in the audience, it was crafted with skill and care, determination and a spirit of bipartisanship for which the entire nation is grateful. This bill met with an overwhelming—overwhelming agreement in Congress, because it upholds and respects the civil liberties guaranteed by our Constitution.

This legislation is essential not only to pursuing and punishing terrorists, but also preventing more atrocities in the hands of the evil ones. This government will enforce this law with all the urgency of a nation at war. The elected branches of our government, and both political parties, are united in our resolve to fight and stop and punish those who would do harm to the American people.

It is now my honor to sign into law the USA Patriot Act of 2001. (Applause.)
(The bill is signed.) (Applause.)
END 10:57 a.m. EDT

USA Patriot Improvement and Reauthorization Act of 2005

120 STAT. 192 PUBLIC LAW 109–177—MAR. 9, 2006
Public Law 109–177
109th Congress

An Act

To extend and modify authorities needed to combat terrorism, and for other purposes.

Be it enacted by the Senate and House of Representatives of the United States of America in Congress assembled,

SECTION 1. SHORT TITLE; TABLE OF CONTENTS.

(a) SHORT TITLE.—This Act may be cited as the "USA PATRIOT Improvement and Reauthorization Act of 2005."
(b) TABLE OF CONTENTS.—The table of contents for this Act is as follows:

18 USC 1801 note.

USA PATRIOT Improvement and Reauthorization Act of 2005.

Mar. 9, 2006

[H.R. 3199]

PUBLIC LAW 109–177—MAR. 9, 2006 120 STAT. 193

TITLE II—TERRORIST DEATH PENALTY ENHANCEMENT

TITLE III—REDUCING CRIME AND TERRORISM AT AMERICA'S SEAPORTS

TITLE IV—COMBATING TERRORISM FINANCING

TITLE V—MISCELLANEOUS PROVISIONS

Sec. 506. Department of Justice intelligence matters.
Sec. 507. Review by Attorney General.

TITLE VI—SECRET SERVICE

Sec. 601. Short title.
Sec. 602. Interference with national special security events.
Sec. 603. False credentials to national special security events.
Sec. 604. Forensic and investigative support of missing and exploited children cases.
Sec. 605. The Uniformed Division, United States Secret Service.
Sec. 606. Savings provisions.
Sec. 607. Maintenance as distinct entity.
Sec. 608. Exemptions from the Federal Advisory Committee Act.

This is an abbreviated version. The official document contains 87 pages and is accessible online.

USA Patriot Act Additional Reauthorizing Amendments Act of 2006

120 STAT. 278 PUBLIC LAW 109–178—MAR. 9, 2006
Public Law 109–178
109th Congress

An Act

To clarify that individuals who receive FISA orders can challenge nondisclosure requirements, that individuals who receive national security letters are not required to disclose the name of their attorney, that libraries are not wire or electronic communication service providers unless they provide specific services, and for other purposes. Be it enacted by the Senate and House of Representatives of the United States of America in Congress assembled,

SECTION 1. SHORT TITLE.

This Act may be cited as the "USA PATRIOT Act Additional Reauthorizing Amendments Act of 2006".

SEC. 2. DEFINITION.

As used in this Act, the term "applicable Act" means the Act entitled "An Act to extend and modify authorities needed to combat terrorism, and for other purposes." (109th Congress, 2d Session).

SEC. 3. JUDICIAL REVIEW OF FISA ORDERS.

Subsection (f) of section 501 of the Foreign Intelligence Surveillance Act of 1978 (50 U.S.C. 1861), as amended by the applicable Act, is amended to read as follows:

"(f)(1) In this subsection—

"(A) the term 'production order' means an order to produce any tangible thing under this section; and

"(B) the term 'nondisclosure order' means an order imposed under subsection (d).

"(2)(A)(i) A person receiving a production order may challenge the legality of that order by filing a petition with the pool established by section 103(e)(1). Not less than 1 year after the date of the issuance of the production order, the recipient of a production order may challenge the nondisclosure order imposed in connection with such production order by filing a petition to modify or set aside such nondisclosure order, consistent with the requirements of subparagraph (C), with the pool established by section 103(e)(1).

"(ii) The presiding judge shall immediately assign a petition under clause (i) to 1 of the judges serving in the pool established by section 103(e)(1). Not later than 72 hours after the assignment of such petition, the assigned judge shall conduct an initial review of the petition. If the assigned judge determines that the petition is frivolous, the assigned judge shall immediately deny the petition and affirm the production order or nondisclosure order. If the assigned judge determines the petition is not frivolous, the assigned judge shall promptly consider the petition in accordance with the procedures established under section 103(e)(2).

USA PATRIOT Act Additional Reauthorizing Amendments Act of 2006.
Terrorism.
18 USC 1 note.
Mar. 9, 2006
[S. 2271]
120 STAT. 279
PUBLIC LAW 109–178—MAR. 9, 2006

"(iii) The assigned judge shall promptly provide a written statement for the record of the reasons for any determination under this subsection. Upon the request of the Government, any order setting aside a nondisclosure order shall be stayed pending review pursuant to paragraph (3).

"(B) A judge considering a petition to modify or set aside a production order may grant such petition only if the judge finds that such order does not meet the requirements of this section or is otherwise unlawful. If the judge does not modify or set aside the production order, the judge shall immediately affirm such order, and order the recipient to comply therewith.

"(C)(i) A judge considering a petition to modify or set aside a nondisclosure order may grant such petition only if the judge finds that there is no reason to believe that disclosure may endanger the national security of the United States, interfere with a criminal, counterterrorism, or counterintelligence investigation, interfere with diplomatic relations, or endanger the life or physical safety of any person.

"(ii) If, upon filing of such a petition, the Attorney General, Deputy Attorney General, an Assistant Attorney General, or the Director of the Federal Bureau of Investigation certifies that disclosure may endanger the national security of the United States or interfere with diplomatic relations, such certification shall be treated as conclusive, unless the judge finds that the certification was made in bad faith.

"(iii) If the judge denies a petition to modify or set aside a nondisclosure order, the recipient of such order shall be precluded for a period of 1 year from filing another such petition with respect to such nondisclosure order.

"(D) Any production or nondisclosure order not explicitly modified or set aside consistent with this subsection shall remain in full effect.

"(3) A petition for review of a decision under paragraph (2) to affirm, modify, or set aside an order by the Government or any person receiving such order shall be made to the court of review established under section 103(b), which shall have jurisdiction to consider such petitions. The court of review shall provide for the record a written statement of the reasons for its decision and, on petition by the Government or any person receiving such order for writ of certiorari, the record shall be transmitted under seal to the Supreme Court of the United States, which shall have jurisdiction to review such decision.

"(4) Judicial proceedings under this subsection shall be concluded as expeditiously as possible. The record of proceedings, including petitions filed, orders granted, and statements of reasons for decision, shall be maintained under security measures established by the Chief Justice of the United States, in consultation with the Attorney General and the Director of National Intelligence.

"(5) All petitions under this subsection shall be filed under seal. In any proceedings under this subsection, the court shall, upon request of the Government, review ex parte and in camera any Government submission, or portions thereof, which may include classified information.".

SEC. 4. DISCLOSURES.

(a) FISA.—Subparagraph (C) of section 501(d)(2) of the Foreign Intelligence Surveillance Act of 1978 (50 U.S.C. 1861(d)(2)), as amended by the applicable Act, is amended to read as follows:

"(C) At the request of the Director of the Federal Bureau of Investigation or the designee of the Director, any person making or intending to make a disclosure under subparagraph (A) or (C) of paragraph (1) shall identify to the Director or such designee the person to whom such disclosure will be made or to whom such disclosure was made prior to the request.".

(b) TITLE

18.—Paragraph (4) of section 2709(c) of title 18, United States Code, as amended by the applicable Act, is amended to read as follows:

"(4) At the request of the Director of the Federal Bureau of Investigation or the designee of the Director, any person making or intending to make a disclosure under this section shall identify to the Director or such designee the person to whom such disclosure will be made or to whom such disclosure was made prior to the request, except that nothing in this section shall require a person to inform the Director or such designee of the identity of an attorney to whom disclosure was made or will be made to obtain legal advice or legal assistance with respect to the request under subsection (a).".

(c) FAIR CREDIT REPORTING ACT.— (1) IN GENERAL.—Paragraph (4) of section 626(d) of the Fair Credit Reporting Act (15 U.S.C. 1681u(d)), as amended by the applicable Act, is amended to read as follows:

"(4) At the request of the Director of the Federal Bureau of Investigation or the designee of the Director, any person making or intending to make a disclosure under this section shall identify to the Director or such designee the person to whom such disclosure will be made or to whom such disclosure was made prior to the request, except that nothing in this section shall require a person to inform the Director or such designee of the identity of an attorney to whom disclosure was made or will be made to obtain legal advice or legal assistance with respect to the request for the identity of financial institutions or a consumer report respecting any consumer under this section.".

(2) OTHER AGENCIES.—Paragraph (4) of section 627(c) of the Fair Credit Reporting Act (15 U.S.C. 1681v(c)), as amended by the applicable Act, is amended to read as follows:

"(4) At the request of the authorized government agency, any person making or intending to make a disclosure under this section shall identify to the requesting official of the authorized government agency the person to whom such disclosure will be made or to whom such disclosure was made prior to the request, except that nothing in this section shall require a person to inform the requesting official of the identity of an attorney to whom disclosure was made or will be made to obtain legal advice or legal assistance with respect to the request for information under subsection (a).".

(d) RIGHT TO FINANCIAL PRIVACY ACT.—(1) IN GENERAL.—Subparagraph (D) of section 1114(a)(3) of the Right to Financial Privacy Act (12 U.S.C. 3414(a)(3)), as amended by the applicable Act, is amended to read as follows:

"(D) At the request of the authorized Government authority or the Secret Service, any person making or intending to make a disclosure under this section shall identify to the requesting official of the authorized Government authority or the Secret Service the person to whom such disclosure will be made or to whom such disclosure was made prior to the request, except that nothing in this section shall require a person to inform the requesting official of the authorized Government authority or the Secret Service of the identity of an attorney to whom disclosure was made or will be made to obtain legal advice or legal assistance with respect to the request for financial records under this subsection.".

(2) FEDERAL BUREAU OF INVESTIGATION.—Clause (iv) of section 1114(a)(5)(D) of the Right to Financial Privacy Act (12 U.S.C. 3414(a)(5)(D)), as amended by the applicable Act, is amended to read as follows:

"(iv) At the request of the Director of the Federal Bureau of Investigation or the designee of the Director, any person making or intending to make a disclosure under this section shall identify to the Director or such designee the person to whom such disclosure will be made or to whom such disclosure was made prior to the request, except that nothing in this section shall require a person to inform the Director or such designee of the identity of an attorney to whom disclosure was made or will be made to obtain legal advice or legal assistance with respect to the request for financial records under subparagraph (A).".

(e) NATIONAL SECURITY ACT OF 1947.— Paragraph (4) of section 802(b) of the National Security Act of 1947 (50 U.S.C. 436(b)), as amended by the applicable Act, is amended to read as follows:

"(4) At the request of the authorized investigative agency, any person making or intending to make a disclosure under this section shall identify to the requesting official of the authorized investigative agency the person to whom such disclosure will be made or to whom such disclosure was made prior to the request, except that nothing in this section shall require a person to inform the requesting official of the identity of an attorney to whom disclosure was made or will be made to obtain legal advice or legal assistance with respect to the request under subsection (a).".

Section 2709 of title 18, United States Code, as amended by the applicable Act, is amended by adding at the end the following:

"(f) LIBRARIES.—A library (as that term is defined in section 213(1) of the Library Services and Technology Act (20 U.S.C. 9122(1)), the services of which include access to the Internet, books, journals, magazines, newspapers, or other similar forms of communication in print or digitally by patrons for their use, review, examination, or circulation, is not a wire or electronic communication service provider for purposes of this section, unless the library is providing the services defined in section 2510(15) ('electronic communication service') of this title.".

LEGISLATIVE HISTORY—S. 2271:
CONGRESSIONAL RECORD, Vol. 152 (2006):
Feb. 16, 27, 28, Mar. 1, considered and passed Senate.
Mar. 7, considered and passed House.
This Act shall become effective immediately upon enactment.
APPROVED March 9, 2006.
Effective date.
12 USC 3414

Patriot Sunsets Extension Act of 2011

S. 990
Patriots Sunsets Extension Act of 2011
One Hundred Twelfth Congress of the United States of America
AT THE FIRST SESSION
Begun and held at the City of Washington on Wednesday, the fifth day of January, two thousand and eleven

An Act

To provide for an additional temporary extension of programs under the Small Business Act and the Small Business Investment Act of 1958, and for other purposes.

Be it enacted by the Senate and House of Representatives of the United States of America in Congress assembled,

SECTION 1. SHORT TITLE.

This Act may be cited as the "PATRIOT Sunsets Extension Act of 2011".

SEC. 2. SUNSET EXTENSIONS.

(a) USA PATRIOT IMPROVEMENT AND REAUTHORIZATION ACT OF 2005.—Section 102(b)(1) of the USA PATRIOT Improvement and Reauthorization Act of 2005 (Public Law 109–177; 50 U.S.C. 1805 note, 50 U.S.C. 1861 note, and 50 U.S.C. 1862 note) is amended by striking "May 27, 2011" and inserting "June 1, 2015."

(b) INTELLIGENCE REFORM AND TERRORISM PREVENTION ACT OF 2004.—Section 6001(b)(1) of the Intelligence Reform and Terrorism Prevention Act of 2004 (Public Law 108–458; 50 U.S.C. 1801 note) is amended by striking "May 27, 2011" and inserting "June 1, 2015."

Speaker of the House of Representatives,
Vice President of the United States, and
President of the Senate.

USA Freedom Act

Summary: H.R.2048—114th Congress (2015-2016)

Public Law No: 114-23 (06/02/2015)

Uniting and Strengthening America by Fulfilling Rights and Ensuring Effective Discipline Over Monitoring Act of 2015 or the USA FREEDOM Act of 2015

TITLE I—FISA BUSINESS RECORDS REFORMS

(Sec. 101) Amends the Foreign Intelligence Surveillance Act of 1978 (FISA) to establish a new process to be followed when the Federal Bureau of Investigation (FBI) submits an application to a FISA court for an order requiring the production of business records or other tangible things for an investigation to obtain foreign intelligence information not concerning a U.S. person or to protect against international terrorism or clandestine intelligence activities. (The FBI currently uses such authority to request FISA orders requiring telephone companies to produce telephone call records to the National Security Agency.)

Prohibits the FBI from applying for a tangible thing production order unless a specific selection term is used as the basis for the production. Maintains limitations under current law that prohibit the FBI from applying for tangible thing production orders for threat assessments.

Establishes two separate frameworks for the production of tangible things with different standards that apply based on whether the FBI's application seeks:

- production on an ongoing basis of call detail records created before, on, or after the date of the application relating to an authorized investigation to protect against international terrorism, in which case the specific selection term must specifically identify an individual, account, or personal device; or

- production of call detail records or other tangible things in any other manner, in which case the selection term must specifically identify an individual, a federal officer or employee, a group, an entity, an association, a corporation, a foreign power, an account, a physical or an electronic address, a personal device, or any other specific identifier but is prohibited from including, when not used as part of a specific identifier, a broad geographic region (including the United States, a city, county, state, zip code, or area code) or an electronic communication or remote computing service provider, unless the provider is itself a subject of an authorized investigation.

Defines "call detail record" as session identifying information (including an originating or terminating telephone number, an International Mobile Subscriber Identity number, or an International Mobile Station Equipment Identity number), a telephone calling card number, or the time or duration of a call. Excludes from such definition: (1) the contents of any communication; (2) the name, address, or financial information of a subscriber or customer; or (3) cell site location or global positioning system information.

Requires the FBI, in applications for ongoing production of call detail records for investigations to protect against international terrorism, to show: (1) reasonable grounds to believe that the call detail records are relevant to such investigation; and (2) a reasonable, articulable suspicion that the specific selection term is associated with a foreign power or an agent of a foreign power engaged in international terrorism or activities in preparation for such terrorism.

Requires a judge approving such an ongoing release of call detail records for an investigation to protect against international terrorism to:

- limit such production to a period not to exceed 180 days but allow such orders to be extended upon application, with FISA court approval;
- permit the government to require the production of an initial set of call records using the reasonable, articulable suspicion standard that the term is associated with a foreign power or an agent of a foreign power and then a subsequent set of call records using session-identifying information or a telephone calling card number identified by the specific selection term that was used to produce the initial set of records (thus limiting the government to what is commonly referred to as two "hops" of call records); and
- direct the government to adopt minimization procedures requiring prompt destruction of produced call records that are not foreign intelligence information.

Allows a FISA court to approve other categories of FBI requests for the production of call detail records or tangible things (i.e., FBI call detail record and tangible thing applications that do not seek ongoing production of call detail records created before, on, or after the date of an application relating to an authorized investigation to protect against international terrorism) without subjecting the production to: (1) the reasonable, articulable suspicion standard for an association with a foreign power or an agent of a foreign power; (2) the 180-day or the two-hop limitation; or (3) the special minimization procedures that require prompt destruction of produced records only if the order approves an ongoing production of call detail records for investigations to protect against international terrorism.

(Sec. 102) Authorizes the Attorney General to require the emergency production of tangible things without first obtaining a court order if the Attorney General: (1) reasonably determines that an emergency situation requires the production of tangible things before an order authorizing production can be obtained with due diligence, (2) reasonably determines that a factual basis exists for the issuance of such a production order, (3) informs a FISA judge of the decision to require such production at the time the emergency decision is made, and (4) makes an application to a FISA judge within seven days after the Attorney General requires such emergency production.

Terminates the authority for such emergency production of tangible things when the information sought is obtained, when the application for the order is denied, or after the expiration of seven days from the time the Attorney General begins requiring such emergency production, whichever is earliest.

Prohibits information obtained or evidence derived from such an emergency production from being received in evidence or disclosed in any proceeding in or before any court, grand jury, agency, legislative committee, or other authority of the United States, any state, or any political subdivision if: (1) the subsequent application for court approval is denied, or (2) the production is terminated and no order is issued approving the production. Bars information concerning any U.S. person acquired from such production from being used or disclosed in any other manner by federal officers or employees without the consent of such person, except with approval of the Attorney General if the information indicates a threat of death or serious bodily harm.

(Sec. 103) Requires FISA court orders approving the production of tangible things to include each specific selection term used as the basis for such production. Prohibits FISA courts from authorizing the collection of tangible things without the use of a specific selection term.

(Sec. 104) Requires a FISA court, as a condition to approving an application for a tangible thing production order, to find that the minimization procedures submitted with the application meet applicable FISA standards. Authorizes the court to impose additional minimization procedures.

Allows a nondisclosure order imposed in connection with a tangible thing production order to be challenged immediately by filing a petition for judicial review. (Currently, such a tangible thing nondisclosure order cannot be challenged until one year after the issuance of the production order.) Removes a requirement that a judge considering a petition to modify or set aside a nondisclosure order treat as conclusive a certification by the Attorney General, the Deputy Attorney General, an Assistant Attorney General, or the FBI Director that disclosure may endanger national security or interfere with diplomatic relations.

(Sec. 105) Extends liability protections to persons who provide information, facilities, or technical assistance for the production of tangible things. (Currently, liability protections are limited to persons who produce such tangible things.)

(Sec. 106) Requires the government to compensate a person for reasonable expenses incurred in producing tangible things or providing technical assistance to the government to implement production procedures.

(Sec. 108) Amends the USA PATRIOT Improvement and Reauthorization Act of 2005 to require the Inspector General of the Department of Justice to audit the effectiveness and use of FISA authority to obtain production of tangible things from 2012 to 2014, including an examination of whether minimization procedures adopted by the Attorney General adequately protect the constitutional rights of U.S. persons. Directs the Inspector General of the Intelligence Community, for the same 2012-2014 period, to assess: (1) the importance of such information to the intelligence community; (2) the manner in which such information was collected, retained, analyzed, and disseminated; and (3) the adequacy of minimization procedures, including an assessment of any minimization procedures proposed by an element of the intelligence community that were modified or denied by the court.

Requires such Inspectors General to report to Congress regarding the results of such audit and assessment.

(Sec. 109) Requires amendments made by this Act to FISA's tangible thing requirements to take effect 180 days after enactment of this Act. Prohibits this Act from being construed to alter or eliminate the government's authority to obtain an order under the tangible things requirements of FISA as in effect prior to the effective date of such amendments during the period ending on such effective date.

(Sec. 110) Prohibits this Act from being construed to authorize the production of the contents of any electronic communication from an electronic communication service provider under such tangible thing requirements.

TITLE II—FISA PEN REGISTER AND TRAP AND TRACE DEVICE REFORM

(Sec. 201) Requires the government's FISA applications for orders approving pen registers or trap and trace devices to include a specific selection term as the basis for the use of the register or device. Prohibits broad geographic regions or an identification of an electronic communications service or a remote computing service from serving as such selection term.

(Sec. 202) Directs the Attorney General to ensure that appropriate privacy procedures are in place for the collection, retention, and use of nonpublicly available information concerning U.S. persons that is collected through a pen register or trap and trace device installed with FISA court approval.

TITLE III—FISA ACQUISITIONS TARGETING PERSONS OUTSIDE THE UNITED STATES REFORMS

(Sec. 301) Limits the government's use of information obtained through an authorization by the Attorney General and the Director of National Intelligence (DNI) to target non-U.S. persons outside the United States if a FISA court later determines that certain targeting or minimization procedures certified to the court are unlawful.

Prohibits information obtained or evidence derived from an acquisition pursuant to a part of a targeting certification or a related minimization procedure that the court has identified as deficient concerning a U.S. person from being received in evidence or otherwise disclosed in any proceeding in or before any court, grand jury, agency, legislative committee, or other authority of the United States, any state, or any political subdivision.

Bars information concerning any U.S. person acquired pursuant to a deficient part of a certification from being used or disclosed subsequently in any other manner by federal officers or employees without the consent of the U.S. person, except with approval of the Attorney General if the information indicates a threat of death or serious bodily harm.

Allows a FISA court, if the government corrects the deficiency, to permit the use or disclosure of information obtained before the date of the correction.

TITLE IV—FOREIGN INTELLIGENCE SURVEILLANCE COURT REFORMS

(Sec. 401) Directs the presiding judges of the FISA court and the FISA court of review to jointly designate at least five individuals to serve as amicus curiae to assist in the consideration of any application for an order or review that presents a novel or significant interpretation of the law, unless the court finds that such appointment is not appropriate.

Permits FISA courts to appoint an individual or organization to serve as amicus curiae in other instances, including to provide technical expertise. Requires such amicus curiae to provide: (1) legal arguments that advance protection of individual privacy and civil liberties, or (2) other legal arguments or information related to intelligence collection or communications technology.

Allows the FISA court of review to certify a question of law to be reviewed by the Supreme Court. Permits the Supreme Court to appoint FISA amicus curiae or other persons to provide briefings or other assistance upon such a certification.

(Sec. 402) Requires the DNI to: (1) conduct a declassification review of each decision, order, or opinion issued by the FISA court or the FISA court of review that includes a significant construction or interpretation of any provision of law, including any novel or significant construction or interpretation of "specific selection term" as defined in this Act; and (2) make such decisions, orders, or opinions publicly available to the greatest extent practicable, subject to permissible redactions.

Authorizes the DNI to waive such review and public availability requirements if: (1) a waiver is necessary to protect the national security of the United States or properly classified intelligence sources or methods, and (2) an unclassified statement prepared by the Attorney General is made publicly available to summarize the significant construction or interpretation of law.

TITLE V—NATIONAL SECURITY LETTER REFORM

(Sec. 501) Amends the federal criminal code, the Right to Financial Privacy Act of 1978, and the Fair Credit Reporting Act to require the FBI and other government agencies to use a specific selection term as the basis for national security letters that request information from wire or electronic communication service providers, financial institutions, or consumer reporting agencies. Requires the government to identify: (1) a person, entity, telephone number, or account for requests for telephone toll and transactional records; (2) a customer, entity, or account when requesting financial records for certain intelligence or protective functions; or (3) a consumer or account when requesting consumer reports for counterintelligence or counterterrorism purposes.

Revises standards under which the government can prohibit recipients of national security letters from disclosing to anyone that the government has sought or obtained access to the requested information.

(Sec. 502) Directs the Attorney General to adopt procedures for imposed nondisclosure requirements, including requirements under the National Security Act of 1947, to be reviewed at appropriate intervals and terminated if facts no longer support nondisclosure.

Removes a requirement that the court treat as conclusive a certification by the Attorney General, the Deputy Attorney General, an Assistant Attorney General, or the FBI Director that disclosure may endanger U.S. national security or interfere with diplomatic relations.

(Sec. 503) Allows national security letter recipients to challenge national security letter requests or nondisclosure requirements under modified procedures for filing a petition for judicial review.

TITLE VI—FISA TRANSPARENCY AND REPORTING REQUIREMENTS

(Sec. 601) Requires the Attorney General to expand an annual report to Congress regarding tangible thing applications to include a summary of compliance reviews and the total number of: (1) applications made for the daily production of call detail records created before, on, or after the date of an application relating to an authorized investigation to protect against international terrorism; and (2) orders approving such requests.

Directs the Attorney General to report to Congress annually regarding tangible things applications and orders in which the specific selection term does not specifically identify an individual, account, or personal device. Requires the report to indicate whether the court approving such orders has directed additional, particularized minimization procedures beyond those adopted by the Attorney General.

(Sec. 602) Directs the Administrative Office of the U.S. Courts to submit annually to Congress the number of: (1) FISA applications submitted and orders granted, modified, or denied under specified FISA authorities; and (2) appointments of an individual to serve as amicus curiae for FISA courts, including the name of each appointed individual, as well as any findings that such an appointment is not appropriate. Makes the report subject to a declassification review by the Attorney General and the DNI.

Directs the DNI to make available publicly a report that identifies, for the preceding 12-month period, the total number of: (1) FISA court orders issued for electronic surveillance, physical searches, the targeting of persons outside the United States, pen registers and trap and trace devices, call detail records, and other tangible things; and (2) national security letters issued.

Requires the DNI's reports to include the estimated number of: (1) targets of certain FISA orders, (2) search terms and queries concerning U.S. persons when the government retrieves information from electronic or wire communications obtained by targeting non-U.S. persons outside the United States, (3) unique identifiers used to communicate certain collected information, and (4) search terms concerning U.S. persons used to query a database of call detail records. Exempts certain queries by the FBI from such estimates.

(Sec. 603) Permits a person who is subject to a nondisclosure requirement accompanying a FISA order, directive, or national security letter to choose one of four methods to report publicly, on a semiannual or annual basis, the aggregate number of orders, directives, or letters with which the person was required to comply. Specifies the categories of orders, directives, and letters to be itemized or combined, the details authorized to be included with respect to contents or noncontents orders and the number of customer selectors targeted, and the ranges within which the number of orders, directives, or letters received may be reported aggregately in bands under each permitted method (i.e., reported in bands of 1000, 500, 250, or 100 depending on the chosen method).

Requires the information that may be included in certain aggregates to be delayed by 180 days, one year, or 540 days depending on the chosen reporting method and whether the nondisclosure requirements are contained in a new order or directive concerning a platform, product, or service for which the person did not previously receive an order or directive.

(Sec. 604) Expands the categories of FISA court decisions, orders, or opinions that the Attorney General is required to submit to Congress within 45 days after issuance of the decision to include: (1) a denial or modification of an application under FISA; and (2) a change of the application, or a novel application, of any FISA provision. (Currently, the Attorney General is only required to submit only decisions regarding a significant construction or interpretation of any FISA provision.)

(Sec. 605) Revises reporting requirements regarding electronic surveillance, physical searches, and tangible things to include the House Judiciary Committee as a recipient of such reports.

Requires the Attorney General to identify in an existing semiannual report each agency on behalf of which the government has applied for orders authorizing or approving the installation and use of pen registers or trap and trace devices under FISA.

TITLE VII—ENHANCED NATIONAL SECURITY PROVISIONS

(Sec. 701) Establishes procedures for a lawfully authorized targeting of a non-U.S. person previously believed to be located outside the United States to continue for a period not to exceed 72 hours from the time that the non-U.S. person is reasonably believed to be located inside the United States. Requires an element of the intelligence community, as a condition to exercising such authority, to: (1) determine that a lapse in the targeting poses a threat of death or serious bodily harm; (2) notify the Attorney General; and (3) request, as soon as practicable, the employment of emergency electronic surveillance or emergency physical search under appropriate FISA standards.

(Sec. 702) Expands the definition of "agent of a foreign power" to include a non-U.S. person who: (1) acts in the United States for or on behalf of a foreign power engaged in clandestine intelligence activities in the United States contrary to U.S. interests or as an officer, employee, or member of a foreign power, irrespective of whether the person is inside the United States; or (2) knowingly aids, abets, or conspires with any person engaging in an international proliferation of weapons of mass destruction on behalf of a foreign power or conducting activities in preparation for such proliferation.

(Sec. 704) Increases from 15 to 20 years the maximum penalty of imprisonment for providing material support or resources to a foreign terrorist organization in cases where the support does not result in the death of any person.

(Sec. 705) Amends the USA PATRIOT Improvement and Reauthorization Act of 2005 and the Intelligence Reform and Terrorism Prevention Act of 2004 to extend until December 15, 2019, FISA authorities concerning: (1) the production of business records, including call detail records and other tangible things; (2) roving electronic surveillance orders; and (3) a revised definition of "agent of a foreign power" that includes any non-U.S. persons who engage in international terrorism or preparatory activities (commonly referred to as the "lone wolf" provision). (Currently, such provisions are scheduled to expire on June 1, 2015.)

TITLE VIII—SAFETY OF MARITIME NAVIGATION AND NUCLEAR TERRORISM CONVENTIONS IMPLEMENTATION

Subtitle A—Safety of Maritime Navigation

(Sec. 801) Amends the federal criminal code to provide that existing prohibitions against conduct that endangers the safe navigation of a ship: (1) shall apply to conduct that is committed against or on board a U.S. vessel or a vessel subject to U.S. jurisdiction, in U.S. territorial seas, or by a U.S. corporation or legal entity; and (2) shall not apply to activities of armed forces during an armed conflict or in the exercise of official duties.

Sets forth procedures regarding the delivery of a person who is suspected of committing a maritime navigation or fixed platform offense to the authorities of a country that is a party to the Convention for the Suppression of Unlawful Acts against the Safety of Maritime Navigation.

Subjects property used or intended to be used to commit or to facilitate the commission of a maritime navigation offense to civil forfeiture.

(Sec. 802) Prohibits: (1) using in or on a ship or a maritime fixed platform any explosive or radioactive material, biological, chemical, or nuclear weapon, or other nuclear explosive device in a manner likely to cause death or serious injury or damage when the purpose is to intimidate a population or to compel a government or international organization to act or abstain from acting; (2) transporting on board a ship such material or device (or certain related material or technology) that is intended for such use, with specified exceptions; (3) transporting on board a ship a person known to have committed a maritime navigation offense intending to assist such person to evade prosecution; (4) injuring or killing any person in connection with such an offense; or (5) conspiring, attempting, or threatening to commit such an offense. Sets forth: (1) the circumstances in which the United States can exercise jurisdiction over such offenses, and (2) exceptions applicable to activities of the armed forces. Provides for civil forfeiture of property used to commit or to facilitate a violation.

(Sec. 805) Includes offenses involving violence against maritime navigation and maritime transport involving weapons of mass destruction within the definition of "federal crime of terrorism."

Subtitle B—Prevention of Nuclear Terrorism

(Sec. 811) Prohibits anyone, knowingly, unlawfully, and with intent to cause death, serious bodily injury, or substantial damage to property or the environment, from: (1) possessing radioactive material or making or possessing a nuclear explosive device or a radioactive material dispersal or radiation-emitting device; (2) using radioactive material or a device, using, damaging, or interfering with the operation of a nuclear facility in a manner that causes or increases the risk of the release of radioactive material, or causing radioactive contamination or exposure to radiation; or (3) threatening, attempting, or conspiring to commit such an offense. Sets forth: (1) the circumstances in which the United States can exercise jurisdiction over such offenses, and (2) exceptions applicable to activities of the armed forces.

Includes such offenses within the definition of "federal crime of terrorism."

(Sec. 812) Amends provisions prohibiting transactions involving nuclear materials to: (1) prohibit, intentionally and without lawful authority, carrying, sending, or moving nuclear material into or out of a country; and (2) establish an exception for activities of the armed forces.

Society of Professional Journalists Code of Ethics

Preamble

Members of the Society of Professional Journalists believe that public enlightenment is the forerunner of justice and the foundation of democracy. Ethical journalism strives to ensure the free exchange of information that is accurate, fair and thorough. An ethical journalist acts with integrity. The Society declares these four principles as the foundation of ethical journalism and encourages their use in its practice by all people in all media.

Seek Truth and Report It

Ethical journalism should be accurate and fair. Journalists should be honest and courageous in gathering, reporting and interpreting information.

Journalists should:

- Take responsibility for the accuracy of their work. Verify information before releasing it. Use original sources whenever possible.
- Remember that neither speed nor format excuses inaccuracy.
- Provide context. Take special care not to misrepresent or oversimplify in promoting, previewing or summarizing a story.
- Gather, update and correct information throughout the life of a news story.
- Be cautious when making promises, but keep the promises they make.

- Identify sources clearly. The public is entitled to as much information as possible to judge the reliability and motivations of sources.
- Consider sources' motives before promising anonymity. Reserve anonymity for sources who may face danger, retribution or other harm, and have information that cannot be obtained elsewhere. Explain why anonymity was granted.
- Diligently seek subjects of news coverage to allow them to respond to criticism or allegations of wrongdoing.
- Avoid undercover or other surreptitious methods of gathering information unless traditional, open methods will not yield information vital to the public.
- Be vigilant and courageous about holding those with power accountable.
- Give voice to the voiceless.
- Support the open and civil exchange of views, even views they find repugnant.
- Recognize a special obligation to serve as watchdogs over public affairs and government. Seek to ensure that the public's business is conducted in the open, and that public records are open to all.
- Provide access to source material when it is relevant and appropriate.
- Boldly tell the story of the diversity and magnitude of the human experience.
- Seek sources whose voices we seldom hear.
- Avoid stereotyping. Journalists should examine the ways their values and experiences may shape their reporting.
- Label advocacy and commentary.
- Never deliberately distort facts or context, including visual information.
- Clearly label illustrations and re-enactments.
- Never plagiarize. Always attribute.

MINIMIZE HARM

Ethical journalism treats sources, subjects, colleagues and members of the public as human beings deserving of respect.

Journalists should:

- Balance the public's need for information against potential harm or discomfort. Pursuit of the news is not a license for arrogance or undue intrusiveness.
- Show compassion for those who may be affected by news coverage. Use heightened sensitivity when dealing with juveniles, victims of sex crimes, and sources or subjects who are inexperienced or unable to give consent. Consider cultural differences in approach and treatment.
- Recognize that legal access to information differs from an ethical justification to publish or broadcast.

- Realize that private people have a greater right to control information about themselves than public figures and others who seek power, influence or attention. Weigh the consequences of publishing or broadcasting personal information.
- Avoid pandering to lurid curiosity, even if others do.
- Balance a suspect's right to a fair trial with the public's right to know. Consider the implications of identifying criminal suspects before they face legal charges.
- Consider the long-term implications of the extended reach and permanence of publication. Provide updated and more complete information as appropriate.

ACT INDEPENDENTLY

The highest and primary obligation of ethical journalism is to serve the public.

Journalists should:

- Avoid conflicts of interest, real or perceived. Disclose unavoidable conflicts.
- Refuse gifts, favors, fees, free travel and special treatment, and avoid political and other outside activities that may compromise integrity or impartiality, or may damage credibility.
- Be wary of sources offering information for favors or money; do not pay for access to news. Identify content provided by outside sources, whether paid or not.
- Deny favored treatment to advertisers, donors or any other special interests, and resist internal and external pressure to influence coverage.
- Distinguish news from advertising and shun hybrids that blur the lines between the two. Prominently label sponsored content.

BE ACCOUNTABLE AND TRANSPARENT

Ethical journalism means taking responsibility for one's work and explaining one's decisions to the public.

Journalists should:

- Explain ethical choices and processes to audiences. Encourage a civil dialogue with the public about journalistic practices, coverage and news content.
- Respond quickly to questions about accuracy, clarity and fairness.
- Acknowledge mistakes and correct them promptly and prominently. Explain corrections and clarifications carefully and clearly.
- Expose unethical conduct in journalism, including within their organizations.

- Abide by the same high standards they expect of others.
- The SPJ Code of Ethics is a statement of abiding principles supported by additional explanations and position papers (at spj.org) that address changing journalistic practices. It is not a set of rules, rather a guide that encourages all who engage in journalism to take responsibility for the information they provide, regardless of medium. The code should be read as a whole; individual principles should not be taken out of context. It is not, nor can it be under the First Amendment, legally enforceable

RTDNA Code of Ethics and Professional Conduct

Guiding Principles:

Journalism's obligation is to the public. Journalism places the public's interests ahead of commercial, political and personal interests. Journalism empowers viewers, listeners and readers to make more informed decisions for themselves; it does not tell people what to believe or how to feel.

Ethical decision-making should occur at every step of the journalistic process, including story selection, news-gathering, production, presentation and delivery. Practitioners of ethical journalism seek diverse and even opposing opinions in order to reach better conclusions that can be clearly explained and effectively defended or, when appropriate, revisited and revised.

Ethical decision-making—like writing, photography, design or anchoring—requires skills that improve with study, diligence and practice.

The RTDNA Code of Ethics does not dictate what journalists should do in every ethical predicament; rather it offers resources to help journalists make better ethical decisions—on and off the job—for themselves and for the communities they serve.

Journalism is distinguished from other forms of content by these guiding principles:

- Truth and accuracy above all
  - The facts should get in the way of a good story. Journalism requires more than merely reporting remarks, claims or comments. Journalism verifies, provides relevant context, tells the rest of the story and acknowledges the absence of important additional information.

- For every story of significance, there are always more than two sides. While they may not all fit into every account, responsible reporting is clear about what it omits, as well as what it includes.
- Scarce resources, deadline pressure and relentless competition do not excuse cutting corners factually or oversimplifying complex issues.
- "Trending," "going viral" or "exploding on social media" may increase urgency, but these phenomena only heighten the need for strict standards of accuracy.
- Facts change over time. Responsible reporting includes updating stories and amending archival versions to make them more accurate and to avoid misinforming those who, through search, stumble upon outdated material.
- Deception in newsgathering, including surreptitious recording, conflicts with journalism's commitment to truth. Similarly, anonymity of sources deprives the audience of important, relevant information. Staging, dramatization and other alterations—even when labeled as such—can confuse or fool viewers, listeners and readers. These tactics are justified only when stories of great significance cannot be adequately told without distortion, and when any creative liberties taken are clearly explained.
- Journalism challenges assumptions, rejects stereotypes and illuminates—even where it cannot eliminate—ignorance.
- Ethical journalism resists false dichotomies—either/or, always/never, black/white thinking— and considers a range of alternatives between the extremes.

- Independence and transparency

  - Editorial independence may be a more ambitious goal today than ever before. Media companies, even if not-for-profit, have commercial, competitive and other interests—both internal and external—from which the journalists they employ cannot be entirely shielded. Still, independence from influences that conflict with public interest remains an essential ideal of journalism. Transparency provides the public with the means to assess credibility and to determine who deserves trust.
  - Acknowledging sponsor-provided content, commercial concerns or political relationships is essential, but transparency alone is not adequate. It does not entitle journalists to lower their standards of fairness or truth.
  - Disclosure, while critical, does not justify the exclusion of perspectives and information that are important to the audience's understanding of issues.
  - Journalism's proud tradition of holding the powerful accountable provides no exception for powerful journalists or the powerful organizations that employ them. To profit from reporting on the activities of others while operating in secrecy is hypocrisy.
  - Effectively explaining editorial decisions and processes does not mean making excuses. Transparency requires reflection, reconsideration and honest openness to the possibility that an action, however well intended, was wrong.
  - Ethical journalism requires owning errors, correcting them promptly and giving corrections as much prominence as the error itself had.

- Commercial endorsements are incompatible with journalism because they compromise credibility. In journalism, content is gathered, selected and produced in the best interests of viewers, listeners and readers—not in the interests of somebody who paid to have a product or position promoted and associated with a familiar face, voice or name.
- Similarly, political activity and active advocacy can undercut the real or perceived independence of those who practice journalism. Journalists do not give up the rights of citizenship, but their public exercise of those rights can call into question their impartiality.
- The acceptance of gifts or special treatment of any kind not available to the general public creates conflicts of interest and erodes independence. This does not include the access to events or areas traditionally granted to working journalists in order to facilitate their coverage. It does include "professional courtesy" admission, discounts and "freebies" provided to journalists by those who might someday be the subject of coverage. Such goods and services are often offered as enticements to report favorably on the giver or rewards for doing so; even where that is not the intent, it is the reasonable perception of a justifiably suspicious public.
- Commercial and political activities, as well as the acceptance of gifts or special treatment, cause harm even when the journalists involved are "off duty" or "on their own time."
- Attribution is essential. It adds important information that helps the audience evaluate content and it acknowledges those who contribute to coverage. Using someone else's work without attribution or permission is plagiarism.

- Accountability for consequences

  - Journalism accepts responsibility, articulates its reasons and opens its processes to public scrutiny.
  - Journalism provides enormous benefits to self-governing societies. In the process, it can create inconvenience, discomfort and even distress. Minimizing harm, particularly to vulnerable individuals, should be a consideration in every editorial and ethical decision.
  - Responsible reporting means considering the consequences of both the newsgathering—even if the information is never made public—and of the material's potential dissemination. Certain stakeholders deserve special consideration; these include children, victims, vulnerable adults and others inexperienced with American media.
  - Preserving privacy and protecting the right to a fair trial are not the primary mission of journalism; still, these critical concerns deserve consideration and to be balanced against the importance or urgency of reporting.
  - The right to broadcast, publish or otherwise share information does not mean it is always right to do so. However, journalism's obligation is to pursue truth and report, not withhold it. Shying away from difficult cases is not necessarily more ethical than taking on the challenge of reporting them. Leaving tough or sensitive stories to non-journalists can be a disservice to the public.

A growing collection of coverage guidelines for use on a range of ethical issues is available on the RTDNA website—www.rtdna.org .

Revised Code of Ethics adopted June 11, 2015

JRN 101 Oral Presentation
(Speech Outline)

Name:
Date:
Presentation Title:
THE GRABBER: *(A line, a quote, an anecdote, a fact -- something that will immediately grab the audience's attention)*
EXPLICITLY STATE WHY THIS IS IMPORTANT OR WHY THE AUDIENCE SHOULD CARE: (Ex: *This is important ... or You should care because...*)
EXPLICITLY STATE THE PRESENTATION'S OBJECTIVE/WHAT IT WILL PROVE OR SHOW: (Ex: *The objective of this presentation is... or Through this presentation I will show... or you will learn...*)
EXAMPLES TO SUPPORT POSITION: (Ex: Personal examples and/or attributed facts or statistics -- *according to PollingReport.com, 70 percent of Americans believe...*)
SIZZLING SUMMARY/INSTRUCT THEM ON WHAT TO DO: *(Sizzle don't fizzle. Close with a strong, memorable ending and/or instruct your audience on what you'd like them to do.)*

Speech Format

Your name   # of words
E-mail address
Speech #
Date

Title of speech

Start the speech halfway down the page. It should be typed double-spaced. Keep it to
no more than 350 words.

There should be a five-space indention with new paragraphs. Use the space bar, not the
tab bar. Margins should be 1 inch on the top and bottom, and 1 to 1-1/2-inches on the
sides.

Please use a good, regular 12-point typeface that is legible. Do not use clever typefaces.
Just use a regular font like you see here. And please don't boldface.

When you come to the end of the first page, place "more" at the bottom of the page if
there is another page that follows. At the top left of the second page, you should include
your name and title of the speech, along with the page number.

At the end of your speech, you should type either "30" or "###." Either symbol signals
the speech's end -- which is where we are now.

###

The Student's Speech, Free Expression

The Hartford Courant
March 03, 2011
By Frank Harris III

Sitting in the North Haven theater watching "The King's Speech" last month brought to mind a former student's speech. A few days before the class was to do the first of several oral presentations, she asked if she could be exempted because she had a hard time giving speeches.

Her request was not completely unusual. The common view that public speaking is people's single greatest fear—more feared than death—has merit.

Public speaking is part of my class "The Media: Freedom and Power," in which students learn about the First Amendment and the challenges that arise when freedom of expression by the news media, citizens or groups conflict with society and the government. Over the years, a number of students have sought to duck the required three-minute speech before their classmates, delivered without notes, prompts or a podium to stand behind.

But with 50 percent of the course based on oral presentations, not completing this meant failing the class.

She asked if there were exceptions, and when I said no, she revealed, before the class, that she had a speech impediment, which was surprising because neither her classmates nor I noted anything when she introduced herself on the first day of class.

It was surprising, too, because she had mentioned that she sang.

She explained that when she sang, there was no stutter, and when she spoke in many settings, she didn't always stutter. But standing in front of a classroom of people—that was different.

I had never faced this before. Yes, in the past there were those who were nervous and scared beyond all belief—but never anyone who asked out because they stuttered.

"All I ask," I said, "is that you just go up and do the best you can. Just try."

On the day of the speech, before her turn came, there was a guy who stood before the class and was having a tough time. I rescued him, telling him to take a seat and try later. Then came her turn.

She spoke in a slow, halting voice about a little girl with her dad in a candy store. The little girl wanted something, but was afraid to speak because of her stutter. Standing before us she described how difficult it was to speak then. As her halting voice grew stronger, she spoke about how those who have no speech impediment take speaking for granted, just as those who have freedom of speech provided by the First Amendment take it for granted. The little girl had grown up and now stood before us recognizing and exercising her right to free speech.

Then in a challenge to her classmates, she said if she could do this despite her stutter, then surely they could take their place before the class and exercise their voices.

It was a stunning tapestry of a speech that weaved her speech impediment with freedom of expression and her personal experience. She delivered it with power and passion and when she finished, there was a moment of silence followed by thunderous applause.

We took a break then. We had to. The class was near tears.

The student who I had rescued came over to me.

"Well, now I have to speak. I want to go next," he said.

When class ended in the late afternoon, we emerged from the building to a misty rain, a bright sun and, like something out of a movie, this huge rainbow in the sky over Southern's campus.

Over the years I have presented her example to students who have given reasons for shunning or shying from giving speeches due to obstacles obvious and obstacles unseen.

There have been speeches before and since that hit on all the elements of what a good speech should be. Yet it is hers that stands out. Hers, I remember.

I think it's because we root harder and appreciate so much more those who—with fear staring them in the eye—stand and try.

Top 100 Banned/Challenged Books: 2000 to 2009

1. *Harry Potter* (series), by J. K. Rowling
2. *Alice* series, by Phyllis Reynolds Naylor
3. *The Chocolate War*, by Robert Cormier
4. *And Tango Makes Three*, by Justin Richardson/Peter Parnell
5. *Of Mice and Men*, by John Steinbeck
6. *I Know Why the Caged Bird Sings*, by Maya Angelou
7. *Scary Stories* (series), by Alvin Schwartz
8. *His Dark Materials* (series), by Philip Pullman
9. *ttyl; ttfn; l8r g8r* (series), by Lauren Myracle
10. *The Perks of Being a Wallflower*, by Stephen Chbosky
11. *Fallen Angels*, by Walter Dean Myers
12. *It's Perfectly Normal*, by Robie Harris
13. *Captain Underpants* (series), by Dav Pilkey
14. *The Adventures of Huckleberry Finn*, by Mark Twain
15. *The Bluest Eye*, by Toni Morrison
16. *Forever*, by Judy Blume
17. *The Color Purple*, by Alice Walker
18. *Go Ask Alice*, by Anonymous
19. *Catcher in the Rye*, by J. D. Salinger
20. *King and King*, by Linda de Haan
21. *To Kill A Mockingbird*, by Harper Lee
22. *Gossip Girl* (series), by Cecily von Ziegesar
23. *The Giver*, by Lois Lowry
24. *In the Night Kitchen*, by Maurice Sendak
25. *Killing Mr. Griffen*, by Lois Duncan
26. *Beloved*, by Toni Morrison
27. *My Brother Sam Is Dead*, by James Lincoln Collier

28. *Bridge To Terabithia*, by Katherine Paterson
29. *The Face on the Milk Carton*, by Caroline B. Cooney
30. *We All Fall Down*, by Robert Cormier
31. *What My Mother Doesn't Know*, by Sonya Sones
32. *Bless Me, Ultima*, by Rudolfo Anaya
33. *Snow Falling on Cedars*, by David Guterson
34. *The Earth, My Butt, and Other Big, Round Things*, by Carolyn Mackler
35. *Angus, Thongs, and Full Frontal Snogging*, by Louise Rennison
36. *Brave New World*, by Aldous Huxley
37. *It's So Amazing*, by Robie Harris
38. *Arming America*, by Michael Bellasiles
39. *Kaffir Boy*, by Mark Mathabane
40. *Life is Funny*, by E. R. Frank
41. *Whale Talk*, by Chris Crutcher
42. *The Fighting Ground*, by Avi
43. *Blubber*, by Judy Blume
44. *Athletic Shorts*, by Chris Crutcher
45. *Crazy Lady*, by Jane Leslie Conly
46. *Slaughterhouse-Five*, by Kurt Vonnegut
47. *The Adventures of Super Diaper Baby*: The First Graphic Novel by George Beard and Harold Hutchins, the creators *of Captain Underpants*, by Dav Pilkey
48. *Rainbow Boys*, by Alex Sanchez
49. *One Flew Over the Cuckoo's Nest*, by Ken Kesey
50. *The Kite Runner*, by Khaled Hosseini
51. *Daughters of Eve*, by Lois Duncan
52. *The Great Gilly Hopkins*, by Katherine Paterson
53. *You Hear Me?* by Betsy Franco
54. *The Facts Speak for Themselves*, by Brock Cole
55. *Summer of My German Soldier*, by Bette Green
56. *When Dad Killed Mom*, by Julius Lester
57. *Blood and Chocolate*, by Annette Curtis Klause
58. *Fat Kid Rules the World*, by K. L. Going
59. *Olive's Ocean*, by Kevin Henkes
60. *Speak*, by Laurie Halse Anderson
61. *Draw Me A Star*, by Eric Carle
62. *The Stupids* (series), by Harry Allard
63. *The Terrorist*, by Caroline B. Cooney
64. *Mick Harte Was Here*, by Barbara Park
65. *The Things They Carried*, by Tim O'Brien
66. *Roll of Thunder, Hear My Cry*, by Mildred Taylor
67. *A Time to Kill*, by John Grisham

68. *Always Running*, by Luis Rodriguez
69. *Fahrenheit 451*, by Ray Bradbury
70. *Harris and Me*, by Gary Paulsen
71. *Junie B. Jones* (series), by Barbara Park
72. *Song of Solomon*, by Toni Morrison
73. *What's Happening to My Body Book*, by Lynda Madaras
74. *The Lovely Bones*, by Alice Sebold
75. *Anastasia* (series), by Lois Lowry
76. *A Prayer for Owen Meany*, by John Irving
77. *Crazy: A Novel*, by Benjamin Lebert
78. *The Joy of Gay Sex*, by Dr. Charles Silverstein
79. *The Upstairs Room*, by Johanna Reiss
80. *A Day No Pigs Would Die*, by Robert Newton Peck
81. *Black Boy*, by Richard Wright
82. *Deal With It!* by Esther Drill
83. *Detour for Emmy*, by Marilyn Reynolds
84. *So Far From the Bamboo Grove*, by Yoko Watkins
85. *Staying Fat for Sarah Byrnes*, by Chris Crutcher
86. *Cut*, by Patricia McCormick
87. *Tiger Eyes*, by Judy Blume
88. *The Handmaid's Tale*, by Margaret Atwood
89. *Friday Night Lights*, by H. G. Bissenger
90. *A Wrinkle in Time*, by Madeline L'Engle
91. *Julie of the Wolves*, by Jean Craighead George
92. *The Boy Who Lost His Face*, by Louis Sachar
93. *Bumps in the Night*, by Harry Allard
94. *Goosebumps* (series), by R. L. Stine
95. *Shade's Children*, by Garth Nix
96. *Grendel*, by John Gardner
97. *The House of the Spirits*, by Isabel Allende
98. *I Saw Esau*, by Iona Opte
99. *Are You There, God? It's Me, Margaret*, by Judy Blume
100. *America: A Novel*, by E. R. Frank

The American Library Association keeps track of the censorship of books in the U.S. This is the most current list as of this book's publication. Learn more at www.ala.org.

"Top 100 Banned/Challenged Books: 2000-2009," http://www.ala.org/bbooks/top-100-bannedchallenged-books-2000-2009. Copyright © 2009 by American Library Association. Reprinted with permission.

"2 Communists Leaders Held as Anarchists," *New York Tribune,* November 15, 1919.

"18 Red Party leaders nabbed on West Coast," *Portsmouth (New Hampshire) Herald*, September 17, 1952.

ACLU. "List of Plaintiffs in Ashcroft (and Reno) v. ACLU." Nov. 23, 1998. http://www.aclu.org/technology-and-liberty/list-plaintiffs-ashcroft-and-reno-v-aclu.

ACLU of Illinois. http://www.aclu-il.org

American Library Association website. *The 100 Most Frequently Challenged Books of 2000–2009.* http://www.ala.org/bbooks/top-100-bannedchallenged-books-2000-2009.

"An Irishman Scourged and Tarred and Feathered," *Charleston Mercury,* December 19, 1859.

"'A Revolutionist, I Ask No Clemency,' Gitlow Tells Jury," *New York Tribune*, February 5, 1920.

Attorney General Ashcroft: Prepared Remarks Senate Committee on the Judiciary. September 25, 2001. U.S. Government Website.

Bagdikian, Ben. *The New Media Monopoly.* Boston: Beacon Press, 2004

"Bostrom is Freed, then Re-arrested," *Tacoma Times,* November 9, 1917.

Bulla, David. *Abraham Lincoln and Press Suppression Reconsidered.* Vol. 26, p. 11, October 2009.

EFF—Section 230: https://www.eff.org/issues/cda230

The Avalon Project at Yale Law School. The Lillian Goldman Law Library in Memory of Sol Goldman.

Blackstone, William. *Commentaries on the Laws of England.* 1769. The Founders' Constitution, 1986. http://press-pubs.uchicago.edu/founders/documents/amendI_speechs4.html

Carter, Barton T., Marc A. Franklin, Jay B. Wright. *The First Amendment and the Fourth Estate,* Third Edition, Mineola, New York, The Foundation Press, Inc., 1985.

"The Case of Debs," *The Washington Herald,* July 3, 1918.

Christopher Collier and James Lincoln Collier. *Decision at Philadelphia: The Constitutional Convention of 1787.* Random House, 1987

Corn, David. "Secret Video: Romney Tells Millionaire Donors What He Really Thinks of Obama Voters. *Mother Jones*. Sept. 17, 2012. http://www.motherjones.com/politics/2012/09/secret-video-romney-private-fundraiser

"Enraged Mob in Front of White House Tears Down Suffagists' Banner Which Attacked the President, *Washington Times*, June 20, 1917.

"Eugene V. Debs Gets Ten Years," *Philadelphia Evening Public Ledger*, September 14, 1918.

Filmer, Robert. *Patriarcha*. 1680. Constitution.Org. http://www.constitution.org/eng/patriarcha.htm

First Amendment Center, www.firstamendmentcenter.org

"12 Communist Leaders in U.S. are Indicted," *Gettysburg Times*, July 21, 1948.

The First Amendment and the Fifth Estate, Regulation of Electronic Mass Media, Second Edition, The Foundation Press, Inc., Westbury, New York, 1989.

Freedom Forum, www.freedomforum.org

Galvin, Katherine M. Media Law, *A Legal Handbook for the Working Journalist*, Nolo Press, Berkeley, Calif. 1984.

"German Editors Fight Treason Charge," *Chicago Daily Tribune*, September 21, 1917.

"Great Excitement at all Points, *The Nashville Union*, April 17, 1861.

Gillmor, Donald M., Jerome A. Barron, Todd F. Simon. *Mass Communication Law, Cases and Comment, Sixth Edition*, Wadsworth Publishing Company, 1998.

Harris III, Frank. The Student's Speech, Free Expression. *Hartford Courant*, March 3, 2011.

"Whom Do We Trust to Tell the Truth?" Harris Poll, #61. Dec. 12, 2001.

"Heed their Rising Voices," *New York Times*, March 29, 1960. http://www.archives.gov/exhibits/documented-rights/exhibit/section4/detail/heed-rising-voices-transcript.html

Hellinga, Lotte. *William Caxton and Early Printing in England*. Chicago: University of Chicago Press, 2010.

Heritage Guide to the Constitution, www.heritage.org

"I didn't raise my boy to be a soldier," 1915. Sheet music from the Archeophone Records collection. https://www.archeophone.com/features/march_to_war/songs/cd1/05.php

"La Follette in 2-Hour Speech Angers Senate," *New York Sun*, October 7, 1917.

"La Follette Talks," *The Washington Times*, October 8, 1917.

Library of Congress, www.loc.gov.

Locke, John. *Two Treatises of Government*. 1823. LONANG Library, 2003–14. http://www.efm.bris.ac.uk/het/locke/government.pdf

London Evening Mail, August 13, 1798.

London Observer, January 27, 1799.

Madrigal, Alexis. "It Wasn't Sunil Tripathi: The Anatamoy of a Misinformation Disaster." *The Atlantic*. April 19, 2013. http://www.theatlantic.com/technology/archive/2013/04/it-wasnt-sunil-tripathi-the-anatomy-of-a-misinformation-disaster/275155/

"Majority Arrested Here are Released," *New York Tribune*, November 15, 1919.

Maryland (Annapolis) Gazette, July 3, 1800.

"May Day Demonstrations Broken up by Mounted Police and Soldiers, Who Ride Down Mobs," *New York Tribune*, May 2, 1919.

Mencher, Melvin. *News Reporting and Writing*. McGaw-Hill, 2010.

Milton, John. *Areopagitica: A Speech For The Liberty Of Unlicensed Printing To The Parliament Of England.* 1644. Project Gutenberg ebook 2013. http://www.gutenberg.org/files/608/608-h/608-h.htm)

"More Anti-Draft Arrests Expected … Heavy Bail Demanded for Men Taken in Raid Last Night. 16,000 Circulars Found," *Philadelphia Evening Public Ledger*, August 29, 1917.

Morland, Howard. "The H-Bomb Secret." *Progressive Magazine*, November 1970,

National Archives, www.archives.gov.

"Negroes in Protest Parade," *Indianapolis News*, July 28, 1917.

"Newspapers, to Succeed, Must Print All the News Available: William R. Hearst Asserts that Censorship Clause in Espionage Bill is Blow at Constitution and Rights of People—Says Congress and Party that Passes it Will be Swept from Power," *Washington Post*, May 7, 1917.

North-Carolina (Halifax) Journal, September 13, 1802.

Overbeck, Wayne. *Major Principles of Media Law*, Harcourt Brace College Publishers, 1999 Edition.

Pember, Don R., *Mass Media Law*, Fifth Edition, Wm. C. Brown Publishers, 1990.

Pew Research Center. *Terror Coverage Boosts News Media's Image,* Nov. 28, 2001.

"Pickets posted outside White House today by women," *Washington Herald*, January 10, 1917.

Pittsburgh Gazette, March 22, 1837.

"Plot to Blow up Munition(s) Train is frustrated," *Washington Times,* Aug. 4, 1917.

"Pro Slavery Mobs," *The Liberator*, November 22, 1834.

Publick Occurrences Both Domestick and Forreign. 1690. National Humanities Center. http://nationalhumanities-center.org/pds/amerbegin/power/text5/PublickOccurrences.pdf

Remarks by the President at Signing of the Patriot Act, Anti-Terrorism Legislation. October 26, 2001, U.S. Government Website.

Roots, TV mini-series. 1977, http://www.tv.com/shows/roots-the-complete-miniseries/watch/.

Scotusblog, www.scotusblog.com, various Supreme Court decisions.

Seldes, George. *You Can't Print That.* 1929. Payson & Clarke Ltd, New York. https://ia600302.us.archive.org/29/items/YouCantPrintThat/YouCantPrintThat.pdf

"Socialist Paper is Barred from the U.S. Mails," *Lima (Ohio) News,* July 7, 1917.

"Speaking Our Minds: Conversations with the people behind landmark First Amendment cases." Joseph Russomanno 2002. Lawrence Erlbaum Associates Inc. publishers, Mahwah, NJ, Chapter 10. 410–468.

Silverman, Craig. *Regret the Error.* Poynter.org.

Supremecourt.gov, www.supremecourt.gov.

Tedford, Thomas L. *Freedom of Speech in the United States,* 3rd ed. State College, PA: Strata Publishing, 1997.

Tell the Truth and Run, 1996 film.

The Liberator, August 24, 1849

The Liberator. June 21, 1850.

The Patriot Act, H.R. 3162, in the Senate of the United States, October 24, 2001. U.S. Government Website.

The War of the Rebellion: a Compilation of the Official Records of the Union and Confederate Armies. Washington Government Printing Office. By an act approved June 23, 1874. http://ebooks.library.cornell.edu/m/moawar/text/waro0115.txt

"Traitors to the Rear," *Harrisburg Telegraph*, April 12, 1918.

"Trial of C.L. Vallandigham—The Specifications and Evidence," *The Daily Ohio Statesman*, May 10, 1863, 1

The United States Statutes at Large, V. 40. (April 1917-March 1919). Washington: Government Printing Office, 1919. 553–554.

"Unafraid and Unashamed in Shadow of Jail Sentence, *Philadelphia Evening Public Ledger*, March 12, 1918.

University of Missouri, Kansas City School of Law: http://law2.umkc.edu

U.S. Patriot Improvement and Reauthorization Act of 2005, H.R. 3199, March 9, 2006. U.S. Government Website.

U.S. House of Representatives, Committee on the Judiciary Website. *Highlights of the New Civil Liberty Safeguards Contained in the Reauthorization of the USA Patriot Act, HR 3199*, signed into law on March 9, 2006.

"War Censorship," *The Chicago Tribune,* April 17, 1917.

"War Department Has Troops Ready to Quell Trouble," *Washington Times,* Aug. 4, 1917.

War of the Worlds. 1939. CBS Radio Broadcast. https://www.youtube.com/watch?v=W6YNHq1qc44

"Watson's Weekly Held up by Federal Order," *Topeka Daily Kansas,* June 29, 1917.

WikiLeaks, WikiLeaks.org.

"Yager Charged with Obstructing the Draft," *Richmond Times-Dispatch*, September 1, 1917.

INDEX